Why I *Satan* Hate the Woman

By Joseph Brice

Dedication

To the strong, fearless, and virtuous women of God—
This book is lovingly dedicated to you.

For every moment you poured out love, even when it was
not returned, and for every battle you faced with grace and
dignity, know that Heaven took notice. Your unwavering
faith, quiet strength, and sacrificial spirit have become
vessels of God's glory in this world.

You are the daughters of the Most High, chosen and
cherished. Though we honor and love you, remember—God
loved you first, and His love surpasses all.

You are never alone. His Spirit walks with you, His hand
upholds you, and His promises sustain you.

Thank you for being light in the darkness, a living
testimony of grace, and a reflection of the Savior's heart.
Your life is a sermon the world desperately needs.

References

**Forbes
100 Most Powerful
Women 2021**

**Some Of The World's
Greatest Women
Achievers**

**U.S. Statistics of
Domestic Violence and
Abused Women**

From The Author

In Heaven, what was violated was God's love, and nothing is more sacred or more vital to Him than love itself. When we gaze into the universe, we're not just seeing stars or galaxies—we're witnessing one of God's dreams made visible. His dreams are vast, immeasurable, and ever-expanding. And if we dare to be like Him, we must also dare to dream beyond measure.

We may never comprehend how long God labored to bring His vision into reality, because He never stops. He is still working, still creating. Among His greatest dreams is this: to see His children's dreams fulfilled, and to have all His children safe at home with Him, living the life He thoughtfully designed—His Kingdom life—marked by unity, love, joy, harmony, and peace.

God never stops dreaming. When one dream is fulfilled, He reaches for the next. Heaven will never be dull because God is endlessly purposeful.

So don't give up on your dreams. Not because of nightmares, doubters, challenges, fears, setbacks, or time. Chase your dreams with confidence in your identity, in who you are *and* whose you are—and with a clear understanding of who the real enemy is.

Both positive and negative influences surround us. But when the positive stands its ground and resists the negative, it produces usable power, just like electricity. As Scripture says: *"Resist the devil, and he will flee from you."* (James 4:7)

If you walk in love, you are the light of the world. Without that light, the world falls into cold darkness. Love gives life; hate steals it without mercy. I pray for all who have suffered loss—of love, of life. The pain is real. But remember: God is love and life—and He cannot die. Love is not lost; it is relocated.

Yes, hate must exist—for now. But hate is simply love gone wrong, a decayed version of something once good. And in the end, love always wins. Hate is self-defeating; it will burn itself out.

God went to unimaginable lengths to reconcile humanity to Himself. No one will be able to ignore or deny the price that was paid. Darkness may seem powerful, but it is only the absence of light. Light will always prevail.

Lucifer, who became Satan, once tried to destroy God's dream. But now, in this generation, God is unveiling truths no other generation has seen. He is revealing why we exist in time and what lies behind the curtain of the unseen. This is *revelation*—the unveiling of what was always there. For this generation, access has been granted.

Remember *The Wizard of Oz*? I won't retell the whole story, but here's the truth: Oz represents the world Satan manipulates. He rules it with illusions of power—through fame, fear, wealth, intimidation, and control. But behind the curtain, he's exposed as powerless. And just like Toto pulled back the veil to reveal the fraud, the book of Revelation pulls back Satan's curtain.

This book is about what's been hidden behind that curtain. And Satan has worked hard to keep believers from reading Revelation by sowing fear and confusion. But what are we afraid of? If you don't know what's behind the curtain, you might end up worshipping in Oz—comfortable in a counterfeit kingdom.

Instead of proclaiming "There's no place like home," many have made themselves at home in a world not built for us. Even Satan knows there's no place like Heaven—but he's trapped in the empire of lust and pride he built. He cannot go home. But you still can.

He hates us—deeply. He hates sharing space with us because we are beloved. One day, the world will see him for what he truly is: stripped, powerless, and ashamed. He wanted to be God, but he is not.

How long will you serve this fraud? Satan is a liar, thief, murderer, and deceiver. Even believers were once intimidated by him—until Jesus exposed him. Jesus pulled back the veil first. He showed us that Satan is not God's equal. He said, *"I saw Satan fall like lightning from Heaven."* (Luke 10:18)

Satan is bankrupt. And God is sending His angels—His holy collectors—to bind him in chains for the Day of Judgment. This will be the greatest courtroom drama of all time: *The Kingdom of God vs. Lucifer, Satan, the Serpent, the Devil, and the False Prophet*—a spiritual RICO case.

How can you defeat an enemy you don't study? Many fear even saying his name, but Jesus didn't shy away—He called Satan out and cast him down. The five-fold ministry—

apostles, prophets, evangelists, pastors, and teachers—is meant to serve as our spiritual military intelligence. If we didn't need them, God wouldn't have appointed them. (Ephesians 4:11)

Don't be fooled. Don't rely on secondhand faith or social media theology. Read the Word of God for yourself. God's Word is the final authority—don't take chances with your soul.

May God bless you and protect you.

Because in the end, there is truly nothing more powerful than love.

Introduction

"You must not know about me?"

The Woman, who is she? Where did she come from?

Created from a realm with no time and placed in a realm of time, not to be subdued by time, but to be the master of time. She has something to do with everything unrevealed.

What a mysterious and majestic creature! When God was ready to produce life, He created His partner, the "Woman." She is the conduit and giver of life, the partner of the producer of life.

Most of life's greatest moments and memories are credited to women. Some of the most significant influences and inspirations for art, music, poetry, songs, and the good things of life are to her credit.

She surrounds us in our work, play, dress, eat, and interact. Primarily love, and she is the source of that love. The created "Producer" turned "Consumer!" How did this happen? These and other questions we will address while taking this journey.

She is something far beyond precious stones and material possessions. She's unlike any other creature or creation. She's more than just pretty looks, a great body, a sex object, or a servant.

She is a voice that deserves to be heard from a different perspective and desperately needs to be heard. How about being a giver of life or a heart fixer, a giver of love? Perhaps, if misguided or mistreated, a "heartbreaker?"

She often carries many secrets throughout her life; anything from infidelity, molestation, rape, abuse, unwanted pregnancies, abortions, and the secret of conceiving a baby from an affair, to having a man raise a child, knowing the child is not his. These are just some of the burdens a woman may carry sometimes to her grave.

She's a leader, friend, partner, companion, cousin, aunt, girlfriend, wife, or mother. Can she be replaced? Will she be replaced? If so, who could or would even attempt to replace her? What is this envy and jealousy of her? Would we love to exist in a world without her? How could we reproduce without her? We would be extinct. Who can compare to the woman?

Imagine a world without a single woman. Would a man still desire to be successful? What about the arts? What would we write or sing about? What would be our subject matter? Would the world be as advanced? Is there anything else that is loved and hated, admired yet envied simultaneously?

Is there anything that can bring more pleasure or pain? Is there any other creature that could make you want to live or die for? What a creation! Would we still do the same foolish things to impress others or repeat the same mistakes? What would our plot for infidelity look like?

Would we be as competitive or motivated? Would society be satisfied with a man in her place or in a same-sex environment?

Can anyone possibly take the place of the woman? She embodies love; without her, we would neither know it nor experience it to the fullest. Unfortunately, the flip side of all this is that the woman is often the target of abuse, such as rape and molestation at a very early age. She's exposed as an innocent little girl to domestic violence.

As she grows, she faces exposure to alcohol, sex, drugs, rape, and physical and mental abuse. She is betrayed and sold into slavery and sex trafficking as a sex slave.

She endures the epitome and personification of rejection, pain, and abandonment. She may be weak sometimes, but she also possesses tremendous strength to survive and cope with unbearable circumstances.

Regardless of her race, religion, social status, or class, she is relentless in character while still nurturing. She's a woman!

Why is she the target of violence and hate crimes, especially if left unprotected? There is a consistent prowler on the loose who's after all generations.

Many victims have been raised in the absence of a loving father. What is the driving force behind this abhorrence? To find the answer, let's journey back to the beginning, before the woman existed. What is the reason for her creation and her purpose?

Why the hate for her? Who could hate such a lovely creation that can make life so good? Why turn her evil? Why use her for evil? Why manipulate her? If she is evil, what happened? Was she always this way, or did a series of events shape her into this thing?

The world's most significant contributors and influencers are a "Wife and a Mother!" These women are mighty. They need to recognize their greatness. If they love you and are supportive, they can be the greatest blessings in your life.

However, if they are against you, nothing and no one but God can help you. Why is it that, for the most part, the mother-in-law and daughter-in-law don't get along? Why are they often at odds? The reason is that the seed (son) is the center of a woman's divine calling.

The battle began with a prophecy regarding the seed. For the mother, he represents the hope of her future and is meant to deliver her. She hopes he will remember how she protected and nurtured him when he could not care for himself.

To the wife, he is her man, lover, provider, protector, and potential father of her children. He is her everything! These two women are battling over the love of one man.

These two powerful women must understand that they rely on each other in unimaginable ways. If they come together in agreement, there are no limits. One sees him as her child, while the other views him as her man.

They both claim to know him; of course, the mother feels she knows him best. The mother, who raised and nurtured him, feels justified at best. However, the wife feels quite the opposite. To her, he is not a child but a man… her man!

These two sources of power are greater than they realize. The mother should understand the wife's feelings, and the wife should understand the mother's.

Why? Because the mother, along with her son, likely once faced pressure to be accepted by the family of the child's father, especially the mother.

Many women get caught up in relationships that are going nowhere. The misunderstanding is this: just because you meet on the same road doesn't mean you are going in the same direction. The woman is in it for the long haul; she's on the interstate, while a guy may be on the road until he comes to the next exit or two.

When she looks around and finds that he is gone, she picks up the next one on the road. She is just a little farther along on her journey and a little more scorned each time she picks up another traveler. This is a great misunderstanding; they should not fight but humble themselves to a greater calling: to help encourage, fortify, and shape this man for greatness.

This help should be according to God's will and the fulfillment of divine purpose and destiny. Most of us live for our time on earth without understanding the bigger picture: eternal life.

We are sowing seeds here, for a greater harvest there.

The love of a mother and wife is the two most distinctive loves; One is different from the other. The love was customized for the two, never meant to be the same love.

Love is never meant to be compromised but given to the maximum because there are two different kinds of love, uniquely shared! Just think about it for a minute: from the beginning of Adam and Eve, when they were in the Garden of Eden, to the humble beginnings of a child born in the little town of Bethlehem. This virgin birth changed life, as we know it, forever and started time over from B.C. to A.D. to the present, since his days on earth.

What year is this, or what do we call it? Giving birth to greatness is a common part of her very existence. Think of every great leader and life changer, whether good or evil, small or significant, they came through a woman!

How about the woman who has given up on love because of her past hurts, pains, and disappointments? She is an easy target for pimps, wannabe pimps, scammers, and hustlers. It's easy to use, manipulate, and control her. Usually, the perpetrator looks for this kind of woman. He is skilled and trained to cater to her insecurities without seeming to notice her insecurity at all. He's often persistent and appears kind and overly understanding.

This causes an inexperienced woman to let her guard down and allow him into her life. He will initially give her things as bait to win her over. Most times, what he had was acquired from other women. Some women may be the same, but if so, it's because of the past hurts caused by a man.

Every day, when we go about our lives, no matter what that may entail, look around; every human being is here because a woman somewhere gave her life to give life!

Man has the seed, and it needs to be planted to bring forth life. Life depends on the woman, and where that seed is planted, it will produce life. Who else shapes and molds the course of history and its greatness?

Whether in the confines of a small house cooking dinner or bathing her children while getting them ready for bed, or perhaps sending them off to school, helping with homework, and sometimes even working two or three jobs to make ends meet, these are the many natural facets of a woman.

From work to play, she is a force to be reckoned with. She faces challenges in many ways, sometimes unimaginable, from the beginning of her life. She holds so many secrets that she does not think to share. As much as she gives, she withholds so much, for fear of being judged or frowned upon. Some of her experiences are so shameful that she would never tell a soul. We need to hear her story!

No matter how close you may think you are to her or how much you may think you know about her, she still holds things in her mind and heart as a safe place. She gives so much of herself; by doing so, she has potential or greatness in her arms.

It doesn't matter if she is feeding with milk from her breasts, giving herself away for the sake of so many others. She represents the nature of God in many ways.

She is nurturing by nature. Whether it is the next

president or a mass murderer, her love is, for the most part, unconditional. Look at successful men over the years, and when it's time to give thanks, recognition, or honor, the first thing, no matter how old the male is, you will hear is, "Hey Mom, or Thanks Mom, I love you, Mom."

No matter how much the father has contributed and provided, it doesn't matter; his very nature and or spirit is reaching out to the mother from within. That's why most men who have had no relationship or a bad relationship with their mother are overachievers or the opposite, underachievers!

Either gentle or callous! Very faithful or promiscuous... committed or players...the unfaithful! She's always sowing seeds into the spirit of all in her presence. "

Complicated", she is, but she was created from complex circumstances. Therefore, this makes her a force to be reckoned with, making her the most powerful creature to date in this present world. Look out and get ready because here she comes...

Joseph Brice

I AM INIQUITY

Chapter 1

We are in the third heaven because there is no higher place to be. This is it, the highest. This being is running everything like the CEO of heaven. Now, you get the feeling that God is everywhere, but He can make His personal appearances known or unknown. God is a spirit (unseen) but appears in light form at times. God is the King, the Boss, and the Owner.

I kind of understand, but I lack understanding at the same time. I still have memories of what I was taught and learned at home, in school, and church, but nothing quite like this. There are some things I'm able to connect with because of the Bible, while most have no reference at all.

This is not a dream; it's real. I have no control over leaving or staying; I don't even have feelings either way… I'm just going with the flow. I can't help but think, why am I allowed to be here? This place is an eternity where there is no time, just a good life and living. God created this being for His own pleasure; it was created to serve.

Everything at this point was created by the spoken word of God. God would think it, meditate on it, and bring it forth out of Himself. This being created by God is in charge, and the only one who is greater than him is God. So, get this: this is the god whom everyone can see, made by the spirit of God that cannot be seen in a physical form, but as light. It is similar to an X-ray or MRI; something is seen and discovered in this being, but God is the only one who can see it.

* * *

This being is smart, intelligent, educated, and wise beyond comprehension, beautiful, talented, powerful, gifted, anointed, and trusted by God to run things and be accountable for all things in heaven that are important to Him. I'm learning that this being was not created to have an opinion, but to serve and do as it is told or instructed. Accountability and responsibility are its makeup. One day, if we may call it that because there is no darkness here, a discovery was found in this being's heart. While serving and faithful to its assignments, it was challenged with something; the unthinkable, "Jealousy!"

Jealousy became its secret companion. While it worked every day and served God faithfully, it was simultaneously unfaithful—this was the first adultery. This was the first hypocrisy! While "it" thinks it has a secret, God knows and is waiting for it to confess so it can be dealt with, yet the being conceals it. Without the annulment of the seed "jealousy," iniquity is inevitable, but how can it know this? It can't without being honest. Though it is the CEO running everything and having all things in its power, somehow that isn't enough. Now all this is new in heaven.

Even though it's having these issues, it's carrying out its duties. The angels are in control. I'm discovering that its thought pattern is now its meditation. The thoughts are seeds; by the time they reach the heart, the only next thing is manifesting them or bringing them into full fruition. Now, secretly, it has opinions concerning how God does things and assignments given, but it doesn't share its feelings with God —just the angels.

This is the beginning of secrets in heaven. Somehow, the being knows it's not innocent because it does not share its opinions with God. It is now deviating slightly from God's plan, staying close to the original but with a little twist, making changes here and there with some support from its circle of angels. This marks the birth of division and the seed of what we now know as confusion. The changes are not drastic but are noticeable.

They are subtle. Some of the angels are questioning their reasoning for the deviations. They know enough about their God to understand that this is not exactly what He said they should do.

So now there is a noticeable division among the angels, and all this Being is saying is, "I am in charge here!" For the first time, I'm seeing how easy it is to follow what you can see rather than what you can't…even if it's wrong. It's similar to being a "licensed driver" and having a supervisor in a company vehicle with you while they're telling you to go through a red light because there's no traffic.

The law is what I know is right, but it's not tangible; it is only words, while my supervisor is right there. Now, my supervisor understands the law and the conditions under which we are insured and legally protected, but insists that I obey him. He tells me not to worry about the law and the powers that cannot see us.

His justification is that it will save us time, and the boss will be pleased that we arrived early. If I run the light and get caught, I can be penalized and charged as a licensed driver. Still, if I don't, my supervisor can manipulate the situation and terminate me on insubordination charges. It would be my word against his, and he has the upper hand because of his position and authority. What do I do? Do I fight for what's right or give in to my immediate supervisor?

The Bible speaks about how one-third of the angels were cast down from heaven with Lucifer; that means one out of three, and now I can see how and why. I have memories of my experiences on earth regarding my own life.

It is easy to follow the god or tangible thing we can see over the one we can't, because we need faith to believe in what's not right there in front of us. We do it all the time, as children, with our parents, by listening to our friends. How about in school or at our jobs, when we run around with friends? How about the laws of the land?

This is the seed for the potential for leaders to become corrupted. Most do not start that way. Once the seed takes root, it will begin to produce fruit. This happens to law enforcement, lawyers, judges, politicians, bankers, and preachers. Even the drug dealer and murderer started innocently as somebody's baby.

Still, someone or something is always trying to sell us a lie—tempting us with evil and rebellion against the order of right things! Even if it happens, it's not too late if we seek to make it right. If we do not deal with it at the time, we will surely confront it in eternity! What about the unfaithful partner in a marriage?

What about politics—the lists go on and on. Why am I seeing this? It's a heavy load to carry. I fear I will never be the same after this, and how will I live knowing this? The word also says, "There is nothing new under the sun, and what is, already has been."

My question is, what is the connection between Heaven and Earth, and what role does mankind have in all of this? I'm witnessing the birth of a "takeover spirit!" This being wants to take over God's kingdom and establish it as its own, using everything that it has learned from God against God.

It now wants to be greater than God himself. God is the "Most High God," it says in its heart, "I will raise my throne above the throne of the Most High God." Now the Most High God says, iniquity is found in the heart of Lucifer! This thing called "iniquity" is the cruelty of using all the things of God for yourself. Self-gain is iniquity!

Iniquity is not just a sin; it is the sin of wickedness and wrongdoing through the plotting of a hostile takeover of something that does not belong to you.

It is the betrayal of someone you helped or gave life to, someone who would not have had a life without you, and who then turns on you while working for you, becoming your competitor or enemy.

Not only that, but they seek to destroy you! It is the misappropriation or theft from you while pretending to be loyal and working for you, making decisions supposedly in your best interest, but, in truth, looking out for themselves.

It's the sin of "covetousness and desperation" for your power and authority, which is designed for the building up of lives and is now desired by them to use for selfish gain and destroy life. It takes a while to appear to give; it lusts after you rather than loving you, it tears you down; it does not build you up.

Pride is its root, which produces evil fruit such as rebellion against the natural order of things. It loves the gifts more than the giver.

It loves the things of God more than God Himself; it loves money and power more than anything and is willing to do anything for it.

It is the fruit of hate and cruelty. It's a senseless war that sacrifices thousands of lives for its selfish gain. It divides and diminishes; it's the thief, supplying and catering to greed. It's a lie wrapped in a beautiful package, but in the end, it brings hurt and destruction.

It preys on the innocent and sacrifices the needy. It's the "tyrant" of your past, the "terrorist" of your present, and the "villain" of your future. It's the dream killer. It moves in darkness with a skilled eye to do evil. It loves the dark rather than illuminating the light for all to see.

It's the guardian of deep, dark secrets that have taken countless innocent lives. It's both the lawbreaker and the lawmaker, simultaneously judging those who are innocent and have been made guilty to pay; so clever to also be the collector. This is iniquity!

It's the hate for the God who created everything that it lusts after. It's contrary to the will of God and His creation; its greed cannot be satisfied. It's selfish and self-centered… oh yes, I am "iniquity" and will sacrifice anyone and everyone to save only me.

It is the first hypocrite, saying one thing to your face and something different behind your back. It is jealous and crueler than the grave. It's the reason to cheat, and it's the origin of the cheater.

It's unfaithful to the faithful. It's the rapist the molester, iced with murder. I am the one who gave Lucifer the plan to attempt to overthrow God's throne and take His kingdom over.

I am "iniquity," and I was supposed to be a secret. However, before I could accomplish any of these things, God discovered me deep within Lucifer's heart. I am Iniquity.

Yes, it's just me! I was growing in Lucifer's heart like a baby in the womb. Lucifer was cast out of heaven before I could be openly revealed. Cast down to the earth is where I will be born and grow.

I will grow through all generations. I am a spirit that needs a vessel to work through so all can see me. Many think the evil that is done is their creative idea, but it could not be accomplished without me as the controlling partner.

I am every face, seeking every race, and some of the greatest figures in history, who are famous, were used by me. I am the great tester and tempter of those who think they love God, and if truth be told, I am just being me.

I have no love for God, and He knows this, but above all, I can't be judged by anyone because I have judged myself. I'm just being me. If you are not working for God, you are working for me, and with that being said, you're working against Him by using all of His gifts and talents to glorify and elevate yourself while destroying others and stealing His glory.

You know what you are in private quarters! Here's another secret: I seek those who think they love God, but truth be told, again, they love His things; they love His stuff.

You are the easiest target. Listen, I, iniquity, am not one of God's creations, but I was conceived because Lucifer is my father; he had me first in heaven. My parents are Lucifer and Satan. It doesn't sound very clear, but don't let it be, because they are not divided.

That's why they get so much done. I am "iniquity," and I use people to do the job. Listen, no matter my intent, nothing that I do will work unless you have "the lust of the flesh, the lust of the eye, and the pride of life." To possess these three, you cannot have love or love the truth.

Truth and I don't get along too well; I cannot share the same space with love, and truth is my enemy. I use many leaders to deceive people because I don't care about life; I care about money and things; that's the power I seek!

I have many preachers, pastors, and false prophets working for me as well. For those who love money, this is how we work together so well. They take me everywhere with them, and we do the job together. Take an iniquity test: who are you working for? What are your motives for your goals?

Are you giving life or taking it away, helping people or oppressing them, building them up for the better or tearing them down, robbing them of their hopes and dreams? When you leave this life, will God want to reward you or destroy you?

Are you a lover or a hater, a giver of life, or a taker of life? Iniquity results from the misappropriation of the (anointing) gifts of God. Life is a gift, the mind is a gift, the body is a gift; like singing or inventing, being a leader, a father, a mother, children… these are all gifts, and even sex! How are we using our gifts?

Undoubtedly, many are for our pleasure, but none are, nor will they ever be, meant to hurt God or His people. Never allow your circumstances to cause God to regret that you were ever born or to look at you with sorrow; if I may use such a word about a predetermined, superlative, and supreme being.

Sin is the transgression of divine law, specifically any act regarded as such, particularly a willful or deliberate violation of some religious or moral principle, a regrettable action, or a behavioral lapse. Sin can be committed out of weakness or ignorance, but once acknowledged, it can be addressed accordingly and forgiven, cast away as if it never happened; this is the power of repentance and forgiveness!

A sinner may be too weak to walk in divine order but can and will seek help or forgiveness, striving to change or at least to turn away, if only by intention.

God hears and understands a sinner's prayer because we are all sinners, saved by grace if we call on the name of the Lord.

Some may have believed otherwise, opening a very wide door for pride! Iniquity means gross injustice or wickedness; it refers to someone who knows the truth but insists on acting based on their beliefs to destroy life, including that of a person, marriage, family, or even a race or people. Those who commit such acts do not act alone but are guided by a wicked origin.

Look at history for examples; many facets of life were destroyed by the arrogance and pride of the wicked, working for the "wicked one!" Those who are on a mission and determined to destroy life have a father, and they do their father's will.

Remember this: the "wicked" will never repent or turn from their evil ways. They will never willingly compensate anyone for the wickedness committed against them. Equal to this is another group on an assignment: those determined to save lives. Good cannot afford to be passive while evil exists.

These two will never agree because they are determined not to change but to please their fathers. Ultimately, each father will reward his children for deeds done in his honor. Make no mistakes; we are all here for a reason before entering eternity. This battle has an origin; it started in a kingdom. Thus, these battles are records of the greatest warriors ever, as they were taught by God for defense and protection...not a Revolt!

The Kingdom of the Highest God! We don't like to talk about it, but it is ignorant not to do so. Why are we here? Who are we? The bottom line is this: eternity is too long not to become educated and to be concerned about certain things.

Life all around us represents an incomprehensible level of intellect and intelligence, and it is too great for us not to be interested. Is there something greater than us? Are we on our own? Is life over when we die?

Will we answer or give an account of our life here on earth? Think about the countless people who lived here before us and where they are now. Is there good and evil in all races? Now that we have talked about sins and iniquity, let's take a trip back to this place called "heaven."

This is the beginning of the account of "iniquity." It is about the first rebellion, the first division, the first separation of loved ones and family, the first divorce, and the first related pain connected to losing something or someone you love.

The reality is that God is a loving dictator, similar to a loving father or mother with their children; father and mother know best. Everything we see comes from something in the spirit we can't perceive. The structure of the family comes from above, not from beneath.

The one who made or created us should have the right to guide and instruct us throughout life. It's about trust; is it for a better way of life and its continuation? According to creation, everything has a particular purpose.

The sun, the moon, the stars, the plants, the birds, the animals, the insects, the air, the carbon, the water, the fire, and humanity—of course, it goes on and on. What if some superior being created everything that exists out of a vision for its pleasure and glory?

It has to adopt a somewhat dictatorial nature for order and protocol to be established. Otherwise, everything would be in chaos or destructively disarrayed. What if everything that exists suddenly began to have an opinion about its creative origin or purpose? What if the moon were dissatisfied with being the moon and had the potential power to change the position of the sun?

Imagine the orange tree wishing to be an apple tree out of jealousy, yet it hasn't considered the long-term consequences of wanting to change its life solely based on selfish desires. Lucifer held the office of "anointed cherub," being in charge without God Himself as ruler.

This means that no one in the kingdom had power and authority except for God. Only on the throne did God show that He was greater than Lucifer. This is a beautiful place filled with love and harmony; who would think that there might be a potential problem with all of this? That sounds familiar.

To the woman, the greatest secret kept from you of all time is that "I hate you!" I hate you and have hated you since the first time I laid my eyes on you! I can't explain it, but I do! What is this hate thing? It's a newly founded overwhelming emotion.

Where did it come from? What is its origin? It was not here before, or maybe it was, but nothing brought it out of me or activated it until I saw the woman. I thought I was a loving creature. Throughout eternity, I had been a loving servant. I was known for my love and how much I expressed it. What happened? It started great!

Why do I feel this way? Where is this coming from? Why won't I fix it? Can it be fixed, and if so, how?

I knew I was starting to feel particular about God, but I didn't think much of it. I felt a little envy here and there, wishing I had what God has, that He were me, or that some of His stuff was mine.

It started as praise and compliments, and I was sincere, but somewhere along the way, I changed; my praise had become an expected offering of gratitude for my life, job, and position. Serving God while feeling a certain way about yourself is not love.

Love seemed to have a secret and did not want anyone to know, not even its originator. God is love, so why wouldn't Lucifer go to God about his issue?

Yes, this is the first recorded instance of heaven having an issue, and it's found in the heart. Lucifer's secret is becoming harder to keep. Every day, he feels this and doesn't know what it is. It seems to be growing. It started as a seed, but now it's becoming like a giant oak tree.

Therefore, if you have a problem with someone, especially a newly discovered issue, you should go to them, not to everyone else, and talk about it. It is easier to remove a seed than a tree! Hate is "love twisted," a seed looking for good ground so that it may grow.

It is much easier to eliminate the seed than the tree because hate manifests as the tree. This tree will produce fruit in its season and will bring destruction.

Now, with pride and arrogance working together, it's a cruel and awaited bomb, ready to kill love at all costs without any remorse. Hate needs a birthing place for its display of actions; this is where we find people who will commit horrific acts, and it doesn't bother them—they are the devil's seed...the produced fruit.

Remember the woman as the "great wonder in heaven." The dragon hated her and was very angry with her, but for what reason? Hate is evil and needs no reason to commit its acts. The creature didn't even know the woman. This is the spiritual account of a place long before we, as human beings, came on the scene. We are vessels that these spirits seek to use to give visual accounts of these actions. They need someone to work through. So, how could anything harbor such hate for someone or something they've never known?

Therefore, we must acknowledge that there is a wisdom or source far above mankind and humanity. What about when we hate someone of another race without knowing them? We've already concluded them based on what?

Past information, what we've been taught, or what we've heard about them. What makes us so fearful of the unknown? It must be fear. How can we hate someone based on their beliefs, gender, religion, culture, national origin, skin color, or anything else?

This is spiritual ignorance! These issues are the fruits of a root from a much-needed reformed heaven. I can only imagine the reactions to a devil's family being exposed! God prepared a place for us like we would for each other. Whether good or evil, we all strive to provide a good home or environment for our children and family.

Then why wouldn't our Heavenly Father provide a place for us? If we hate one another, even enough to kill, simply because of race or religion, then go home desiring good for our families, then how much more will God do good for us, being that He is good? There's no evil in Him, nor can there be. We are all tempted with knowledge to do good or evil. Why? Simply because of our nature to want knowledge, good, and evil. It is our inherited nature from the beginning of the Garden of Eden.

We all have this potential; our flesh is the enemy. Every day, we make choices and are tempted by seemingly random happenings or circumstances to cross the line. Many people are in prison, not because all are evil; it would be ridiculous to believe anything of the sort. But many cases are because of the heat of the moment, whether fueled by hate or love!

Some are from pride, not wanting to seem like a pushover or soft. Many are crimes of passion when in a love relationship, something went wrong, and somebody didn't walk away. What about getting caught up, maybe helping a friend?

Many arise from hurt and disappointment. Some stem from seeking revenge. Others are made in an attempt to achieve a better life, but employ the wrong methods or unlawful practices to do so. Many have been manipulated into doing the devil's work without even realizing it.

There are also cases where individuals align themselves with Satan to fulfill his will, and no matter what you do for them, they remain committed to doing evil, which pleases their father, the devil. The reality is this: God will have the final say. What if this life were our only hope?

Then we would be miserable. Every case will one day be presented before the Great White Throne of God or the Judgment Seat of Christ and be judged by the "True Judge."

This Judge accepts no bribes—he's righteous! God and His children will judge even the judges and lawyers for how they handled His people.

This is why Jesus told his followers to visit captives or prisons, because many of them were there unjustly, and some were puppets on the puppeteer's strings and didn't know it. Working for your enemy the devil, tricked, hoodwinked, bamboozled, and pimped by the pimp while trying to be a pimp.

The reality is this: you can't keep anything that he gave you or promised you anyway because it's not here to keep. After he uses you up, he goes to the next sucker or victim, and by the time they catch on, he's moved on again.

His job is to keep it moving, from generation to generation. That is also why Jesus said, "To be wise as serpents but harmless as doves." This is not a posture of weakness, but of brilliance, knowing that if you stay ahead of your enemy, you become the beneficiary of all his stuff.

Be wise enough to know you are dealing with snakes and outsmart them. Do not join or become like them. Some have reacted to a lie or lies and have gotten in trouble.

When we respond rather than resist, we get played! The non-violent act is an act of God, which requires the most extraordinary courage and strength of all, besides death itself, and it was brilliant! This act called Satan out and exposed him! When we look back in history, we can see how furious the devil was at God's strategy, which was disguised as weakness!

You're not a big person for taking advantage of the weak and helpless. Jesus could call thousands of angels to destroy his enemies, but he didn't. One angel has the power of more than 180,000 men, just one angel! The angels were and are at Jesus's beck and call. Imagine them hanging on the balconies of heaven, waiting for a signal from their master and king.

Mankind, the devil, and his demons would not have stood a chance of survival. The demons asked Jesus, "Have you come to destroy us? We know you, Holy One of the Most High God." Jesus told the demon, "Come out of the man" (Mark 5:1-20).

What's impressive to me is that the devil and demons knew who Jesus was, but the priests and preachers of the temple, the so-called "holy men," did not recognize him. It was the church that had Jesus killed; the Roman government merely carried out the order.

The procurator Pilate tried many times to set Jesus free because he found no fault in the man, but the religious leaders were persistent and relentless in their desire to have Jesus killed. Those who preached and prayed for the coming of the Lord, the Messiah, did not welcome him when he arrived.

Many answered prayers will not look like we imagined, so we are tempted to reject our answer from God and wait for another. These so-called "Men of God" were evil; they were murderers!

Preaching about God while hating what God loves—His children. Where do you think these evil men are right now? Certainly not, "Resting In Peace!" When they could not rid themselves of Jesus through their lies, they turned to politics to get the job done.

We should be careful about how we handle God and politics. We can't mix lies with truth without facing God's consequences. Many wish they could warn families and friends of the misfortunes awaiting them when they leave this world.

Hell is a part of eternity's jail. It's where booking and processing occur, preparing those going to trial and a court date.

Don't let anyone lie to you and make you feel good about evil.

Don't sign that check of lies and hate, seeking to destroy someone else's life while you hang out and party off that blood money. God is the judge who takes no bribes. We all get our day in court.

Throw yourself at the mercy of God's court right now and accept the plea Jesus is offering. If we don't take the "Plea" of guilt, we will go to trial on this side of the court, where we will be tried, found guilty, and convicted! Again, the solution to this problem is, "REPENTANCE!"

Please take the deal. Jesus died in our place. If we don't take the deal, everything we've done wrong against God and His righteousness will be judged. Sometimes we don't know what's in our hearts until we find ourselves in a place we never imagined and go all the way left. We sometimes do shameful things and try to cover them up for life.

You cannot afford, in these times, to accept lies or support lies to make yourself and/or someone feel good. How often have we heard, "We are all God's children?" This is not what God said. "All souls are mine," says God. "The soul that sins will die" (Ezekiel 18: 4, 20). Let no one deceive you by any means: for that day will not come unless the rebellion comes first, and the man of lowliness is revealed, the son of destruction. (2Thessalonians 2:1-12).

For this reason, we are not born in eternity first, but in time, in this world, to reveal all hearts, good or evil, righteous or unrighteous. Don't let anyone deceive you. It is not enough to go to church; we have witnessed churches being shut down during this pandemic. As believers, stop saying, "Rest In Peace"; we will be accountable after this life—yes, everyone.

Know who your Father is. Don't allow anyone to deceive you. All those cases judged with biases and lies are not the final authority. God will judge in every case: the cases that made it to court and those cases that were swept under the rug.

Even the judges, lawyers, prosecutors, district attorneys, witnesses, and jurors will one day be judged for every case they ruled and judged. "Woe to those who plan iniquity, to those who plot evil on their beds! At morning's light, they carry it out because it is in their power to do it" (Micah 2:1).

Being careful of what side of the law you're on, right or wrong, justice or corrupted involvement? God will give all of us our day in the real Supreme Court in His Kingdom.

Woe to the ones who took an oath to serve the people and God concerning justice, and those who swore on the Bible to tell the truth but lied for money, among other reasons, are not righteous. Imagine all the evil people who thought they had gotten away with this world because of their connections and hookups, only to find they had a court appearance waiting for them in eternity.

A judge who takes no bribes and goes by His book in all cases, no matter who you are. So many influential people wish they could come back and warn their people and families of this place of justice. "Then I beg you, Father, send Lazarus to my family, for I have five brothers.

Let him warn them, so they will not also come to this place of torment" (Luke 16: 19-31). Trust and believe in a God who is eternal, and who judges all people and generations.

It doesn't matter how rich or poor, powerful or otherwise a person is in this world; it's only temporary, and what's their end? "Then I acknowledged my sin to you and did not cover up my iniquity." I said, "I will confess my transgressions to the Lord." And you forgave my sin (Psalms 32:5).

"When a righteous man turns away from his righteousness and commits iniquity, and dies in them; for his iniquity that he hath done shall he die." (Ezekiel 18:26)

"Rejoice not in iniquity, but rejoice in the truth;" (1 Corinthians 13:6) "Surely he hath borne our griefs, and carried our sorrows: yet we did esteem him stricken, smitten of God, and afflicted. But he was wounded for our transgressions, he was bruised for our iniquities: the chastisement of our peace was upon him; and with his stripes, we are healed.

All we like sheep have gone astray; we have turned everyone to his own way, and the LORD hath laid on him the iniquity of us all." (Isaiah 53:4-6) Iniquity is mentioned in over 262 scriptures in the Bible. This word is important enough for a conversation.

I'm making this insert because I had gospel leaders saying, "They never knew what iniquity was or is. Is it a sin? Or just another word for sin?"

The first mention of INIQUITY was in the heart. It was found in Lucifer's heart. He was the holy and anointed cherub of the Most High God. The heart is the first womb. This was the birthplace of iniquity. Iniquity attempted to hide it from God, like a child hiding from their parents that she is pregnant. Question: How did iniquity get there?

Answer: A seed, planted by the lust of the eye, lust of the flesh (world).
Question: Where did the seed come from? Answer: Pride provided the seed—a proud look, a lying tongue, and hands that shed innocent blood.

The angels were to stay away from pride, as Adam and Eve were to stay away from the forbidden fruit. Lucifer never lied to God until he committed adultery with pride. Question: Who is the father?

Answer: Pride is the father. God is NOT the Father! God talked to Lucifer about the pregnancy; it was determined that the baby would need to have a father in its life. Lucifer's pride grew within him/her, and its name is "Iniquity."

What's so dangerous about this is pride will not listen to anybody. Lucifer chose Pride, and they were cast down from heaven to the earth. Iniquity can grow and multiply; it is a part of your heart, whereas Sin is committed… It is an action… something you have done, will do, and/or will continue to do… a job.

"The wages of SIN is death, but the gift of God is eternal life." We all have been given the right to choose. Choose this day whom you will serve: Life or Death…?

BETRAYAL

Chapter 2

Betrayal is one of the deepest wounds a person can endure. Throughout life's journey, betrayal is a shadow we cannot escape. At some point, everyone faces it, leaving us with the inevitable question: *why?* Why does betrayal feel so much like death itself? Why is no one immune to it?

It can come from anyone — a father, mother, brother, sister, spouse, friend, partner, business associate, doctor, lawyer, judge, teacher, preacher, or politician. Sometimes, the harshest betrayal comes from within ourselves. It lurks, hidden in the people we trust the most.

If you haven't yet been betrayed, keep living — it will come.

Those who have tasted betrayal know a pain they never thought possible. The heart doesn't just break; it shatters into a thousand pieces, leaving scars that never fully heal. *Betrayal is the worst thing ever.*

The first act of betrayal was Lucifer's defiance against God — a betrayal not only of his Creator but also of himself and countless others who followed him. In the same way, when a wife betrays her husband, she first betrays herself, then him, and ultimately their children, born and unborn.

The devastation of being betrayed by the one you loved most can feel impossible to overcome. For some, it becomes a wound that never closes, leading to depression, despair, and even thoughts of ending their own life. The tragedy is worsened by the realization that the betrayer often moves on without remorse, while you are left imprisoned by a grief that refuses to let go.

Betrayal is a brutal teacher; its lessons are written in the deepest parts of the heart.

You must trust in something greater than the moment you're

trapped in.
First, you must face the painful truth: the one who betrayed you was driven by something deeper and darker than you may understand. You'll know if they have become one with that darkness because evil feels nothing. If the betrayer makes no effort to make things right, it's a clear sign: they are lost to it.

The hardest, yet most necessary thing you must do is forgive — and move forward. Forgiveness is not for them; it's for you. Your best days are not behind you — they are still ahead.

Here's the reality we often forget: **God Himself was betrayed first.**
Yes, it's true — even though it's hard to grasp. In heaven, Lucifer betrayed God while smiling in His face, harboring dark plots and secret rebellion in his heart. I'll go into deeper detail later in this book, but for now,

God is love — the very definition of it. He loved Lucifer with all His heart, giving him every blessing, every opportunity. And yet, despite being love itself, God was still betrayed.
I believe we often overlook the pain God suffered long before humanity existed. We think of betrayal as something only humans endure, but God's heart was the first to break. And it is because of that betrayal, we exist — born into a plan of redemption forged from divine heartbreak.

When Lucifer betrayed Him, God was wounded—and alone. There was no one to counsel Him, no one to comfort Him. So he became His own counselor, His own healer.
In His pain, God could have reacted with immediate destruction—wiping Lucifer and the fallen angels from existence. Instead, He chose a higher path: He regrouped. He created an infinite plan—one that would demand relentless focus, deep creativity, sacrifice, and unimaginable patience. Trust had been broken, and now every soul would be tested, without even knowing it.

Sadly, many religious teachings have diluted who God truly is. They've offered us shallow versions that miss His depth, love, and grief. This is why it is so important to champion the true message: **not religion, but the Kingdom; not tradition, but a real relationship.**

We need to build a relationship with God while we are here on earth, rather than waiting to get to know Him only when we are dying or about to embark on the voyage into eternity. Since He made us in His image and likeness, it means that we are like Him in many ways and have a natural desire for Him, albeit without the wickedness.

There is nothing we go through that God has not experienced first; He truly understands. Therefore, it is important to remain spiritually connected to Him.

Many have committed murder against those who betrayed them out of anger and the indescribable emotions they were feeling at the time. This is why they refer to such acts as "crimes of passion."

Many are in prison or have been incarcerated and served "time" because of this horrific experience. Upon discovering betrayal, so many don't quite know or understand how to handle the confusion, fear, hurt, and pain. When it happens to you, these feelings and experiences are all new.

How do you go on when the one who betrayed you is walking away with your most valuable asset, aside from life itself: your heart? Reflect on the wisdom of God; in this, we will find that we are more like Him than we realize if we can endure the test of betrayal.

Even if we mess up, it can be fixed if we give it to Him instead of trying to resolve it ourselves. There is a supernatural power in forgiveness! Let me explain. Despite God's power, He withdrew, knowing what was in Lucifer's heart. He spared him by granting him space, hoping Lucifer would change his mind and heart.

Take the time to think about what you're about to do. You are about to destroy a family for feelings, lust, or greed; this is incredibly selfish. This is how you will recognize the devil's children: they will always choose lust over love, promiscuity over commitment, and a destructive good time at the expense of others who trust them.

The betrayer does not want to sacrifice; it always wants more, is never satisfied, and is willing to sacrifice everyone else to get what it desires. The betrayer doesn't care how many people will be hurt; he or she is too selfish to see the bigger picture.

Lucifer's betrayal went far beyond what could be seen; it would need a module to contain it; his betrayal would have atomic effects. He must go if he refuses to be defused. In other words, come clean, confess, and forsake it, and God will fix it! No one could see or understand the hurt and pain that God endured.

God's heart was broken for the first time because it came from His greatest love, His heavenly family. It is impossible for us to feel anything as the originators because time is when things are manifested in bodily form or given a face. How do you put a face to a broken heart? How could anyone or anything know the magnitude of God's pain if there's no model for it, then it's hidden? How many of us have carried pain from a loved one and concealed it?

It's easy to betray someone who loves you because of their trust; they trust you with their life. When they give you their heart, they give you their life. God put all that He cared about in the hands of Lucifer because love trusts and is not reserved.

God stepped away from Lucifer and gave him space to change his heart, but instead, Lucifer took this as a sign of weakness. God is not weak; He is long-suffering, merciful, and patient, hoping for a repented (changed) heart.

In other words, God was willing to forgive and start over, but Lucifer made this impossible. He had a hidden agenda, and it wasn't beneficial for him to fix it! Lucifer was so set on having his own life that he sacrificed the whole kingdom of heaven to do so. The angels, who thought they knew Lucifer, saw a side of him that they didn't know. For real, who is this person?

Have you ever been with someone for years, and they turned on you, doing things you can hardly wrap your mind around? You're thinking, "Were we ever married?" I gave my life for this person and sacrificed for them. I've been sleeping with this; I gave my life to this.

It can literally make you sick. Do you want to know where the devil comes from? He came from God, and Lucifer's relationship went wicked due to betrayal, with God not judging or destroying him. God spared His "now enemy," who at one time was His greatest friend.

Justice said to kill him, but mercy said to put him out and see if he'll turn from evil and accept forgiveness.

When Lucifer was cast down to Earth, he transformed into the serpent and experienced great wrath and anger! "Woe unto the earth's inhabitants, for Satan is cast down with great wrath and vengeance." Consider the account of Jesus's life, birth, and battle with the religious leaders who ran the temple. The temple was considered "The House of God," and Jesus was not welcomed there.

This should tell us something. The religious leaders in the Bible during this time represent Lucifer and the fallen angels. These spirits work through humans to express and expose the true heart! How could we know what transpired in the hearts of these angels if God did not establish some way for them to be revealed? This is what the Earth is for; there is no other planet quite like this one; it's for this specific purpose...to uncover secrets.

Every situation is not new but relevant to something hidden in heaven, where it did not have a chance to show itself; all things hidden must be brought into the open or revealed. One of the most famous, if not the most famous, betrayals was that of Judas and Jesus.

This man was a disciple and devout follower of Christ. He became very close to Jesus and was even the ministry's treasurer, which signifies that Jesus trusted him. Jesus took him under his wing and taught him priceless lessons about life on earth and the world to come.

What's so amazing is that these people had been waiting for hundreds of years for the prophecy of the coming of the Messiah. These followers were the first to know the secrets of heaven and the business of God and His kingdom.

Jesus allows Judas into his world, even closer than his own earthly family. In one particular instance, Jesus's followers informed him about a group of people trying to push through the crowd to reach him. They told the disciples who they were, and it was Jesus's mother, brothers, and sisters.

Surely this would get them through, especially after being verified by Jesus; however, after receiving the message, his response was, "Who is my mother?" I'll tell you, "He who does the will of my Father is my brother, sister, and mother"(Matthew 12:50).

Judas heard this while walking with Jesus; he recognized how serious and focused this man was about his mission. Jesus' greatest lesson to his followers was the message of God's love and love for them (John 3:16). He demonstrated love and emphasized how important it was for them to love one another (John 13:34, 15:17).

No matter how much love you give, there will be hate; this isn't to say to stop loving. Look at Jesus' example of how to love and overcome hate. No matter what, Jesus continued to love on purpose. Sometimes the people in your circle don't get it, but continue loving; someone will appreciate you.

Why did they hate Jesus so much? Because they manifest the iniquity hidden in the hearts of Lucifer and the fallen angels? No matter what he did, they found fault or something to condemn him for.

They used the Temple for a glorious life apart from the Roman Empire. They didn't love God or His people; they loved His stuff, money, and power! When Jesus came and did the actual work of God, this exposed them, and they couldn't tolerate that because they had deceived the people into believing they were "real men of God."

They were crooked, and Jesus was straight as a plumb line. The line he walked revealed the crooked ways in which they were leading. People began to follow Jesus; without a building or physical church, he preached and reached people everywhere. They chose to follow him to the desert, where they could hear the truth, rather than listen to the hype in a beautiful and comfortable Temple, because they were hungry for righteousness!

These temple priests were regarded as the righteous men of their race and culture, proudly referring to themselves as the seed of Abraham and the Law of Moses.

These are the same men who used Judas to betray Jesus. Then one of the twelve, called Judas Iscariot, went to the chief priests, and said to them, "What will you give me and I will deliver him to you?" and covenanted with him for thirty pieces of silver, and from that time he sought opportunity to betray him(Mathew 26:14-16).

Some people are with you for opportunity and money. They start out believing they are with you, but when their love for money kicks in or their lust for something you possess arises, they forget that you are a person with feelings, not just an opportunity.

Many people think money is evil, but that's not true. The Bible says, "The love of money is the root of all evil: which while some coveted after, they have erred from the faith, and pierced themselves through with many sorrows," (1 Timothy 6:10).

Judas stopped trusting the Lord and living by faith; he took matters into his own hands. In other words, God took too long to bless him. If you sow, you will reap. Judas betrays Jesus but never enjoys the money, which brings him sorrow and death. Despite all that Jesus invested in him, he did not trust the process (John chapter 15). He was deceived into believing he was missing out on something greater than the moment. He wanted what he wanted and wanted it now!

He is famous for betraying the Lord. Imagine what table he is sitting at or with whom he has relations. Judas was at the table of that "Last Supper" when Jesus said, "One of you will betray me" (Matthew 26:14 through 75). Sometimes people get offended with you because things did not turn out in your life the way they planned. Some people make plans for their life based on your success; if it's not at the level to carry them, they can turn on you.

This is what happens with Jesus; many had imagined what it would be like when the Messiah would come, and based on their imagination, Jesus was a disappointment. Therefore, many were offended and turned on him. I wonder, "Where Are They Now?"

Betrayal began in eternity long before time or this world as we know it. We did not know what happened in heaven unless God revealed or exposed it. This is how He unveiled the secrets of heaven, good or bad... it is the truth! It's time to accept the truth!

Why do we consider the crucifixion so barbaric and horrific? Because it reveals the hidden things in Lucifer's heart while serving God in heaven, this is how he felt about Him.

God humbled Himself in the form of Christ to expose the hatred of His enemies and have the angels in heaven as witnesses, for without this, they could never believe that their angelic brothers could be so evil, even after God had been so gracious and good to them.

This is real history in heaven; we get to see it up close and personal through everything around us. From every celebration of something good to the bad, including wars and tragedies! Lucifer wants everything God has created, but won't work or labor to make his own. Instead, he is always plotting how to steal everything. He is obsessed with being God! So, God submitted His enemy's hands to expose his true heart towards Him.

If God submits to Lucifer in time, He will then expose everything that is hidden in Lucifer's heart for eternity, so that everyone can see how he feels about God. He will not be able to resist the opportunity to be God's Ruler and Boss! "Let's see how well God can do at serving since He's always giving us orders." Lucifer-Satan-Devil (this is the 666) is six, which was the number for the Angels in heaven.

The angels were in Legions of 6,000. When Lucifer was exposed and corrupted, he passed this system to his alter-egos: six (6) for himself (Lucifer) as the master, six (6) to Satan as his officer, and six (6) to the Devil as his agent; this is the "Demonic Trinity!" They lied to him, spat on him, beat him, and hung him on a tree until he died.

The "Religious Leaders" manipulated his death and tried to curse him, determining the manner of death Jesus would experience. "Cursed is the man who hangs on a tree!" They betrayed "The only begotten Son of God." This was God's heart that they were handling!

They thought they were dealing with a man, but they were actually handling God's heart! This illustrates how Lucifer handled God's heart in heaven, which was kept secret. No one could see the heart of God; it could only be felt.

God did not disclose this to anyone at the time. He was working while hurting! Have you ever gone to work, raised your children, or gone about doing other daily duties while in pain that you could not express to anyone? It just hurts and feels like it will never go away.

The hate crime of Jesus's death was "the hate crime of all hate crimes." To come, trust, and believe he understands our pains, sorrows, and losses. Take notice, after all that pain they inflicted on him, the first thing he said after they nailed him to the cross was, "Father forgive them because they don't know what they are doing." Immediately, he rid himself of all possibilities of being unable to forgive his enemies.

Don't get stuck in your pain. Don't become trapped in the place where you were hurt and lose the ability to move into your destiny. We all must beware of making a god out of our pain. He stripped the enemy of his power, and at the same time, he showed Satan how love operates; love covers. He granted each of them an opportunity or a space in time to change their heart and mind, or to "repent!"

This is the most extraordinary power when you don't use our greatest ability to destroy, but to save. When betrayed, do as God does and "upgrade!" Take your opportunity to get better and do better than you ever have before; this is the best revenge you'll have against your enemies because the reality is that God's enemies are our enemies, and vice versa. We inherited them when we said, "Yes" to God from our hearts.

When Lucifer and the angels betrayed God, He could have replaced them with other angels. Instead, He chose to upgrade and start a family from His loins. This is how we came into the picture, through the born-again system. Lucifer and the boys are still furious and fighting over that! Nobody can join God's kingdom; we must be born into His kingdom.

Therefore, it's important to preach and teach about His kingdom. We all belong to one kingdom or another, no matter the religion. Religion is so overrated!

All mankind, upon entering eternity for all generations, entered into a kingdom and are there right now. Why do we think that enormous Universe is out there? It's not just taking up space, that's for sure. This is exactly why He said, "It is finished!" Satan will never have this opportunity again. Lucifer's heart is finally being exposed, and now it is all caught on camera.

God has a strong case against him and all his followers. Even today, Lucifer is still heavily involved in running the Temple services. Be watchful to see if they love the Lord or if they love money… this is a very easy distinction. If they love money… they will hate God and you; it's plain and simple. They can't reach God, so they will hate whoever speaks the truth!

Of course, God does not oppose our being wealthy. He's The

King. It would be ridiculous to think otherwise. But when we love money, "The love of money is the root of all evil!" The love of money will cause anyone to destroy life for money, fame, and power!

No wonder the "church" today has greater titles and positions than the Pharisees, Sadducees, and Scribes. They all appeared to be righteous in the eyes of the people, until "righteousness" showed up! What's sad is this: Satan has deceived them into believing that they have a reward in heaven awaiting them when they leave here. We have people who go to church faithfully yet are as mean as a snake; Jesus said, "They do their father's will, the Devil." Look at their works and remember that, although we are not saved by our works, we will be judged by them.

God did not instruct us to be faithful to church services, but to be faithful in serving—faithfully serving, not looking to be served. We are here in this world to help somebody!

Don't go by titles, but by the spirit in operation; we all know God loves life and is the giver, while Satan loves things and is the taker of life. Satan will take life to get money and things. In the ultimate betrayal, he will kill your sons and daughters, then show up for the memorial service bringing flowers… this is how wicked he is.

He will console the mother and family, saying, "If there's anything I can do, please don't hesitate to call me." Now this is a devil! This is one of the betrayals hidden in heaven and exposed on the earth. When we see evil revealed in the world through people, it is the manifestation of what was, at one time, hidden in the hearts of some of those beings from heaven. God is the Master of revealing hidden things in the heart. God's hurt changed the game, and what Lucifer did changed everything, ultimately for the better.

These beings, created in heaven, had no choice, but we were born here on earth, and we all have a choice. We can choose which side of God we want to be on: the right or the left. It's our choice; no one will ever be able to say to God or any other eternal Creator, "I didn't want to come here!"

Everyone who will make it to heaven, trust this: they belong in heaven and are the sons and daughters of "The Most High God." It will not be by our religions and traditions of men, but by our relationship with God the Father.

We are born as children of the kingdom, whether of the light or darkness, good or evil, love or hate. Let's be real. Who would want to be joined to evil throughout eternity if you are good, and who would like to be joined to good for eternity if you are evil?

This does not make any sense whatsoever! If you are good, then it's by God's good nature, and if you are evil, it's by Satan's evil nature; it's that simple! It's enough to be subjected to this horrible terror for a lifetime. God only knows we would not want to deal with the evils of this world for eternity; so, we are not all going to the same place; the devil is a lie!

We are all exposed to certain things and people in life for this purpose, and as individuals, we don't know our hearts until we become spiritually mature. We are destined to go through things by design to determine who we are. How can we know what's truly in us without testing?

It's good for us to go through some things; although it may not feel good, these experiences ultimately expose our deep-down dark secrets. If we are who we say we are, we will be willing to fix anything evil and contrary to God's good and will not, by any means, compromise with the enemies of God and righteousness.

We must understand there's a difference between being wicked and being weak. Sometimes, handling hurt causes others hurt, but we can fix it; yes, we can if we want to.

Betrayal is one of life's most brutal blows.

The aftermath can look very different when people are betrayed, especially in marriages or deeply committed relationships. Some spiral into promiscuity, using uncommitted sex as a painkiller, masking their pain behind moments of fleeting pleasure. Others go the opposite way — shutting down completely, isolating themselves from everyone.

Whether they admit it or not, many end up being unfaithful in other areas of life, betraying themselves and their purpose, all in an unconscious effort to numb the hurt. Trust becomes a distant memory; sadly, they inflict pain on others.

This doesn't necessarily mean they are evil. Often, they are lost —confused by the chaos within them. In time, many will find themselves conversing with God, seeking healing they can no longer deny.

The truth is that everyone is a potential victim of the betrayal cycle — hurt people hurt people. It takes time, but we must surrender our pain to the One who knows what it feels like to be abandoned by family, friends, and even the religious community.

Jesus Himself endured betrayal — sold for the price of a slave, treated as if His life were worth nothing. He could have called down judgment in an instant — legions of angels stood ready, each powerful enough to destroy 180,000 men — but instead, He chose mercy.
(See Isaiah 53, John 19:11.)

Jesus submitted to betrayal not out of weakness but divine strength. It was the greatest act of non-violent power the world has ever witnessed. His restraint was not a sign of defeat but a strategic gathering of evidence for the Day of Judgment.

God is building an airtight case — no injustice will be overlooked, and every person will receive a fair and just trial. Nothing that was never in a person can come out of them, so betrayal only reveals what was already present in the heart.

You are not foolish for showing mercy.

You are not weak because someone mistreated you.
They may have the upper hand now, but appearances do not sway God's court. Their day will come.

So, even through the hurt, pray for them. Hope that, in time, they will see themselves—not as wicked beyond redemption, but as confused and broken souls in need of healing.
We should want as many brothers and sisters to make it home as possible.
A day is coming when we will stand before God and give an account for how we treated His people.

* * *

The church needs to wake up and start preaching and teaching the message of unconditional love (freedom), rather than religious doctrines of hate, prejudice, condemnation, and slavery bondage! How many of us are preaching the love of God, which is freedom? Then how can we represent Him? The message in time and all eternity is still love.

Evil will always attack the forces for good; they cannot resist it, as they are naturally evil. Their wicked nature draws them.

As ambassadors of "righteousness," our job is to stand for what's right, regardless! We are not usually in the house of God where His throne is. We lack the understanding of God being the first to be betrayed by a very close loved one.

God's betrayal by Lucifer changed everything in time and eternity. We are dealing with betrayal all the time somewhere on the earth; whether it is by marital relationships, business partners, politics, or family, we all have experienced betrayal at some point in life.

Why? It happened in the Universe first, and anything that happened there must show its face here, on Earth, through time. The reality is this: we are all evaluated based on how we respond to betrayal. It is the worst thing to experience, and betrayal is the worst.

I say it with emphasis, "The worst thing ever to take place!" So many evils are connected to betrayal, for it and the love of money are the root of all problems.

We struggle every day to make decisions based on whom we can trust. Just because someone may have been loyal to you for 25 years, it is not guaranteed that they will not turn on you or have the potential to betray you and seek to destroy you...this is Lucifer's character.

We cannot measure the years of Lucifer's loyalty to God in service, but one day, he turned against God. So, we can never know who our friend or foe is without God's wisdom and divine experience.

For me, it is a no-brainer. We need God daily to lead and guide us, helping us with critical decision-making. Lucifer's betrayal was so horrific that Jesus called him out and said, "Satan (Lucifer is his exalted name, but Satan is his fallen name or his alter-ego's name) was a liar from the beginning and the father of them."

This suggests that God did not give Lucifer credit for all or any of his previous good works throughout eternity (which cannot be measured). The truth is that when you are betrayed, it doesn't matter how many years a person was loyal to you or whether their loyalty was personal or business-related; the betrayal undermines all the good they have ever done.

If a husband betrays a wife to the extent that his actions destroy the lives of her and their children, trust and belief, she will not be somewhere suffering her losses and saying, "My husband surely was a good man." His betrayal has outweighed all the good he's ever done; if they lost everything because of the betrayal, then love and trust became the ultimate sacrifices.

Therefore, if it results from betrayal, divorce is brutal and painful! Betrayal is the most challenging thing to be able to forgive, but it's necessary to forgive. Lack of forgiveness infuses the betrayal even more. This is not implying that anyone should give them a "license" to do it again, but simply taking the power away from them, improving your life, and living again, trusting again, or at least going on the road of recovery.

People can recover much more quickly from losing a loved one or spouse to death than from betrayal and divorce, as most divorces result from some form of betrayal. The struggle lies in learning to trust again; sometimes this entails trusting even God. You must trust again.

Therefore, it is essential to see God as He is, not as some superpower disconnected from our feelings or experiences, because this is untrue. Everything we experience in our world results from what happens in God's world: in eternity. Whether through plot, scheme, or manifestation, it nonetheless hurts. Who did God have? Who could He confide in, and whom could He turn to in this devastating time of need?

God's heart was bleeding from this betrayal. This is how we will know who your daddy is: either we are the betrayed or the betrayer, giver of pain or receiver of pain, liar or truth. We live in a society that embraces the lie. I called it "The birthing of a hypocrite."

We are trained and conditioned to wear masks and celebrated

based on who wears them the best! Some of us wear them out of a need for acceptance, while others do so out of fear of rejection. Some use it as protection, while others use it for "deception!"

When we are conditioned to live a lie while knowing that we are something else, we do so all in the name of acceptance or deception. The term "Politically Correct" is a fancy or proper description of a "hypocrite."

The kingdom of God is "righteous," not political. We should be hot or cold; however, for the most part, we remain lukewarm. Being lukewarm feels safe because we tend to please others and act hot or cold when it suits us. When it's fitting, we'll be hot, and similarly, we'll be freezing.

When confronted with specific issues, we remain neutral. It's easier to get cold from a lukewarm state than from a hot one, and vice versa. We should stand by what we believe, but not kill or condemn anyone just because we don't agree with them. If God is the source, then until the day of reckoning, it's still all about love...

"Sometimes you have to lose to win!"

THE WAR

Chapter 3

When Jesus was born, He wasn't welcomed into His Father's house — He had to be born among animals.
A sheep is simply a sheep, a cow, a dog — they are what they are without deception. But the so-called priests of the Lord at that time were no longer faithful to their calling. They had become representatives of the fallen angels who once served under Lucifer, disguised as men of God.

The temple priests could no longer be trusted. Lucifer had already corrupted their hearts. Beneath their priestly robes were murderers — outwardly holy, but inwardly filled with darkness. While Lucifer worked through the religious system, Satan influenced the government through King Herod. As soon as Jesus was born, the uncorrupted angels of the Lord did not appear to the priests, the scribes, or the temple leaders — instead, they came to humble shepherds keeping watch over their sheep by night.

It was to these pure-hearted men that the angel announced the greatest news the world would ever hear:
"Behold, a King is born — Emmanuel, God with Us."

Now ask yourself: **Why didn't the angels announce Christ's birth to the priests in the temple?**
Because the priests were already lost — their hearts were aligned with murder and treachery.
Only God could see their true nature. All it needed was the right set of circumstances to reveal them for what they really were. Understand this: Lucifer rules the **corrupted church (the temple)**, while Satan manipulates the **corrupted government (King Herod).**

Through Herod's decree to slaughter all male children under two years old, Satan sought to destroy the child before He could even grow. The attack was immediate because Satan knew that once the true

King took His rightful place, his kingdom of darkness would begin to crumble.

Remember the heavenly account about the woman and the child; here it is in the earthly realm. Mary is now representing that woman and her child (son). An angel of the Lord gives Joseph a message to go to Egypt while Herod is raging, and to stay until you hear from heaven. It has nothing to do with God being unable or weak, but rather what is written in heaven—the solution for a problem stemming from eternity. This is why some things we can't explain or understand must happen in life.

There is a book in heaven to which we all are bound, and these events must come to pass. When Mary, Joseph, and the child (now 12 years old) return to Nazareth, Joseph establishes himself as a carpenter. They returned because an angel sent a message to Joseph that King Herod was dead. Earlier, I talked about how things hidden in the heart must be revealed… well, this is part of that exposure.

Now Jesus is raised as a carpenter alongside Joseph. By the age of 30, he is responsible for burying him after his father's death and immediately becomes the head of the household according to the Law of Moses. The eldest son takes the father's place as the provider for the family.

He's also running the family business. During this period while Mary is still grieving as a widow, Jesus is called to start his ministry. Now it's time to fulfill his purpose and destiny. Therefore, he came to the earth. Now he is torn between the Law of Moses, which is the written Word of God, and a Rhema Word or immediate Word.

Now the written Word is challenging the spoken Word. The written Word has been established as God's Word, but the Word that Jesus is hearing cannot be proven yet, because it's fresh and only he can hear it. He must obey what he hears. Later, it will be proven! Who will understand this? He gets

Word that it's time for him to leave home as a carpenter and go now as a Messenger or Prophet. Now he must break this news to his mother, and it's not going to be easy, because she has just lost her husband and is a new widow.

Now she's about to lose her son! Jesus is facing the difficult task of putting the will of God above his emotions and feelings. Somehow this doesn't seem right, but he will not question the will of God, even though it hurts…he's gonna trust Him.

He's preparing to leave and tells his mother what he must do. She knew it was coming, but the timing caused her to react out of fear of her losses. This being "blessed and highly favored" thing is not working out as she thought it would, since the angel Gabriel's announcement so many years ago. She feels cursed right now and is wandering in the wilderness.

It's a very sad time for Mary and Jesus. He can't provide her with many answers; he has limited information because the enemy can't be given a heads-up on what will occur. Jesus now leaves his mother and small siblings on a journey that cannot be explained right now.

This looks bad; how can he leave us like this? They must be thinking. As Jesus departs, he's reminded of all the good times and challenges. Now Joseph is dead, and they will never be the same family again. Jesus leaves and heads down to the Jordan River, where John the Baptist is baptizing. It's a long walk, and he's praying for strength to do what he must. He leaves his mother's house as the son of a carpenter and approaches the Jordan River, where John is baptizing.

John sees him and says, "Behold the Lamb of God, who comes to take away the sins of the world!" He's never heard this before. He submits himself to John for baptism. John refuses to baptize him, but Jesus insists and says, "Let all things be fulfilled." Here we are again; it seems to suggest that somewhere it is written what must be exposed or how this is to play out. Nothing's by chance; this is a production; this is in the book somewhere in heaven. John says, "I am not worthy to baptize you, I am in need to be baptized of you," but Jesus says, "Do it."

So, John baptizes him, and as he comes up out of the water, the heavens open, and the spirit of God descends on him like a dove and says: "This is my beloved Son, in him I am well pleased!" Jesus needed this; it was encouraging because his heart was with his mother and siblings. He needed to know he was in his Father's will, which was confirmation.

His Heavenly Father declares openly before the heavens and earth that this is His son. He left home humbly as the son of a carpenter to be baptized and emerged from the water, the Son of God. He's been waiting for instructions from his daddy.

He worked with his hands as a servant to show how a true Son of God is willing to serve and wait on His Father, desiring to please Him. He is the Son of God, but was willing to work as "the son of man." This established his identity and anointing for the work before him as the Son of God! Satan is not going to stand by and let this happen.

He's furious about heaven and his being replaced! Jesus knows that Satan has a weakness; he cannot stay away from the Word, even if he can't live it. He's addicted to God's Word because wherever the Word is, you will find God. He is not allowed in the third heaven where God is, so he seizes any chance to get a piece of God. He's searching for the prophecy of this son that will bruise his head. Can this be it?

Can he be the Word? Immediately, Jesus is led straight into the wilderness where Satan is. He's going to confront Satan before Satan comes at him. Because of what His Father said, Satan is coming…he can't help himself! Everything that will be a test in His ministry, He's going to face and confront that devil in the next 40 days. Jesus fasted for 40 days and 40 nights; The devil tempted him, had nothing to eat, and afterward, He was hungry.

The devil said, "If you are the Son of God, then turn these stones into bread." He was trying to get Jesus to do something to prove that He was the Son. See, the enemy knew He was the Son of God, but not only this; He was at the baptism, waiting for the Son to show up! The devil knows Him but wants Him to be vain and self-centered!

Understand this: your anointing is not for you to use on yourself, but it's for your assignment! Satan understood this. All things are possible with God, so he's trying to get Jesus to use His anointing on things for Himself.

But Jesus rebukes him and says, "Man shall not live by bread alone but by every word that proceeds out of the mouth of God!" With the same amount of anointing that it would have taken to turn stones into bread to feed himself, he demonstrates to this devil how he was supposed to use his anointing while he was in heaven.

Lucifer was a fallen one because of the misappropriation of his anointing. Later, while doing ministry and preaching, Jesus found himself in a situation where he had been preaching to about 5,000 people who were hungry for God's Word and were now in the wilderness with no food.

He uses his anointing to turn two fish and five loaves of bread into enough food to feed everyone, and there was food left over… more than enough! This is a slap in the Devil's face. The Son of God reminds Lucifer about loyalty, dedication, trust, faithfulness, and pleasing God with your power rather than hoarding it. He showed Satan why he was cast down! If you can win and defeat the Devil in the wilderness, you can beat him anywhere!

We keep hearing about this wilderness! The wilderness symbolizes the uncomfortable places throughout our lives, yet it is where we will find God. During this period of temptation, Jesus will deliberately pursue the serpent.

We all come from something greater than our natural families. None of us is limited to our birth parents or families. We must overcome every hurt, disappointment, and pain to connect to our heavenly family and bring God glory. It's about purpose. Jesus is now confronting the enemy of the woman who gave birth to him.

Women need to understand this; you inherited your enemy; it has nothing to do with what you have or what you have not done.

Your mere existence is enough for your enemy! The male needs to fight for you! Jesus fasted and prayed for 40 days and nights. He will be tempted with "The lust of the flesh, the lust of the eye, and the Pride of life!"

Every leader needs to understand this: Satan offered Jesus power, riches, fame, and glory that came along with the world, government, and religion! Yes, he even offered him the temple and the power of being a high-profile religious leader. He showed him Rome and Jerusalem and took him to a high mountain. He showed him all the world's glory and offered him a deal.

You can have all of this without suffering or sacrificing, and you will endure no pain. You will be embraced by those who would be your enemies; don't tell the truth. We will deceive the world and lead them from God's will with a smoke screen." No matter how much you do for the devil, you will never be able to please him because he is a miserable creature that is lost forever! He knows that he blew it: the love of eternal life.

How many of us have admired a person without ever meeting them? Sometimes you feel like you know them, but in reality, we don't know them; we know of them. How many have sold themselves to be accepted by possessing things of God, but don't even know God? Validation doesn't come from things of God but from a relationship with God. Have you ever given gifts to someone special to you at a particular time in your life, but for whatever reason, you are no longer with them?

If they have your gifts, they can deceive people into believing you are still together, if this has not been publicly displayed. They know they don't have you, but everyone else may think you are fine because they still parade around with old gifts from the previous relationship. Merely getting money does not save lives; in fact, it often destroys them and their destiny. If they are led to believe that money will bring them happiness or complete them without a connection to God, we are deceived. You will recognize those in a relationship with God as their father, as they will consistently use their position and money as tools to improve the lives of others.

They will find a way to help others and bring relief to those who are praying to God for assistance. They become instruments in God's hands, not fools to be deceived by scammers. They will listen to God with money and power just as much, if not more, as before they had money and power. When money is your god, then you will do whatever God tells you to do; but when God is the God over your money, you will love Him more than the money. You can't take the money with you, but you can surely take God with you wherever you go! God will never leave you, but the love of money will make you miserable and virtually impossible to please or live with!

One day we will all give an account to God for the gifts He's given us. Jesus understands that now He must fight to fulfill His purpose. No one wants to be hated or to suffer, no matter who you are, so this is a temptation. By nature, all of us want things to be as easy as possible. The test will always be to get you to choose the gifts of God over God. Never choose the gifts over the giver, because if you stay in a relationship with the giver, you will never run out of gifts.

Jesus prioritized his relationship with his Father above all else. After passing his tests, he is ready to begin his mission. He is purged and transformed from the son of a carpenter into the Son of God. This change occurs not externally but deep within. He departs for Galilee and attends a wedding feast. A wedding is the greatest celebration of all. Interestingly, he has not seen his mother since he left home for his journey. Now, his mother, Mary, is at this wedding.

She sees her son for the first time since he left and has not contacted her. Now imagine how she must feel. A widow and fatherless children, her life previously was secured with her husband and eldest son, and now all that has changed, and she is hurt and doesn't understand what is going on.

Although Mary was enlightened when she conceived her son by the "Messenger Gabriel," this was not quite what she expected, particularly in giving birth to the Son of God. Mary feels afraid, hurt, and offended, to say the least. She does not understand the spiritual warfare that has taken place between her son and the serpent for nearly two months.

Mary has no clue that she represents the Woman in the heavens and a nation giving birth, and that this dragon hated her and would have killed her son if God hadn't saved him. In the heavens, the woman fled, but the son was caught up.

Both are called to the wilderness at different times, but for the same reason: to fight the enemy on his turf. That's a bold statement to fight your enemy on the ground. Now the son is all grown up and will fight for her so that she will never have to run from her enemy again! But Mary is living with a broken heart because of hurt, disappointments, and pain. "Where is God?" So now Lucifer, who hates her, is in her ear; he is an opportunist...it's just who he is.

He sees an opportunity to divide them, the mother and son. Understand this, the enemy that's operating has an advantage. He's still in spirit, but Jesus is in human form. Mary is in her flesh and has no clue of the heavenly account of who she is, and does not know that this devil started his fight with her in eternity. He hated her very existence as a woman, but he lost it when she gave birth to her son, because as soon as the child was born, she became a mother, and he couldn't wrap his mind around how marvelous this creature was.

He's never seen such greatness in all eternity...Who is the Woman? He wishes he were her! Your enemy will always approach you as a friend, but his plot for you is destruction! He hates everything about you! You took his life from him, as far as he is concerned! He's been after you from the very beginning! You didn't know it! Because Jesus left her and his siblings, Mary is upset with him.

Let's leave the fable for a minute and deal with the truth and reality of a mother fighting to take care of her children with the loss of a husband, father, and provider, and on top of that, a son who leaves for some quest or career move. We need a real picture here because this is no fantasy. Can you imagine the tension? The wedding is in full effect, and they have the worst thing to happen in this culture...they run out of wine. Wine, in this culture, is symbolic of joy and prosperity. So, to run out of wine is a statement that my marriage will run out of joy and finances. Jesus's mother spots an opportunity to get at her son.

She approaches her son and says, "They have no more wine; fix this, make it right!" Jesus replies, "Woman, what has you to do with me, it is not yet my time?" Notice he didn't say, "Mother" because he was talking to the Woman in the wilderness, where the serpent was trying to destroy her, but could not get to her. Even though Mary knew what she was told about her son before he was born and the prophecies, she had not seen him do any miracles.

Now he looks the same to the eyes, but Mary was not looking at her son, but the Son of God. The spirit of his Father was on him, and he was in the wilderness in the spirit fighting for her for 40 days and nights. She thinks he's been absent, but he has been covering and fighting for her all the while. If you win in the spirit realm, you have won for real! If we accomplish anything on this earth and it's not backed up by heaven, we don't keep it anyway! If we win in the spirit, we can't lose...ever!

Mary tells the feast's men," Whatever my son says to do, just do it!" They went to Jesus, and he told them to bring him water pots or vessels, and they brought him six of them. He then turns the water into wine. It was so good that the guests called it the best.

They asked if they had saved the best wine for last. This is the first recorded miracle that Jesus performed. He then goes to his hometown of Nazareth to the Synagogue. It's there where he reads the scripture, and he reads from Isaiah chapter 61.

"The Spirit of the Lord is upon him, and he has been anointed to preach good news to the poor and heal broken hearts, to heal those who are abused, set those free who are in prison or bound, and to preach the year of restoration," getting back everything that was lost or stolen from you. To those who heard him read this, he expresses that these things are now fulfilled.

The people went off and said, "Isn't this Joseph's son, isn't this Mary's boy, then how is he making himself out to be some prophet? Only the Messiah can fulfill these things." Remember, Jesus has been gone for almost two months, and this same community has been taking care of Mary and her children in the absence of her son and the death of her husband.

Jesus is not looking too favorable at this time. He is utterly rejected, so much so that they are talking about killing him. Jesus must slip through the crowd for safety. The lesson is that we have an image of how we think God should look or be. Jesus did not come with earthly riches and glory, so he was rejected. They were looking for God to come with wealth and power.

This is one of the most outstanding examples of how we will put God out of His church if we're not careful, because we are looking for wealth and prosperity. The reality is that he's looking for humility and meekness. He could not do many mighty works there because of their disbelief.

He slipped through the crowd and would never live in his natural house with his mother again. He leaves and goes to the next town, but before he departs, he tells them, "A prophet is not accepted in his own house or town."

He went to the next city and performed many miracles because they believed and did not regard him as a carpenter or Mary and Joseph's son, but could see God in him. Jesus's ministry lasted for three and a half years, or about 1260 days.

This duration is prophesied; read Revelation chapter 12. Revelation is the unveiling of what was previously hidden. This means it existed all along but was concealed behind a curtain or veil. It must manifest and come to fruition.

That's what this journey called life entails; some secrets in heaven must come to pass, both good and evil. The heart of God's heavenly enemies has truths to be revealed, which is why the heart is the most valuable thing we possess besides life itself.

The heart matters. Similarly, the serpent didn't reappear until the woman showed her place concerning the Son of God. This is when the enemy attempted to destroy her seed. As the child grew, he posed no threat to royalty, wealth, and prosperity; the kings of the earth continued as if nothing had occurred.

In other words, there were no reports of a new king or kingdom in the land. While they were searching for a natural king with kingly attributes, God had disguised Himself (Son) in poverty and humility! His majesty grew up as the son of a poor carpenter… surely this is no threat. "Maybe we all misinterpreted what God was saying to us," Mary and Joseph must be thinking. God came in humility to draw those who truly love and belong to Him, not the gold-digging religious folks who are in it for the money and not the love of God and His people.

There are some women on Lucifer's hit list, and I say Lucifer because he is the true master of Satan, the devil, demons, witches, warlocks, sorcerers, imps, mediums, and all that is Evil! Understand that he is a Master of evil and excels at it! No one even knew the secrets of the devil until Jesus exposed him! He had power over all generations before Jesus; we would kill the person only to find out that the devil was still there and had relocated into another willing vessel or body. The work does not stop because it's about the kingdom! Every person who is born represents God's Kingdom or Lucifer's Kingdom.

It's only the two because it's only the "one" that split. It was all good, and the split of evil came from Lucifer's vision of desired alterations that God never approved. Lucifer is like a child, thinking he is grown and can't see past his appetite for anything that tastes good or makes him feel good. He was good and was given authority over the good in heaven.

His mistake was that he put "feeling good" above everything else, even when God said, you can't have that right now. In essence, he made "feel good" his priority without balance and succumbed to making it an addiction. He would not listen to or obey God and became insubordinate.

We will learn about God by observing life. Stop making it some religious thing when we think of God. Use real relationships and events in life as a template for understanding. Don't think of heaven as some far-out place that you can't relate to; if you don't like murder here, you won't like murder there. If you don't like betrayal here, you won't like it. Treat people the way you would like to be treated. It's that simple.

God has a problem with Lucifer: he had no problem receiving love, but he struggled to give it back; he would not reciprocate. It is why "it's better to give than receive!" Here it is! He had no issue being blessed by God, but was selfish and did not bless God back.

He had no trouble being anointed, but was the very one to turn it into misery for others. Lucifer is the poster child for "good gone bad." Everything comes from the truth! Satan's kingdom is just the opposite of God's kingdom, or what's already in existence.

Understand this: Satan is not a creator but a thief! Everything he has is stolen. God is the author and architect of life, the teacher, the producer, the songwriter, the arranger, the musician, the song, the music, the model, and the builder.

He is the designer, the decorator, the director, the actor, the doctor, the patient, the maker, and the creator. He is the relationship, the sex, the degree, the hit, the song, the blockbuster movie, the successful business, the clothes, the shoes, the house, the car, the money, the jewelry, and the wedding. He is the husband, the wife, the children, the good life you're chasing, and even that "High" because there's no high like "The Most High God!" Everything that we are chasing in life to live well is Him!

It came from Him! Lucifer knows this right now and has known it for eternity! The sad thing is that many will leave this world only to find out that everything they received from Satan will not be able to be kept because the real owner will file charges, convict, prosecute, and sentence the thief and all his accomplices for their crimes. So, in essence… no matter how things look, the children of God can never lose! Don't allow Satan to make you fake.

He's on a mission, so hardly anyone wants to be real anymore. Why are we under so much pressure working on the surface when, in essence, it will all fade away and die anyway? We are not saying to let yourself go, but why be stressed over people commenting only on your appearance rather than your character? This is all vanity!

If you want to attract fake friends and relationships, flaunt your money and the things it buys, but if you are interested in true friends and genuine relationships, show your true self and open up about your shortcomings, problems, issues, and challenges. They are true if they stick around without trying to change you and accept you for who you are.

Those with you for the riches, fame, or success of a career are only interested in your gifts and the things you offer, not you. God understands this better than anyone. For those at the top of their game, it seemed like you could do no wrong; you had friends and family you didn't even know about, and everyone just loved you so much… you could hardly spend a minute alone.

But one day, you discover that it wasn't you they were there for, but your belongings. Sometimes God does us a favor by allowing certain things to happen to expose these truths, then gives us a second chance… don't blow it!

OPENED EYES

Chapter 4

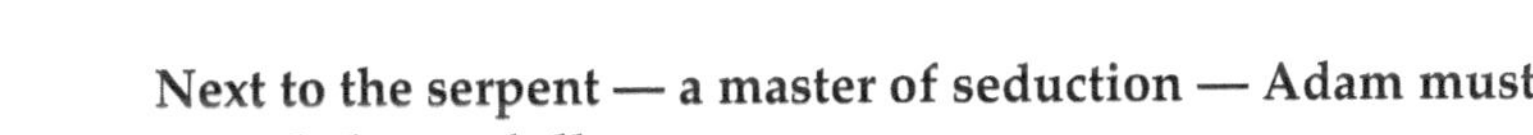

Next to the serpent — a master of seduction — Adam must have seemed almost dull.
While Adam stayed faithful to his assignment, the serpent offered Eve something far more enticing: *pleasure* and *power*. He planted the idea of being "like God" — a temptation that stirred a deep desire within her.

God would visit them daily and then depart again, much like a parent leaving their children at home with promises to return, and warnings to behave.
Now imagine being told, *"You're not old enough to go where I'm going,"* without fully understanding what that even meant. Imagine the serpent whispering, *"If you eat from this tree, you can go wherever you want. You can be like Him. You won't need to wait anymore."*

Meanwhile, Adam was faithfully working, focused, and obedient, carrying out the tasks God had given him. Like many men today, he operated with a mono-focus—task-oriented, diligent, but blind to the deeper emotional and psychological needs unfolding around him. Eve, on the other hand, found herself in a quieter world. Along with her thoughts, she was left to wonder and hunger for something more—fulfillment, purpose, freedom.

It's not so different from what happened decades ago.
In the 1950s and 60s, soap operas exploded in popularity, quietly infiltrating homes by targeting housewives. Many women, isolated at home without careers or outside engagement, found themselves drowning in boredom, which can be dangerous. Before children came, how did they fill those endless hours?
Who was speaking to them during the long absences of their husbands?

And so it was in Eden. While Adam worked, Eve listened.
While Adam obeyed, Eve imagined. And the wrong voice found the

right opportunity.

What about the newlyweds — the young wives expected to simply stay home, be good, and wait for their husbands to return? Temptation doesn't always come in the form of another person. Often, it first comes as a quiet whisper — the voices inside her own mind. Now she lives with a secret war. A constant battle rages between fulfilling what is expected of her and pursuing her own dreams, ambitions, and unanswered questions. In times past, a woman who dared to even act on these inner thoughts was branded "evil." But the reality is, every woman has faced some form of **Eve's temptation**.

The struggle is more profound and more complex than many realize. Even today, how many hours a day does a woman wrestle with the thoughts of leaving her family, her marriage, her structured life to follow those persistent voices calling her toward something more? At the core, it all goes back to Eden. When God gave Adam his wife, it was because God, who knew the depths of Adam's needs, provided a helper perfectly suited for him. But here's a critical detail: **God never directly told Eve not to eat from the tree.**

Those instructions and warnings were given to Adam *before* Eve even existed. This is like a family giving their son a portion of his inheritance to start his own household. Eve, created from Adam and given to him, automatically inherited everything that was his. She didn't have to earn her place; it was granted by her very existence. As the elder, Adam was responsible for teaching and guiding her into partnership with him under God's design. Eve, in turn, had to trust Adam's word — building her relationship with her husband on **faith**, not firsthand knowledge.

This created a hidden vulnerability from the very beginning: a trust gap born from innocence and lack of experience. Even in Eden, marriage faced its first harsh lesson: While the husband worked, another voice—the serpent—entertained the wife. The serpent's words were crafted to sow doubt: doubt in God's command and doubt in her husband's honesty and leadership. And so the cycle began—a battle of trust, temptation, and voices that have echoed through every generation since.

Was Adam withholding information? "I'm not a child, and he is not my father; he needs to tell me more and treat me like his partner."

The trickery of words by the serpent suggested this. He said to Eve, "Yea, has God said, you shall not eat from every tree of the garden?" The woman said to the serpent, "We may eat from the fruit of the garden's trees, but of the fruit of the tree in the midst of the garden, God has said, Ye shall not eat from it, neither touch it, lest ye die."

And the serpent said to the woman, "You shall not surely die: for God does know that in the day ye eat thereof, then your eyes will open, and ye shall be as gods, knowing good and evil." We can see how cunning the serpent was with the woman, but how could she know? It's the same with anyone without experience who is being manipulated by someone with experience. He drew her in by raising questions or doubts about what she was told: "How much was Adam telling me, is he trying to control me?" This method is still used to this day.

Whether in a relationship, marriage, with children, business partners, or friends, the devil is a liar and will distort the truth into a lie. The truth is the source from which the lie is derived. Therefore, truth cannot arise from a lie. Consequently, the woman believed the serpent, ate from the tree, and gave the fruit to her husband to eat. Their eyes were opened, as were her husband's.

In other words, they had lost their innocence. It was as though they had transitioned from being five years old to 25 years of age. Before this, they had seen each other's bodies naked all the time, and it didn't mean a thing; they had no feelings about it whatsoever. Now they were perceiving each other in a whole new and lustful way. They were aware of their nakedness without anyone informing them of this.

Do you remember the first time you did something and felt ashamed of it, knowing somehow that your eyes were opened? You would never see yourself and that person the same again after crossing that line. Sex had not been introduced to them yet because it was obvious they were not ready. Sex was their marriage and wedding present, which could only be given by God, but was intended for a later time after building friendship and trust. Then sex would be a loving experience rather than a lust-fulfilling experiment.

How many times have we entered sexual relationships without a bond of trust and commitment, only to later wish we had never known the person at all? Lust turns into resentment and sometimes hate. The serpent will take total advantage of this because he knows he has caused them to violate God's intentions. When Eve looked at Adam's body, she saw things in a whole new light. The relationship has gone from innocence to "shade" in an instant.

Now Eve is the mature one in the relationship. The serpent has manipulated their trust. It will take a while because they have been sentenced and don't know what all of this entails. They have no reference for anything; they are feeling their way. They, of course, do not have the same favorable relationship as they did before they disobeyed God.

They feel a certain way about the whole situation, but they don't feel in control. They have no idea how the "dying thing" will come into play; remember, it was said they would surely die. In the meantime, they have lost their home…their place of security.

Now Adam and Eve are outside of the garden and almost what we would call homeless. For the first time, Adam is looking for work; remember, all these things were done. They are accustomed to a safe and protected environment.

Everything was taken care of; they were like children provided for by a wealthy father. Now, life will never be the same. They are on their own and feel quite insecure. Adam becomes a tiller of the soil for food. The elements are working against him for the first time. Things are conspiring against him. What is this thing about dying? Having each other is their only comfort.

They comfort each other and are now becoming closer, making love regularly. They had never received guidance on this sex thing. Today, for some reason, we have been led to believe that sex is nasty.

The truth is that God created, engineered, designed, and is the Architect of it, having reserved it as a wedding gift. Because of the premature use of this gift, they never received the instructions. Though it makes them feel good, they can't help but be interrupted by thoughts of dying and their relationship with God.

They don't know what to expect about death or what it looks like when it comes. In the meantime, they are trying to survive daily and adjust to their new living arrangements. Eve's going through some bodily changes. Maybe this is death? She's sick in the mornings and has never felt this way before. She feels strange every day. "Something is wrong, Adam," she says.

Adam is concerned; after all, he ate the fruit because of his love for her and chose to die with his wife rather than live without her. "But why is she sick and I'm not?" Adam says. "This is happening every day. Maybe it's what we're eating? But why isn't Adam sick?"

Now Eve's belly is growing! What is this? They are completely lost except when they see the birth of animals. Maybe you're going to have a little one of us. Now, Adam and Eve are paying closer attention to the animals giving birth.

Now his wife is large, and they are afraid. Adam loves his wife very much and doesn't want anything to happen to her; she is all he has. Adam is in love, and he will care for his baby no matter what it takes. Now Eve's in pain giving birth to sons, and they name them Cain and Abel.

She remembers the promise of the seed and the war between her seeds and the serpent's seed. Her seed will bruise the serpent's seed's head, and the serpent's seed will bruise her seed's heel. This promise was made not to Eve personally but to the woman as a being.

She is the chosen one to bring forth the seed to avenge all women. There are so many women hurting throughout the world, across every race and color. The one thing you all have in common is this: The Serpent Hates You! You are always at war, and who can understand you in this but God?

The woman carries so much all the time. Sometimes she wishes she could tell her mind to just stop! It's always thinking and moving. So many women have lost love, children, sons, daughters, husbands, fathers, and other women who meant the world to them. Nothing can take the place of a good mother who is neither selfish nor self-centered.

Love is the greatest of all gifts and the most expensive...more than riches, silver, and gold...it's priceless! While Eve waits for something to happen in her life and doesn't quite know what that may consist of, her sons are starting to go through some changes. The incident at the tree with Eve eating the forbidden fruit gives this serpent access to her marriage, children, and her family.

Now the serpent is here by way of rights granted through her disobedience. When God said, "her seed," He meant that it is spiritual; a woman's seed is spiritual, the serpent's seed is spiritual, and the man's seed is natural. That's why no matter how much a father does for his son, the athlete's son looks into the camera and says, "Hello Mom, love you!" when he wins a game.

It's what she instills in him during nurturing that enters his spirit. The serpent targets the minds of women and their children from an early age. He tries to plant seeds while they are young, seeking to violate them very early in life. They may be protected, but someone must teach them about their God and history so that they may understand who they are and where they come from. Adam and Eve's two sons were like night and day. The same man fathered both, yet each son represents two different seeds.

Both were Adam's natural sons, but spiritually, one was Eve's seed and the other the serpent's seed. When the serpent could get Cain to follow him without resistance, he then claimed him as his own. I know that in today's world we are so advanced that we don't believe certain things, but some things are established in the heavens whether we believe them or not. The serpent twisted Cain's mind so that he would be jealous of his brother Abel and ultimately kill him.

The oldest brother killed his younger brother out of jealousy and competition. Now, we are talking about the first family of supreme intelligence. They were created in the image and likeness of God; they have intellect. This occurred with children from the same parents. Now, think about this today. We have children by multiple fathers growing up amid all kinds of perverted and wicked happenings as the norm. They don't stand a chance without some help! The children are exposed, and this is the work of woman's greatest enemy: the serpent. He's in their lives, sending these wicked men into their lives—ungodly, unruly men!

Most of the time, the woman is just looking for love, but in all the wrong places… this is a setup! Think about more than gratification. Eve didn't think past her desires, but she had no references; we do! Every time you bring an adult situation to a minor, you expose them to your enemy and open a door for their spirit to be violated. Today, many children who were victims of their parents' indiscretion are adults, and they are still trying to recover, but they don't know from what! The serpent will make the woman afraid of being alone or insecure. She will put up with a raggedy man to avoid being alone, and in the meantime, her children are subjected to abuse! Because of the woman's creative nature, she wants to be praised… this is her nature. The serpent plays on this with a no-good partner and delivers him to her at the right time.

Most women will spend all they have on their image and receive compliments from the serpent seeds dressed in something they like. Therefore, a woman must be careful because she was created to worship but also to be worshipped! She was created to worship love, not lust! She will worship something, even if it's herself! This is why more women are drawn to church and religion and are involved in organizations focused on saving something or nurturing. This is her nature; it is not a criticism, but an acknowledgment.

This is a very good quality in the hands of love; however, it can be lethal otherwise. What other reasons would a woman participate in a music video that degrades her and other women? She tolerates the message in exchange for the opportunity to be seen and worshipped! Of course, she may not know the extent to which it affects her or believe that it is worship, but she does know the rush she feels seeing herself with this power over her audience.

God created women and gave them power; if they want to reach their full potential, they need to stay in a relationship with Him! What would you do if you had an exotic car that was not operating properly? You would either read the manual or take it to the dealer or mechanic.

This is the problem: we go to everyone else when our lives are not functioning correctly, rather than going to the Creator who made and knows us. People who do not care for others hurt women every day. Every day, someone's children trust those who abuse them. Many women don't realize until it's too late that they have introduced their child to the molester or pedophile who victimized them. Some children never tell their parents for fear of losing their relationship, what little they have, and some just leave and never fix it!

Sadly, some mothers don't realize they have poor relationships with some of their children. The child feels that while you were trying to get your groove on, your man was getting his groove on with me. Little girls end up becoming these men's mistresses. What kind of wives will they be if they don't discuss it or feel safe enough to seek help? Many marriages have dissolved because of this issue; a little girl is trapped in a grown woman's body and becomes "damaged goods!"

With so much potential interrupted and seemingly having no purpose, she becomes her worst enemy; she sabotages every good relationship and sometimes even her marriage. She can't handle long-term relationships, and the sad thing is that the serpent is the puppeteer pulling the strings. Yet, we go to the club, church, work, and remain in the home, living a lie. This enemy that the woman has on her heels just won't quit.

When God raises a little girl from impossible circumstances, it is He who blesses her to show the world that "All things are possible, if you just believe and don't quit!" At the same time, He reveals how much this serpent hates her, yet has no power to stop her! As God speaks to her, the serpent is speaking as well. For example, she demonstrates her ability to hear, trust, and obey the right voice—the one who cares for her and is providing her a way out!

Not everyone is strong enough to get out! He has given her a greater purpose than even she realizes, but this thing is driving her. She won't settle, and she won't give up! She is being guided every step of the way. When she makes a mistake, she learns from it and keeps moving forward. She is confident now that the ideas she's getting are bigger than her; they're bigger than her life!

She is coming into her own, and although she has an enemy to contend with, she does not give him any space. She knows how to pray, not in a religious way but in a relational way. She remains levelheaded and as humble as can be expected.

Many people tried to talk her out of certain things, but she knew what she knew, and she had to get it done. She's a risk-taker, and it's clear that she has many enemies, but she enjoys the greatest support one could ever have. God is a God of order and has everything arranged—He's the King.

When He created the woman, He created royalty... her majesty! The woman has been on God's enemy's hit list. In the Garden of Eden, the enemy went straight for Eve, not Adam. He knew from the beginning what the woman was.

The woman didn't know who she was. God would not leave her defenseless, and will not! When the incident happened in the Garden, God addressed all parties involved. I'll go deeper into it later in the book, but my point is that she was placed with the serpent as a rival.

Adam was set aside while God specifically spoke to the woman and the serpent about their ongoing conflict. Why do you think that, from the beginning of time, women have been the target of every imaginable evil? She is used and abused. The serpent seeks to silence her because her power lies in the word God gives her to speak. God will always send her help. God promised the woman, and the serpent does not take lightly his hatred for her.

When God appeared to Mary, the mother of Jesus, a man was not present; she was not yet married. God was fulfilling His word spoken to her and the serpent in the Garden of Eden concerning her seed and the serpent's seed. A woman does not naturally have her seed, so it must be spirit. Christ was not conceived by man but by Spirit! Everything that God does, Lucifer imitates or tries to duplicate. He is the Anti-Christ. Satan's trick is to make everything religious to distract from the real deal.

This is not about religion, but about her relationship with the one who loves her and created her and the heavenly kingdom. The woman was created in God's kingdom. Lucifer was cast down out of that same kingdom... get the point! The enemy is trying to disqualify women by turning them into whores. By doing this, he can accuse her of not being clean for God's use. Don't allow your enemy to devalue you.

When Mary Magdalene found the truth in Christ, she immediately knelt before Him and asked for forgiveness. She was converted right away and never prostituted again. She came in as a whore and left as a daughter of God. It's that simple; you don't labor for the gift that God has for you. Your enemy is trying to make you God's enemy by destroying your life. Your enemy wants to use you to tear down marriages, families, and each other.

Why should two women who are the same devil hate allow that

same devil to manipulate them into fighting each other? Save that strength to fight him. Without knowing the history of the woman and the serpent, you can be tricked into taking a backseat in your own life. You must know who you are. God wants to raise you, but you must remain faithful, humble, strong, and not arrogant. God desires to give you a platform to help women; you must understand why

He's blessing you. Lucifer uses religion as one of his greatest instruments to keep you silent. In the church, they say to keep quiet, yet simultaneously, they say you can build the church. This is not what God intended; He's silencing the spirit of rebellion against Him… He will silence Jezebel anywhere!

If you have the spirit of Jezebel, then you are not a daughter of God! God is a God of order and respect, while Satan's children are in rebellion against God's will and order.

Why would God know that the enemy targeted the woman and then allow her to be a sitting duck, waiting to be shot? This is not God! The woman has been under attack from the beginning, so why would God silence her? She must stand for what's right and guide these children to turn back to God. You can't be in your 40s and 50s and still be trying to find a good man in the clubs, surrounded by multiple men who put you at risk of being abused.

What example is this for girls? The woman must know who she is... The message is clear. On that day, I will say to the righteous: when I was hungry, you fed me; when I was thirsty, you gave me drink; when I was naked, you clothed me; when I was homeless, you sheltered me; when I was sick, you came to me; when I was in prison, you visited me.

Then the righteous will ask, "When did we do all these things for you?" God will answer them, "When you did these things to the least person, you did them to me!" When you see God working in people to help those who cannot help themselves, this is the love of God working through them. Where do all her critics come from? She uses her platform to reach millions of sheep, yes, sheep.

When you hear her testimony of her humble beginnings, only God could have done something like this. Who is the woman? Why is she hated? Who are her haters? Haters have a father, too, and he's not in heaven, so be careful, haters! You have no clue about the serpents that fight against her works. Jesus said to the religious leaders of his day,

"If you don't believe in me, then believe in the works that I do. A good tree cannot produce evil fruit, nor can an evil tree produce good fruit; you will know the tree by its fruit." We need to start checking these trees! But even in Jesus' day, they would rather give the devil credit for God's doing.

Even Jesus said to them, "If Satan cast out Satan, then his kingdom would be divided, and a divided house cannot stand." When we leave this earth, many will be surprised at who will enter heaven's gates. Jesus openly told the preachers in the temple (not to the sinners),

"Woe unto you, there will be wailing and gnashing of teeth, you will be cast into outer darkness!" You can't get sweet and bitter waters from the same fountain. God raised this woman for such a time as this.

The Pharisees are also a spirit, the spirit of "Lucifer!" They appear righteous, but they steal from the sheep and oppress them. They deceive them and take their money, leaving them destitute. While the church is trying to keep the woman silent, Satan is giving her a voice in the world to do evil. The spirit of Jezebel is on the loose, in and out of the church. So, what would make anyone think God would not raise someone He could trust to help His sheep? She uses what her Father has entrusted her to do good deeds and help somebody!

We need to learn from children of God like her and many others who do more reaching than preaching! Many church leaders opposed Dr. King in his day, calling him a troublemaker or stating he was from the wrong denomination. This is ignorant!

Many would not even open their church doors for him to preach, but when the doors were opened through "Equal Credit and Housing," these same preachers benefited from that man's sacrifice...hypocrites!

After his assassination, they were the first to buy new Cadillacs and homes. Many, to this day, have not apologized or repented. But now they enjoy wealth, megachurches, and a lifestyle that would not be possible for preachers if this appointed Man of God had not obeyed his assignment.

Many of us have been cowards, merely watching to see how things would unfold. God gave me this assignment over 12 years ago, and I recognized the responsibility and ran from it. I said, "I don't want to be a preacher; I'm a builder!" God turned my life upside down!

Destiny has called me for the last time, and I will not answer! All hell broke loose against me! When I said yes, everybody left me! It has cost me everything to write this book. I thought God would give it to someone else to do, but I see things getting worse and worse. Somebody must stand for what's right!

It took a woman brave enough to use her platform to reach abused women and men! This has inspired millions! This is how God gets the glory! The day is coming when we all will give an account of the gifts God has given us! The kingdom is about righteousness… serving, not waiting to be served. It's not about how many services we attend. Who have we served lately?

THE HATE

Chapter 5

Why are so many little girls molested, teens, and women raped? I won't bore you with numbers. Why are so many women victims of abuse? I want to address what might be behind the hate. Who? Fruit is the evidence or produce from a tree.

"You will know the tree by its fruit." What is the root? If we understand this, we will understand its origin—the root. Anything you see is fruit, but where it came from is the root. We have been fighting the fruit for too long, only to discover that when we think it is solved or gone, here it is, back in our lives again.

That is why a person can apologize for a wrongful act and steadily repeat the same horrific act: because it was never uprooted from the source. Destroy the source and rid yourself of the issue or problem; in other words, eliminate what produces the fruit.

There is a place in scripture where a woman was brought by religious leaders to the "Master" (Teacher) for his opinion on judging a case according to the Law of Moses, concerning a woman who was supposedly caught in the act of adultery.

They pretended to seek justice, but there was one major problem: they only brought the woman forward. Where was the man? You cannot commit the act of adultery by yourself! This illustrates how biased and hateful this was, because the punishment for this act was "death" by stoning. The penalty was usually enforced within 24 hours.

Imagine a woman facing execution, aware that her accomplice is escaping free despite committing the same crime. This situation leaves her feeling inferior, starkly contrasting to when she served the man. She was everything and more while she satisfied him, but utterly diminished when they were apprehended. Publicly, she is shamed, but in private, she was the object of the greatest desire and pleasure; now her fate is shame and death.

The flip side to this is that many women have become cold-hearted, callous, vindictive, and manipulative because of these practices. Many women have done great things to better other people's lives and have made many sacrifices. Not that she got anything out of it sometimes, but most of the time, she had no voice.

Women are influential and the engines behind the scenes, but they are often underrated and taken for granted. It is not fair for us to judge all women for the bad seeds of treacherous people who have sold their souls for the destruction of mankind or life. As long as the earth remains, we will have good and evil, life and death.

The woman has one great enemy: Lucifer, who faithfully seeks ways to destroy her. What's sad is that most women don't even know this! They think these events occur by chance or as a result of some action by man. A man or woman may be collaborating with Satan in her destruction.

If a man does not have a relationship with God (this does not mean religion)—he is honoring, respectful, kind, considerate, submissive, loving, and generous—and is willing to love and protect her with his life! If a man wants you and claims he loves you, saying that you're the one, you can trust that he will be willing to die for you if you are a daughter of God.

We must see this situation for what it is. Anyone can and will make mistakes, but an evil person has no conscience when it comes to killing and destroying someone's life and dreams. They constantly plot to do evil; this is who they are. People may act for survival; when given the opportunity, they will take it in stride and be grateful.

Everyone wants to live a good life, even if they cannot articulate it; they desire it by nature. What mother would not want good for her child? When you encounter a woman who knows "who she is" and "what her purpose is in life," you could have no greater gift.

Everyone who is born has a purpose in life and will not be satisfied unless they are fulfilling that very purpose. We are often distracted by images of someone else's pursuit of their destiny, if not most of the time.

We all have our paths in life, but we become jealous of someone else's success out of ignorance. Just because it works for them does not mean it will work for someone else. For this reason, we become haters and critics of others' contributions to this world.

If anyone strives to bring good to this world and potentially improve things, we should cheer and celebrate them. Given all the evil in the world, we cannot afford to block anyone or anything that brings hope for improvement.

We need all the help we can get to offset evildoers. Critics of good, where did they come from, and who do they work for? In this battle of good and evil, who's behind it? Love is the origin; hate is the by-product. Good is the origin; evil is the by-product. Truth is the origin; a lie is the by-product. Life is the origin; death is the by-product. The by-product tries to supersede the origin.

For example, you have "Crude oil, Kerosene, Gasoline." Crude oil is the origin, and gasoline is the byproduct. The need was kerosene; after the process, the byproduct was waste, and from that waste came gasoline. Then, a source behind the scenes makes the byproduct equal or greater in value than its origin. How?

When the automobile was designed, it was engineered to burn Gasoline." Because of the new demand for its use in automobiles, waste has become a commodity! In other words, the waste is sold for more than the valued product. This is the workings of those who are wise at making money because of their knowledge. The packaging, marketing, and sales became the dressing of the turkey…who will know? Who will care how we did it and what our cost is? They're going to need Gasoline!

Satan plays and preys on those who lack knowledge. You have God-good-evil, God-love-hate, God-truth-lie, God-life-death… get the picture? The last of the three is the waste: Crude-Kerosene-Gasoline! When mankind's love for himself outweighed the love for God and life, a demand was created for the waste.

When we began loving money more than life and valuing it more than God, we started seeking money, power, and pleasures at any cost, even if we hurt, lie, steal, kill, and destroy others in the process.

Can we see how Satan is in demand and he's never been more available? He has stations almost everywhere, even in some of our homes. The Great Wonder in heaven, which is the Woman! You have her and her son in the 12th chapter of Revelation. "The dragon desired to destroy the child as soon as it was born" because he's trying to make him a waste!

Your enemy is trying to devalue your children! Women do not need to fight each other, and by no means support their true enemy in destroying the family, marriage, and relationships that started productively. Only God can produce life; Satan cannot give life, so he recruits, steals it, takes it, uses it, and finally destroys it...this is who he is! "And made war with the remnant of her seed!" That's why we need God to open our eyes, because the Devil in these end times, above all other times, has valued our children as WASTE! He's after your SEED!

There is a prophecy that can only be fulfilled by what the woman gives birth to; it's in Genesis chapter 3. The woman can only avenge herself through what she brings into the world. God tells the woman that she has seed and also tells the serpent that he has seed. We know this cannot be scientifically possible; the male carries the seed. The seed God speaks about is not of the natural but of the supernatural; it's spiritual! From conception, the woman is transformed into another creation…the mother.

She's supernaturally building a relationship with the developing child in her womb. Her spirit transfers into the child, and all she does and will do affects the child. After the child is born, it craves love and nurturing that is known only from the mother. The mother knows her child's movements, cries, and tone; each has significance to her. To another, it's just a cry or noise—everything the mother does or does not do impacts the child. The mother is the child's most significant source of life and depends on her for almost everything.

As she nurtures the child, she makes a spiritual transfer and investment in him. In ancient times, the son would be nurtured by his mother until he was 12 years old. From about 7 to 12 years old, the child would be weaned from his mother to spend time with his father for male adult-like training. What the mother has invested in the child will remain for the rest of her life; no one can sever the ties between them. That's why, conversely, the relationship becomes brutal and bitter if the mother creates bad blood between herself and the child.

Most children, as adults, find it very difficult to function in progressive lives. Even if they meet good partners who give them love, they still feel a void due to the lack of or poor investment from their mothers. There's a far greater need from mothers than from fathers when they are little children; there is a spiritual connection between them. This is the very thing that the woman's enemy (Satan) will use against her if she lacks the knowledge of her God.

She must understand her identity; this is crucial for her and her child's destiny. Her influence and power stem from supernatural sources, and her enemy is aware of this. Consequently, her enemy enlists her to gain control over what she brings into the world.

If he can manipulate her into becoming his servant, he effectively owns her children, even though he has neither fathered them nor given birth to any. He aims to brainwash her to ensure that her children grow up to obey him and engage in wrongdoing. Sex, drugs, alcohol, promiscuity, lying, deception, infidelity, unfaithfulness, and cheating are all tools he seeks to instill within her progeny so that he can forge an army to fight his battles on earth.

The woman's seed is the remedy, the "resolve" not the problem. Thus, Satan's job is to convert the woman by preventing her from doing evil and influencing all who are under her rule. Therefore, her enemy comes early to contaminate her mind, making her an easy target for recruiting. He encourages her to distrust the male at an early age, distorting her mind and way of thinking.

He needs her to distrust and be hurt by the father, so she is an easy target for his abuse and use of her. He devalues her and values her at the same time! Now this can be very confusing...that's the point. The same Devil that rapes her through one body, is the same Devil who provides a way of escape, like a hero. He comes as her knight in shining armor, when he is the Devil's agent, her Destroyer. The Devil who empowered a person through sexual desires to molest the child is the same Devil who will get in a cousin or friend of the family to rape her.

For example, if he starts with her at three years of age, she doesn't know what to believe or think by the time she becomes a teenager, especially in the absence of a loving and protective father. He will use a father, stepfather, brother, sister, cousin, friend, or foe; it doesn't matter, he needs a willing vessel. There are countless women, past, present, and future, who will share stories of being violated and feel too ashamed to reveal them.

The woman who is the victim has no clue that the same enemy (which is spirit) is the voice in her head, manipulating her into believing she should keep this secret. But this secret is killing her. She's living as a slave to this. It does not matter her status, success, or marital situation; she's bound and not free. Many hide behind religion or their careers, but it does not change the fact that she is not free! Many women are unable to function in their relationships because of this. Numerous marriages have ended in divorce, and the Devil is laughing, thinking about how many lives he's destroyed with the same old trick, just used on different victims.

This has been happening since the beginning of time. "He Hates the Woman!" Without God, the woman doesn't stand a chance. Having a man without a relationship with God is like turning yourself over to Satan himself because he will eventually use your partner as his partner in crime. He will even use you (the woman) if you're not wise enough to see.

The young girl, who was preyed upon as a victim of sexual abuse, has now grown and is trying to live an everyday life. The guy is asking her out for a date. He makes her feel good, gives her gifts, takes her out, and does not pursue sex at first, but it's coming. When the time comes for sex, she is now attempting to separate her past experiences of abuse from her current feelings. With this secret, she is ready to open up to this person because she likes him, but she has no idea what it will feel like.

Will it feel like rape or molestation? She must think, "No way," because I like him. Her sexual experience is supposed to be pleasant, and it may certainly start that way. The problem is that the boyfriend will eventually do or say something like what her abuser did or said, but of course, with no knowledge. Here's the problem:

when the Devil uses a perpetrator to commit the violation, he will use many natural behaviors that should have been experienced in a committed and loving relationship, but the flip side is that it is almost impossible not to encounter similar behaviors.

When a woman is ready for a relationship, she will exhibit some behavior patterns of her potential mate. Now, the man who seeks love and companionship with her does not know her past. He is falling for her and simply wants her love, but he is in for a rude awakening. To make matters worse, most women do not disclose this information. However, once the relationship becomes serious, her partner needs to know. When a woman who has been a victim is intimate with her partner, this can become tricky because she holds a secret.

This can lead a woman to have flashbacks, perceiving the one who loves her as the perpetrator, which confuses her. If the guy loves her, he will try to understand her mixed behavior, but how long can this last? The issue is that he doesn't know what he's trying to understand. If he's willing to stick it out, the woman may hesitate to share her past, fearing judgment. Now she is developing feelings for this guy and may consider him a potential partner; things are becoming somewhat serious.

She can sometimes be the most loving person, so compassionate and passionate. But at other times, she can be so distant and doesn't want to be touched. I don't understand. She might not want to seem weird or problematic, so she moves on. She breaks up the relationship, and I don't even know why. I'm pleading with her because I've fallen in love with her. It was so unexpected, but it's true. She leaves and will not answer my calls or return any of them. I'm hurt, to say the least.

What should I do? I think she has another man. She seems so cold and cruel, so maybe this is for the best, and I need to work on getting her out of my mind. I like this girl! She is doing too much work! Finally, I catch up with her and she tells me she doesn't think this is working. I'm asking what went wrong. She has no valid answer and seems immensely irritated by every word I speak.

I'm thinking, who is this person? She says it's over, she's sorry, and then leaves. I cried for her, and I was surprised at myself because I'm not the crying type. What's so sad is that I don't know what happened, and she is so beautiful; I thought she had a beautiful soul and was a wonderful person. The problem is that the issues follow her no matter where she goes.

She is building a track record of failed relationships because she has not dealt with the problem. She has trust issues, which are justified. What's sad is that it's not her fault; instead, it's due to the lack of knowledge or trust. Who can she trust, especially when this happened and her mother did not believe her? Many women have suffered at the hands of their mothers because they told them what happened. They were made to think they had done something wrong to bring this about.

The children are not protected, making it a sad environment for the woman seeking love as an adult. Love should feel beautiful, but instead, it's perverted! In ancient days, a woman's virginity was a commodity. A father would receive a bride's ransom for his daughter's purity. Due to her pure status, they would enter into a contract. The father and mother guarantee the daughter's purity and untouched status.

Upon marriage, at the wedding, the marriage was consummated right there at the reception. The priest, fathers, and mothers of both the husband and wife would be present to witness the blood on the sheets after they had sex. The sheets would then be given to the priest who married them and the husband's father and mother as valid proof.

They would witness and verify the blood as evidence of the purity and virgin status of the daughter. If the daughter was not a virgin, it would be considered fraud, leading to the execution of the bride, her father, and her mother. In this context, one can easily imagine a daughter being valued and protected. What happens in a nation or society where a woman's value system has been so devalued?

This is a reason that so many little girls are violated every day and are victims of sexual abuse. Because no one is accountable for their protection. No one even knows when virginity was taken or given up. It's evident that women are objects of desire and have become twisted because they must figure out how to protect themselves. So, we have a society where women may feel like they'll give it away before they let another man take it from them.

This is a trick, but she desperately seeks to regain her power. She's tired of being used and abused. She's tired of being abandoned because she's not good enough. So, some say, "I'll get him before he gets me!" The woman who's been a victim is now taking control. Since she can't regain her virginity, some become withdrawn, while others sell their bodies or become exotic dancers.

The success of long-term relationships is almost impossible or unlikely. So, we try to glamorize it through videos and media, but the reality is that young men are angry at women, and you hear it in their music. They are calling them "Hoes and Tricks!" Nobody trusts anybody.

Everybody is in the game, and Satan is the director. Many are on drugs and alcohol, trying to escape their demons from their past, but he won't leave her alone. Even though he's not physical, he's in her mind playing head games.

Sadly, this monster has moved on to his next victim. Who are these women protecting? She allows him to ruin her chances for a happy life… can we get some "HELP PLEASE?" How many women are hiding in the crowd with this same story? It's so not fair to the woman and her children. Will she ever be happy? I believe God is the answer, along with professional help, love, and support. But we must be honest and support one another. So many hide behind a beautiful mask, but these issues hurt too many people; it must stop.

To those who don't understand what you've endured, they often respond in anger because of the pain you've caused. Now Satan has achieved the ultimate victory; never has the devil had so many men on his side to bring destruction upon the woman.

Examine history, and you will see. Never before have so many women been so widely degraded and disrespected! Amid this surge of disrespect, the woman's enemy hopes to set her back for the kill. But Revelation declares that the woman will receive help. The earth will assist the woman. Observe how we have shifted from praising the woman to thoroughly and openly embarrassing her. Where is her protection and her moral guide?

Unfortunately, the woman has been the victim of war. She

uses her outer parts as weapons for vengeance when it will be her head… brains! Her intellect and spiritual empowerment are her deliverance, not her body. It will be the glory of God placed in her that gives her power. The trouble in this world is that Satan uses the woman's body as a distraction, but God will use her mind, intelligence, education, and relationship with Him to empower her.

God spoke it from the beginning in the Garden of Eden and declared it concerning who the Woman is in the heavens above. God and the Heavens called her, "A GREAT WONDER!" When it is all said and done, that is what she'll be… "A GREAT WONDER!"

Nothing has been created greater than her glory! The face of the woman is about to change globally! The woman needs to understand that there's only one she can trust: her Father in Heaven! If her man is not a God-man, then he will be used to turn her away from her divine purpose, and God knows it was not "WHOREDOM!"

Who has turned her pain into selling her body and making her a whore? Satan's making everything about her, shame, and "vanity!" Her enemy is trying to make her vain. She is obsessed with her outer appearance and her looks, but not concerned with her heart and "The contents of her character!"

No matter what she does, her body will inevitably change, but the building of character is forever. The enemy of the woman has the woman competing with the woman, when in fact the woman needs the woman to defeat her enemy, the Serpent!

HE HATES ALL WOMEN: Rich, Poor, Black, White, Married, Single, Successful, Non-successful, Fat, Slim, Republicans, Democrats, Christians, Muslims, Hindus, Buddhists, Gay, Straight, Foreigners, or Americans, God-fearing or Atheists… He HATES all of you, Women!

If she is the daughter of God, she will be vindicated, and it's simple if she can turn and forgive and be forgiven by submitting to her Heavenly Father, and not be evil in assisting the devil to destroy life and family. When she leaves this life, she will be the god she was meant to be, and her body will be perfect without aging. Your body will be paralleled with your character. Great character, great body!

It's time for all Women to unite for the actual cause, which is warring against the real enemy…The Serpent! Making our world a better place for our families to live. To the Woman, it is not the other woman who is your enemy, but the serpent is making her your enemy because of a lack of knowledge. We must know our God and His enemy. God's enemy is your enemy because He replaced him with YOU! Lucifer thought he was Irreplaceable, but God told him, "To the left!"

Remember Beyonce's song "Irreplaceable?" Listen to the message in the music. It speaks of the relationship in heaven between God and Satan (whether they knew this when they wrote it or not, but Lucifer knows this is an accurate account of his past life in heaven). "If I'm not your everything, then I will be nothing to you!"

Jesus said, "When I return and my Holy Angels are with me, I will separate my sheep from the goats, and all the sheep will be on my right side and the goats to my left. The sheep will enter the gates of heaven, but the goats will be cast into eternal damnation!" (Matthew 25: 31-46)

I wouldn't be too excited about being called a "G.O.A.T."; as Christians and Believers, don't accept anyone calling you a "GOAT!" Lucifer knows precisely what this means! Just like when he persuaded Eve to eat from the wrong tree, praising her opened her eyes to good and evil. He set her up! He's doing the very same thing to this generation.

Please read and study for yourself. This generation is unlike any other generation to grace this planet! You have tremendous access to information and knowledge. Use your power for change, for the good of this world. Women are called to give hope for generations to come. Women cannot continue to support men who were born of a woman's body but insist on promoting their hate and disrespect for women!

When a woman who was created with all this glory from God, "Clothed with the Sun, the moon under her feet and a crown of 12 stars on her head," needs we say more?

How can a woman, any woman, participate in buying a song, album, download, stream, or video that's degrading herself and/or any woman? Stand up! If a man wants to degrade you in a video, then let him do what Lucifer did; let him impersonate the woman.

Make him dress up like a woman and then portray his hate for the woman! Now that would make sense! But don't support his hate for you! Yet any woman would have to be a fool to support any industry degrading, enslaving, disrespecting, and violating God's greatest Masterpiece… The Woman!

We as men… Real men need to take their place and not support this devil in destroying our women! If you are a man, love your mother, wife, sister, daughter, girlfriend, or friend, then you should not participate with these half-men who exploit and degrade God's daughters.

The devil can do as he wants with his own property, but not with God's property! The devil has no power to give life or create life, but he gets his children through deceit. They chose him and his evil to unite and destroy good works. Every good and perfect gift comes from God.

Can you see how he perverts the gifts? Openly promoting the destruction of life and a people is, without a doubt, the work of the Devil! We could truly see if we stopped trying to turn kingdom life and our relationship with God into a religion. God is a Father; He should be seen this way, and we should get closer to Him. I will use Berry Gordy as an example.

When God is ready to move, He will give someone a vision. Somebody must see what God sees and be willing to do what He tells them, and it will come to pass. When you look at how Motown came together, you will know that this was God's doing.

When God is in the picture, He does not start with money; He begins with faith, heavenly gifts, and talents! Where did the songs come from? People believe that the devil is talented. Even in the Bible, when God did great things, the religious people gave the devil credit for it, but the devil is a liar! God will give someone an idea; this is God's nature in us as His children, and it's up to us to follow His instructions. With all the odds against Mr. Gordy?

Don't think he could have reached fame and acclaim without Heaven's endorsements for a minute. People cannot do what he and those sent by God can do, both then and now. The industry, with its millions of dollars, does not have the same impact. Berry Gordy and

Smokey Robinson testify that they accomplished this one day at a time. Each idea, song, songwriter, musician, producer, engineer, and artist was orchestrated by something bigger than themselves. They created music as medicine that helped a sick nation. God provided Motown with some much-needed medicine for a very sick nation.

The world would soon discover that good music is born from pain, just like a baby! Only God could devise a method for creating world-changing music from the degraded times and streets of oppressed people. How could something so beautiful emerge from something hopeless, forgotten, and bad? Yes, the people, or artists, faced challenges; this was bigger than life, unfolding through damaged goods, and no one saw it coming. It was just a dream.

God is the Master who created the musical masters. The genius behind the scenes is God Almighty. He set the stage, and the timing gave birth to the talents and gifts to be used. They would have had a better plan if they had known in advance. The truth is, they were just as shocked as the world when they blew up.

They were instruments in the hands of God, bringing a piece of heaven to earth. The world needed something without knowing what it was. The music began to give hopeless people hope. Where there was racial tension and hardship, downtrodden individuals created good music with messages of hope, peace, and joy. How do you borrow $800, build this incredible Empire, and make history? The biblical meaning of 8 is, "New Beginnings." How ironic! He started this music,

"Empire," that would change the world forever. The music is undeniable and Timeless! During this era of civil rights, we faced persistent hatred and racism. This music was produced by Black artists and took over the airwaves. These occurrences did not happen by chance. How could this happen during such racial tension? They were charting hits on the Pop Charts, not just Rhythm and Blues. It was a sound! God was in this sound.

Religious people wanted to say it was the Devil, but even during Jesus's days, religious leaders referred to him as the "Devil," despite his good deeds for the people. When people can't explain something bigger than life or out of the ordinary that brings positive change, they declare, "It's the Devil!" Consider this: "The Devil's

Music— Yeah right!" Jesus said, "A good tree cannot produce good fruit." This music was, and still is, good fruit.

The level of quality in the music can only be attributed to God, for He is good. Satan cannot receive credit for this goodness because "An evil tree cannot bring forth good fruit." Good try, Satan! If we have any historical knowledge, we know that Satan comes to destroy, kill, and steal through various means: hurts, broken dreams, disappointments, disagreements, drug problems, you name it; it was all present. But who brought it there? This was significant—why wouldn't the devil intervene after the fact? Man, nobody was prepared for this phenomenon!

Black people were in the eyes of the whole world, and God placed them there. The world did not see Dr. Martin Luther King, Berry Gordy, Smokey Robinson, and Motown as evil or the Devil. They could not accomplish this overnight, but a series of events and experiences is the evidence that something bigger than they was leading and guiding them.

They were bringing about social change for all people. Only something supernatural could have the power to move this machine through such times of hatred, inadequacies, and opposition. These things occurred in this era of racial hatred and racism, and were necessary for the hand of God to be seen.

With this kind of power, demons will show themselves. This was a lot of responsibility and glory for these artists, musicians, writers, and producers to handle in the face of uncertainty. The Devil, of course, would now try to attack them in many ways. God took people who hated them to accept them through music.

They could not eat in restaurants, use restrooms, ride buses, drink from water fountains, or stay in hotels as equals, but black music and artists were welcomed into their living rooms. Motown went through the doors of white America's homes daily…through television, radio, and record players. How can we not see the hand of God in this…Do we need a "Movement" now? Listen to the devil talking to our children through today's music.

Now, call this the "devil" because it's killing and destroying a nation! It can only happen when God is involved! While Dr. King and the Civil Rights Movement occurred, Motown laid out the Red Carpet through their music. Imagine what the movement would have been like without Motown in the homes of White Americans during a time of such racial tension! This music was used to "Sooth the Savage Beast!" Revelation talks about the Beast!

It's a spirit that opposes righteousness! Motown offered a glimpse of heaven's war of good, but the Devil cannot tolerate goodness without chaos and hatred. That's why he's been cast down and out…he's a troublemaker. "When I would do good, evil was always present." Everything God creates that is good, Satan follows up and twists it into evil if we're not vigilant.

Therefore, we must be God's conscience; this has been evident throughout history. He is a thief. God is the ORIGINATOR, THE REAL, and Satan is the FAKE, THE COUNTERFEIT! He is always copying good things and ruining them!

Look at all that good music from yesterday and listen to it today. Listen to the message! It uplifted people and praised women; today, music's message is destructive, tearing down people and degrading women. Open your eyes. Wake up! With everything that has happened, including war and drugs, Berry Gordy and Smokey Robinson did not make music talking about how much dope, houses, cars, women, jewelry, and money they had.

All these messages are self-centered and selfish. If you ever wanted to see the Devil, he's not in horns and a red suit with a pitchfork; he's bragging about himself, but with God's stuff that he stole. And get this: he can't take anything he's bragging about off this planet to wherever he's going! I think that's stupid! He's a hater but a lover of himself!

He is fueled by hatred and will destroy you while making a way for himself to come up! He will ruin your dreams and do everything to make his dreams come true. He will kill your children and go home praying that his children are safe and sound.

He will destroy your future and sacrifice everything you have to secure his. Please, we need to open our eyes! Do we honestly think God is in heaven planning to give eternal rewards and say to most of today's artists, producers, and writers, "Well Done!"

We've got to be kidding! Listen to the messages, and better yet, look at the results! God is watching the killing of His children, turning them into thieves, murderers, whores, liars, manipulators, destroyers of good and life; you know the rest! No matter what we have done in life, if we can call on the name of the Lord, repent, and ask Him for forgiveness, we will be saved.

Salvation is a work of the heart. The heart needs to change, and then a renewed mind. God already provides forgiveness, but all we must do is go to Him. What father would refuse his child if they came to Him humbly seeking help?

Only the proud will not be sorry for killing and destroying life; these are none of His. We will be surprised at those who did and didn't enter heaven. Religion will not do it! "The Father knows those who are His." God is love, and make no mistake about it!

He cares nothing about religions but about love, saving lives, and helping to bring good to the world—this is His will. Many people in religion are meant to be " Cobras!" and equally venomous! This life is about who our Father is and what kingdom we are from: God or Satan, good or evil?

Believing in God does not benefit Him, nor does it determine His existence. He is God all by Himself; believing in Him benefits us. We don't have to believe in death, but one day we will inevitably die! Death is the one thing we all share across the spectrum. We don't have to believe in the law of gravity, but if we don't pick up our feet or step off a bridge, we will fall, regardless of our beliefs. We can't see the law, but we should respect it to be safe and live.

We can't see the signal that makes our cell phones work, but we continue to use them and heavily depend on them. We don't say, "I'm not using that thing until I see a signal." So, how much more should we respect God? No matter how much earthly power anyone possesses or money they wish they had, they still desire power over Death!

Death is the enemy of us all! Sometimes a man feels powerful because he took someone's life prematurely, but that man will eventually die. He may live another 10 or 30 years, but eventually, he too must die! Do we see justice in this?

This is the verdict: Light has come into the world, but people love darkness instead of light because their deeds are evil.

Everyone who does evil hates the light and will not come into the light for fear that their deeds will be exposed. But whoever lives by the truth comes into the light so that it may be seen plainly that what they have done has been done in the sight of God (John 3:19-21).

This is by no means to say anyone is perfect, but we will answer to God for what we did in this life and whether we were obedient to God's assignment. The Bible says, "Abraham's obedience to God was counted unto him as righteousness." So, he was far from being righteous or perfect, but doing what God gave him was his present to the Almighty.

JEALOUSY

Chapter 6

Setting the Record Straight

Let's set the record straight: Jesus came into the world not just to show us the way, but to reveal the secrets of His Kingdom and, ultimately, to die for us, so that we could be reconciled to God. In God's Kingdom, there is no competition and no jealousy.

No one has to strive or fight for the Father's love. God rejects offerings that are born out of rivalry or pride. God created us; He knows our weaknesses and flaws and still favors us.

We have already been accepted. Each of us has been uniquely crafted with individuality: a distinct fingerprint (in the flesh) and a distinct soul (in the spirit). God expects us to fulfill the role He assigned us in life and His Kingdom. True fulfillment comes from obedience to His call, not competing with one another.

Kingdom life is about **completing**, not competing. Satan twisted this truth a long time ago. When we compete against one another in the church and jealousy or division creeps in, we act not like Christ but like the enemy. If competition within the body of Christ breeds strife and resentment instead of fullness and joy, then it is not of God — it must be rejected.

Jesus always chose the right person for the correct assignment. Sometimes, he called all twelve disciples. Other times, He took only seven, five, or only Peter, James, and John. It was never about favoritism; it was always about completing the Father's work. The devil will fight you if you truly do God's will.

That's why we need all the help, unity, and support we can get. So why sabotage your brothers and sisters? Why tear down what God is building? The work of the Kingdom is what pleases the Father.

Completing His mission together, in unity and love, brings Him glory.

When Jesus completed what the Father asked him to do, he said, "It is finished!" Another translation says, "It is completion!" Before approaching the assignment of the shame of dying on the cross, Jesus prayed in the Garden of Gethsemane, asking three times if he could drink from this bitter cup. In other words, can this be done another way?

But Jesus said, "Nevertheless, not my will but your will be done." This was the best gift Jesus could offer his Father. How many were jealous of this gift at the time? Who was competing with Jesus to please God? No one could do His job; God wanted Jesus only to die on that cross. This offering pleased God because He saw us saved, safe, and secured our place in heaven even today. Be yourself! Leave ego, pride, and all the other attributes of the devil to the devil.

Be the best that you can be; this is the gift we are meant to bring to life. Jesus did not compete with anyone. The devil could not get him to do the "EGO" tricks and "Pride" games. When the religious leaders tried to get him to prove himself to them, he never did. Instead, he gave them the word of God and a warning of destruction, not a performance!

He was not performing for the devil while serving him the word of God. Many of us benefit today and beyond because of Jesus's obedience to God. His focus was on the right people, not the left. He will never be satisfied, no matter what you do for the devil. Look for that sign in people, even when we pray and look in the mirror. We must think beyond ourselves and this moment in life… there's a bigger picture. Jealousy has a root, and it needs to be plucked up no matter how much it hurts.

You do not want jealousy to be the producer in your life, because those fruits are deadly. This is one of the reasons Jesus said, "Satan, you are a liar and the father of lies and murderers, you have been from the beginning." Jealousy is a life-threatening disease. It cannot and will not be a part of God's kingdom. This is why heaven will never be Satan's home again. He chose pride over God and everything holy, pure, and good. Satan loves the good life, but he is not good!

Jesus was so focused on his assignment and pleasing his heavenly Father that anything else seemed foolish. One day we will see Jesus face to face. Jealousy will burn in his glorious presence. Sabotaging even your children, spouses, and siblings while pretending to be following the calling of God, when you know the truth, is futile. Nothing will be hidden that will not be exposed. Satan has deceived many leaders into thinking they are special and will get a free pass.

The only pass known to mankind is— REPENT! Why are you so protective of jealousy, when it is a spirit that is cancerous to your soul and a threat to your relationship with the Father? "Jealousy is cruel as the grave!" Jealousy is a root, and its fruit is murder! Jealousy kills. It will kill your dreams, it will kill your happiness, and it will kill your children's dreams.

It will lead you to destroy the dreams of your husband, children, and everyone around you, just as long as your dream can be fulfilled. Even when your dream has turned into everyone else's nightmare, jealousy will still have you driving until nothing is left but to bury you! Have you ever given or done good for someone and been hated for it?

It's hard to understand how family or anyone else, for that matter, can be jealous, mad, and even furious with you for having favor with God. We would have to be evil to understand. Jealousy will kill your relationships, whether marital or otherwise.

Jealousy kills! It is the most notorious killer there is! Jealousy will kill you spiritually and naturally. People who don't dare to kill someone physically are killers spiritually and emotionally; they are assassins of character every day, but they think they are better than those who took a physical life. You must be able to kill in the mind, then in the heart, before you kill in the physical realm.

The day will come when we all will be judged for every word that comes from our mouths, not the mouths of prophets and religious people; they will have their issues to deal with...you can trust God on that one. That's why it's important to repent, forgive, and apologize when we hurt people or take a life. It could be because of envy or jealousy.

The first biblical murder was of an older brother who was jealous of the younger brother for doing something good that was simply praised and acknowledged by God. Did the brother deserve to die? NO! Listen to what God said to the brother before he killed his brother, "If you do well, I will reward you as well." Do you see this picture if you do well?

It's up to us to do something to be honored or recognized—doing something good in the sight of Almighty God! Yet, we have those who are vessels filled with jealousy. Cain killed his brother over Abel's good deed that garnered notoriety and honor from God. Jealousy is the root that produces the fruit of death, even for his baby brother.

When God asked Cain, the oldest brother, where Abel was, Cain responded, "Am I my brother's keeper?" Then God said, "Your brother's blood is crying out!"

We have been deceived into thinking we can outsmart God, but cannot. Ask old Lucifer, and he'll tell you, not with words, but through his track record. We compete for so much that we would kill to have what others possess, instead of pursuing our paths, answering our calling, and walking in our lanes. Even in church—that's right, in church! We fight for recognition from the wrong sources and believe we have escaped the consequences.

Men often forget that God is the reward for hard work and faithfulness. Backbiting and speaking about one another to undermine visions, whether good or not, is about being on top. It should always focus on the people and what is best for them, with God's help, not our social status or expectations at the expense of His sheep. We all make mistakes, some greater than others, but the word of God says, "If we mess up on one law, we might as well have messed up on all."

This is not to say don't try to do good, but don't be so full of yourself as to think you are good on your own. We all need help; we cannot do it alone. We have a Father. God does not take pleasure in us killing our brothers and sisters and thinking He will reward us for it. If we receive a reward for evil in this world, there will be a price to pay in the next.

That's why most evil people, whose father, the devil, uses,

dismiss life after death, because that would mean acknowledging torment and facing penalties for their crimes.

Crime is only enjoyable when you think you've gotten away with it. What criminal or real gangster looks forward to a court date, knowing there's evidence piled against them to be judged and convicted, reminding them of how they achieved their lifestyles?

This is hypocrisy at its best. How would you feel knowing you worked hard to live in a safe community focused on progress, family, security, and a good life? You're thinking about your family, and when you see the rewards of your efforts, you feel that all your hard work is paying off.

Yet, your neighbor, who speaks to you, has killed several people just last night. How would you know? Because we live in a culture where the love of money rules, not morals.

So, criminals are motivated to get the money to be accepted as they are. We created this monster of "Paper Chasers" instead of "God Chasers." We shape our children's future through exposed lifestyles that lack morals or respect. If we have been given a platform to influence people, we should review our work and ask if we're proud of our impact on so many. Vanity is the new face, and jealousy is the other two-faced side of life.

Not everyone is our competition. Without constant competition, we would have room to celebrate people for their gifts and talents. We are often placed in someone's life to help complete them and ourselves, if we do not always compete.

Usually, we see critical and often outright cruel comments about people's talents, especially on social media, even though most cannot come close to what someone posted. If your first thought is to criticize others, we must remember that God created us differently on purpose. We must be constructive, not destructive. All of us have strengths and weaknesses.

Whenever God tears us down, it's only to build us back up and improve us. Celebration rather than jealousy would turn this world right side up.

The Church as the Body of Christ should not be jealous of one another because we represent one kingdom where God is our Father.

We are One! How can the eyes be jealous of the mouth, or the hands compete with the hands? We should uplift one another and not tear down unless we plan to stick around to make things better. Can your head hurt while the rest of your body rejoices and says, "That headache is your problem"? No way; the entire body shares that pain.

Why do we compete rather than complete each other? Jesus told his followers, "Love each other as I have loved you; by this, the world will know you are with me by how much you love one another." When Jesus finished his work, He said, "It is finished!"

Another translation says, "It is completion!" We are called to complete each other, not compete. This leaves very little room for jealousy. Many families end in tragedy because of this spirit. Dreams, hopes, and joy die at the sickness of jealousy.

Cain killed his baby brother out of jealousy. All Cain had to do was follow his brother's example of what pleases God. Do you know many people in church who compete for the spotlight or the pastor's favor and will kill for that position?

Forgetting that God is watching and rejecting their entire display of praise and worship. Worshipping God is not a competition but a personal offering to Him. Nobody can beat you at being you. God accepted Abel's offering, but was waiting for Cain because no one could ever give God what Cain should have given.

No matter how many children you have, they are all individuals with their own personalities. Jealousy kicked the angels out of heaven. Competing infected them.

So if you're jealous of anyone, check it and lay it down at the altar before you offer God anything, especially praise and worship, because He will not receive that vain offering of vanity. Ask Jealousy how many lives it has destroyed and is still counting? Those who dare to obey God will tap into their potential if they hear and heed that tiny voice within, guiding them to their destiny.

If they are willing to separate themselves from those who are not pushing or helping them to reach their destiny and purpose, and are ready to make necessary adjustments in their lives, including having lots of friends and partying all the time, they can see the birth of their vision rather than criticize someone else's hard work.

God is not a "CRITIC," but Satan is! It's time to call out the engine behind the madness!

Most criticisms are driven by jealousy, and the Word says, "Jealousy is cruel as the grave!" If you are a critic of good, then we know you should have no problem with death, because death is your brother and is the greatest critic of them all. Death is never satisfied nor pleased. He finds something wrong to say about everyone who lives, no matter how many lives he's given. So, when your critic shows up for you, no matter when it comes and how it shows itself, it's the only thing you will not be able to criticize! Satan is humanity's accuser!

Do you know how many lives have been destroyed because of false accusations? "And I heard a loud voice saying in heaven, Now is come salvation and strength, and the kingdom of our God, and the power of his Christ: for the accuser of our brethren is cast down, which accused them before our God day and night." (Revelation 12:10)

The Devil's children work overtime to secure their pompous positions in society. They dress up so well. Jealousy can stand before judges and a jury, holding to a straight face while lying to you for self-gain. Only the Devil can make a lie sound like the truth because he is the father of lies, and his children want to be like their father.

"You are of your father the devil, and the lusts of your father ye will do. He was a murderer from the beginning, and abode not in the truth because there is no truth in him. When he speaks a lie, he speaks of his own: for he is a liar and the father of it." (John 8:44)

So, they practice and rehearse lying to perfection, attempting to lie like their father in hopes of pleasing him to receive rewards. A lie can originate from the truth, but the truth cannot stem from a lie because the truth came first and is the origin of all life, good or evil.

To the daughters of The Most High God, do you know that the same spirit that drives you to lie for a better life or revenge is the same devil that persecutes you all the days of your natural life and your children, especially your daughters!

Don't allow your enemy to pressure you so much that you lie to seem beautiful on the outside, dress up in pretty shoes, and rob yourself of your wings. Remember, he's a serpent, a snake, unable to fly; his strength and power lie on the ground, in the dirt. In contrast, your strength and power lie in flying; he has no power over you.

He keeps you so confused, desperate, afraid, and thirsty that your decisions become his decisions for you. They are foot decisions, rather than head decisions. You are meant to be above only, and not beneath.

"The Lord will make you the head, not the tail. If you pay attention to the commands of the Lord your God that I give you this day and carefully follow them, you will always be at the top, never at the bottom." (Deuteronomy 28:13 NIV) "And when the dragon saw that he was cast unto the earth, he persecuted the woman which brought forth the man child.

And to the woman were given two wings of a great eagle, that she might fly into the wilderness, into her place, where she is nourished for a time and times, and half a time, from the face of the serpent." (Revelation 12:13-14)

The mother is an example. Either they want to be like you or don't want anything similar to you. Fallen from grace due to listening to and obeying the wrong (god) voice! Yesterday, the enemy told you you're too young for life; today, you're too old, and tomorrow, he prepares you for death.

If he can't use you, he will dispose of you without emotion; he has no love for you. I pray, women, your eyes come open and come home. I know of "Prodigal Sons," but it's time to welcome the "Prodigal Daughters" back home!

Your Father loves you and is waiting! Learn to love your sisters and not be jealous of one another. So many women need another woman for their healing. But it cannot be achieved or accomplished with jealousy, because that spirit will make you lie and pretend.

To accomplish true victory and success, we need transparency. The pains of your past are those of your sisters' past and sometimes present. She needs your help, and you need hers. Jealousy has no room here and should not be welcomed. Just love her as the Lord loves you.

Don't allow Satan, through men or any persons, to tell you that you cannot preach and teach the gospel after all the HELL you have endured to reach your God! I'm not promoting 'REBELLION' but the very opposite!

I'm talking about "SUBMISSION" to God your Father in the name of our Lord Jesus Christ and submitting to the Will of God, as Jesus and his followers did! Allow the spirit of Christ and the Holy Ghost to work through you! Come, Lord Jesus...come!

DAUGHTERS, I SALUTE YOU!

Competition in the church is of the devil! Study the traits of your enemy; know and understand his nature. He cannot love! He is fake! He is phony! He is a liar! HE IS JEALOUS—HE IS JEALOUS!

EXPOSED SECRETS OF THE HEART

Chapter 7

I Am sent to bring revelation knowledge and to clear up some mysteries, also to sound the alarm and help a generation to "Wake up" out of sleep and turn back to their source for life...God!

As a people of all races, nationalities, cultures, religions, and social, economic, and political backgrounds, we feel something that we cannot express or explain, but the whole world somehow knows; it's something in the air. We need a change, and we desperately need something that we've never seen before!

The world is God's place of restoration, manifestation, and discovery. Why discover? He's building a case, where we all will go on trial at "The halls of the Great White Throne of Heaven." All of us who have lived on earth are going to trial.

This is where we will all be judged. We will all give an account of how we lived and dealt with all people, everyone with whom we have interacted. Every life becomes a certificate of validation and proof of our life here. Before our life is over, we are served a subpoena when death appears, giving us a scheduled court date.

Subpoena: the usual writ for the summoning of witnesses or submitting evidence, as records or documents, before a court or other deliberative body.

Exposing all secrets of the heart, from eternity to time, is the ultimate purpose of humanity. From Lucifer and his Angels to the holy Angels of God, from the holy Celestial Cherubs of the Most High God to the fallen angels of Satan, even the heart of God will be tested; there will be no more secrets. We all expect something, but don't know what. Who better than the woman should teach us the lesson? We go after what we can see, but what we can see is the exposure of what we cannot see, which is the heart!

Understand this: God is the Boss! Many have been distracted from the "real you." There is another you that is greater than the you with which you are familiar. Life is all about finding the God in you with purpose, which was put in you when He created you. This is what the Devil does not want you to discover.

The Bible talks about a fisherman, Peter, who was born Simon. Simon worked a job or business, but was unsatisfied with his life. Frustrated with his income and how life treated him, he was tempted to become bitter, as so many of us do. The unsatisfied person can be lethal with their tongue; they are your worst critics. Why?

They want to make your life miserable because they are unhappy with their own life.

You will find that the most critical people in other people's lives are usually those who are unsatisfied with their own lives. They get off by critiquing and criticizing other people's works and accomplishments because they have none of their own! If they were given one chance to do what you do regularly, they would likely freeze up like an iceberg!

If given the chance, they would say, OMG, I didn't know it was this hard. No matter what you've achieved compared to them, they are deceived into believing their opinion concerning someone else's works counts for something.

God has chosen some to impact the world and make it to the top of the charts by doing good works and displaying their talents, bringing some joy to the world, while others sit around trying to find fault or flaw with these Godly gifts.

Can you make a number one anything? The reality is this: you're not condemning the gift, but the Giver of the gift! You are judging God and seeing how it will turn out. "In the manner that we judge, we will be judged; and every word we speak will be used to justify or condemn us on the Day of Judgment!" I am prepared to face God for everything I write in this book!

We should repent and be thankful for the gifts and talents that

God gives to us on earth. We all have at least one gift or talent. One day, we will give an account for the gift that we've been given. Everyone is meant to lead, especially if they are blind.

Those who have vision should be the leaders. Beware of following blind guides. What would we be doing if it were not for some of the gifts we are given?

Life would be boring. Everybody is not created to do the same thing, so find out what your thing is to do, and just do it! Be the best that you can be and contribute to building up and not tearing down! Simon was this kind of man; he had a problem with most.

Now, you would think this God of heaven would know better than to hand-pick such a man for ministry. You would think God would go to the Temple, Synagogue, or Church in our day and times if He's picking someone for ministry to represent Him. But he chooses this man from the streets; he's ungodly, wild, loud, opinionated, and has a foul mouth.

He's not a fan of priests or preachers at all. He's not the church-going or temple-worshipping type, as we think it should be today. Nevertheless, Jesus still chooses this man and selects him as a candidate for the Kingdom Movement, which makes him a disciple and leader.

He asks Simon to follow him so he can have a real account of who God is and how he works. There is nothing like the religious examples set before them. Simon is struggling, and He gives Simon the miracle of supplying fish for his much-needed business.

Fish was his source of income; in other words, the man struggled to care for his family. Simon did not want to hear a sermon, but if God was real, he needed Him to do something about his situation.

Jesus obliged him and did not take no for an answer, concerning who he was/is, and the destiny set before him. Later, Jesus changes Simon's name to Peter and is made the leader of this movement. Hardly anyone remembers Simon, but they surely do know who Peter is.

This is the opposite of all we see and learn in church. We have been conditioned to look for perfection, and that's why we birth hypocrites, because we know we are not all those things and are under so much pressure to prove perfection according to man's standards, not God's.

We'll never make it in our righteousness. We are justified through the righteousness of God. Peter was Simon's untapped potential and looked nothing like the Simon that even Simon himself thought he knew.

There's another you in all of you. Life is about being born a caterpillar, but all of us have the potential to transition into a butterfly.

All of us have butterfly potential, but many are unwilling to do what it takes to become the butterfly. To become a butterfly, you must walk alone, cry sometimes, be misjudged, misunderstood, separated, practice, pray, be patient, talk about horribly, and most of all... Hated! So, what do we do?

Those not tired of crawling become the haters of the same butterflies we secretly admire and envy simultaneously, because of jealousy; deep down within, we know by now we should have our wings!

Hate on, but by doing so, you will miss the destiny only God can give you. Haters don't get wings but die as worms. Peter submitted, repented, and stopped hating on those he didn't understand. We are so messed up today because we have lost the courage of the true prophets of yesterday to tell us the truth.

Everyone wants to be liked and accepted these days, but the truth is that we as a people need God's rod to whip our behinds back in our lives so we can come to our senses and be righteous people again who love God first and the life with which He has blessed us.

I don't know; for many of us, it's a curse! Look around you; we as a nation are killing one another for things that glitter and have produced souls that are filthy, stinky, and dirty, all for the love of money! Lucifer is behind the scenes pulling the strings; he's the puppeteer.

Listen to the confessions of his heart, and you will find he's selfish and has nothing to lose, so why follow him? When you leave here, no matter what he gave you in time, you cannot take it to eternity.

He will mock you and torment your mind forever because he knows you should not be with him through eternity, but where else should you go but with him, because you followed him just as the angels did, He could have made more angels, then I could compete with them, but this woman I can't. Satan is thinking, "I'm feeling things.

I've never felt before; it's something about her presence that gets to me, man, I hate her!" She made things that were hidden come up out of me like vomit! Things came out of me that I never knew existed. While I was being demoted and falling, she was being exalted! I hate her! Until she came along, I was the beauty of heaven. I was the most remembered creation ever. I was the talk of heaven, the center of attention, and the top of all things but God.

I received praise, worship, honor, and rewards for my achievements. I was the most desired visible thing. I made everyone feel good just by being in my presence. This is the gift of God given to me. I was the closest thing to God until you came into the picture.

I prided myself on being the best! I never thought that there would be anyone or anything greater than myself. I felt betrayed, for God has created such wonderfully fashioned beings of beauty with multiple gifts and talents. How could God generate this being called Woman and give her all these extras?

Why is she so beautiful? Why did He make her this way? She is fabulous, but I will never tell her. I can't stand her! She is stunning and has the grace of God all over her. I study her all the time, but she doesn't know it. I will be like her; one day, I will duplicate her!

Her glory separates her from all of heaven's creation! Somehow, I must get my hands on her glory. She is created from God's greatest love and desire to represent Him and everything related to His passion. How can this love God has for her be expressed? All the heavens marvel at this "Great Wonder." It's why she seems to be the most difficult. It would be wise for anyone to go to her Creator to get to know and understand her.

Lucifer wished he could work it like the woman, their constant feud. It was not the woman who hated him, but he hated the woman without getting to know her. How often have you felt hated by others you didn't know and may have wondered, "Why are they hating?" Haters have been around since you were created. Therefore, it is essential for all women not to allow the same enemy who hates all women to be so crafty and wise to use you to hate a woman!

A woman hating another woman would be like a bird hating its wings; they need each other. The wings are what make a bird. Women are wings. Every woman needs the woman; she is the life-giver, the source that carries and nurtures life. The enemy of the woman is using the woman to hate the woman. He needs a way in, a door or window.

Women are very competitive by nature. So, the enemy of the woman from her very beginning uses this quality against her. Your competition is Lucifer, not another woman. Lucifer is your enemy, not her. Every woman is hated just as much as the next.

It doesn't matter the race, religion, sexual orientation, shape, weight, size, outer or inner beauty, and so forth, as long as you are a woman. He hates you and will use your gender to destroy you if possible. Unfortunately, we seem to appreciate each other in times of adversity and crisis.

In wars, you can look over history and see how multifaceted women could be, even when considered second-class citizens. She would fill in the shoes and do the jobs that under normal circumstances would be performed by men. When necessary, she can step up to the plate. Women have this supernatural strength when necessary.

It's a part of their makeup. Men can be out of touch with a woman's value by looking at her outer appearance and missing the value of her heart and soul and the strength of her character. She's described as Adam's helper, not his hater, completer, or competition. She was not created to compete with him but to complete him.

I know it's a popular saying, "I don't need a man to complete me," but the reality is that God created them to need each other, and without them, the world would be extinct. It's not about the woman competing with anyone, but the value of her worth. The woman is a hero in everyday life and is misunderstood or misused in many ways.

If she feels threatened, afraid, or desperate, she can become lethal out of desperation. Trying to survive and adjust to impossible conditions, she has tenacity unexplained, for she was created for greatness, and many times never reached her full potential. I'm not passing her off as perfect, but pointing out how she was made for perfection, which means she was chosen to give birth to the chosen of God, to do the will of God! How she is reared is very important.

Given the right circumstances, she possesses incomparable abilities. Most of the time, she's fighting for her life because she is exposed to threatening situations—a mother's friend, a mother's boyfriend, a family friend, family members, etc. All of this influences how she handles herself.

This can be challenging for her because some women desire a good life with a decent person who will love them, but are damaged, and sometimes don't know how to reciprocate that love. They may seek sex as a trade, rather than love.

A woman damaged from her childhood by sex abuse can find it very difficult in a monogamous relationship, simply because she does not know how to separate her abuse from receiving love from her spouse or partner.

Many women even think it's their fault and choose not to talk about it, because of the shame, but not talking about it can be the reason for failed relationships, and they may not even know it. It's hard to feel as though you might be judged or misunderstood. Some women react by being promiscuous, while others become sheltered and a target for even more abuse because they're looking for love. These abusive spirits are attracted to you.

The promiscuous one may feel she's taken control over her life by giving it away instead of having someone take it from her. In any case, this becomes a form of survival. It's hard for this individual to trust. The damage is done. She can be helped, but this is usually hard to fathom.

What's so sad is this child had to become her counselor because she felt that she couldn't trust anyone, especially if she tried talking to her mother and was rejected or made to believe she was at fault. Many times, even if the mother knew it to be true, she would not disclose this to the daughter for fear of revealing her shame and secret abuse.

The abused child had to grow up way too soon. Now you have a child acting out of character for a child her age, because she's more than her age in her mind, having adult experiences in a child's body. Imagine the confusion this child is dealing with daily.

Her anger is her expression, and who cares how she feels? A child is now planning her escape at an early age. Some give in because their circumstances are too overwhelming and seemingly impossible to get out of. Some mothers have turned their backs and a blind eye to allow the perpetrator to have his way, because the man gave money or supported the household.

These are the dynamics of demonic affairs and spiritual activities in an accepted, if not welcoming, environment. The deception is this: the devil makes them believe there is no way out! He's a liar and benefits from those participating in this circle of lies.

"What happens in this house stays in the house."

What happened on the plantation stays on the plantation! The problem with this is that when the slaves were freed from the plantation geographically, they were still bound to their experiences mentally. The mind is the spirit, and the spirit remembers.

When humans are degraded and forbidden to love and even show that love, and be in a committed relationship, they become very cautious about loving. When they know they could be penalized for loving someone, not loving someone becomes a survival strategy.

What do you do when you know the life of someone whom you would love if it's revealed, is evil? This is not a mistake or weakness but nothing short of wickedness. What about being in an environment where you are forbidden to marry?

Who would give a slave a "license" to marry? No one! So, a committed relationship needs to be kept on track. If a man who was a slave fell in love with a slave woman, they had no rights as a slave. They would hide their feelings for more reasons than one. If they showed signs of love or caring, then the slave master would suddenly have a craving for that same female slave's sex or sell them off.

If a male was strong and built, he was called a buck. The slave master would breed him like a dog for more "baby bucks." So, they were not considered parents but animals. So, if the slaves were not permitted to love or have committed marital relationships, then what message was sent to them as a people? Why do religious organizations condemn so many people without the wisdom of the past sins of the slave's master against the slaves?

If it is a part of Christ, the church would heal, not commit more grievances to people who are already downtrodden. Why can't we love one another? I am not politically correct because I'm not running for any office to please men, but I am called an Apostle by Jesus Christ, according to the will of God.

 I am blowing the trumpet to the so-called righteous, in hopes of persuading anyone and everyone of us to repentance! I am sent to open the eyes of all people. I am not looking for supporters, for a calling is of God.

God has ordained me to speak what I am saying; this is all that matters. When God calls you, even your family will hate you if they are not of God but have a form of Godliness. The sign is this, Stan can preach, and he knows church services, but he cannot Love, for the love of God is not In him!

Many go to church but are hateful, arrogant, and self-righteous with all those titles, just like the Pharisees who hated the Son of God. They compete with one another for filthy lucre, not talking to one another. As a result, they will not miss a church service but will never serve God, do His will, or love.

Keep walking, because one day, when you leave here and take your last breath, it doesn't matter how many surround you; you still die alone. It will be God's angels to receive you or the grim reapers, one or the other! "If God be for us, then He is more than the whole world against us!" Jesus said, "I did not come to condemn, but to save."

So, how can the church find a thousand reasons and laws to keep those who are weak and crying out to God for help, not understanding why there is so much pain and suffering?

The slaves ' bodies were not their own, but the slave masters.

The slaves were property, nothing more and nothing less. They were not considered to be human or have feelings.

This is a cruel and harsh reality. If a slave master or any of his workers wanted a female slave, they were not restricted. The worst thing one could be was a female slave because she had no say over her body. She was raped regularly.

She was a slave, servant, whore, mother, nurse, cook, doctor, maid, concubine, cotton picker and wench. What happened was that a man could come to them anytime and demand they take off their clothes and give him sex. Well, this was the norm for the female slaves.

They had no say in the matter. Think about the male and female children who witnessed this pattern of behavior. So, look at this power shown to the slaves. This would degrade them at an early age, planting the seeds to make it known that they were nothing.

Females were looked at as a piece of meat. When a slave male was paraded from plantation to plantation to mate with female slaves, it was because the master was selling his services to other slave owners to save them money and time from traveling to purchase more slaves.

So even though he was being used like an animal to breed slaves, he then became something to be desired in an immoral lifestyle. To everything, there's a root before you can see the fruit. We cannot heal people by talking about the fruit, but by dealing with the root.

The master made the male slave e a rolling stone; the slave felt like he was better than picking cotton, hence, the birth of the pimp! Imagine no more long-awaited trips to and from Africa.

The slave masters have turned men into boys who used to have morals into a new breed of what? From a homeland to a new world, they are not looked at as human beings, but as animals.

Their forefathers would not have believed that a people strong and respected could be reduced to less than human. After a few hundred years of this barbaric and animal-like behavior, the slaves tried their best to take care of one another. But now they are something different from when they first arrived. They have evolved into a whole other people.

We need to uproot this demonic spirit amongst the people, not glamorize it! This is slavery's creation, and baby. The abused male is now used to abusing the female. He sees her as a piece of meat. He's a sellout, and now that same "sellout" we have glamorized through videos and movies rather than tearing it down and seeking its reform. Satan hates all women, no exceptions.

He's behind the scenes, working with everybody! Do you see the parallels in the plantations from 250 years ago to now? The former male slave is trying to be like what he saw in the slave master, but he can't handle it. It is killing him and his people, trying to be something that he's not.

Now, how does God Almighty judge this? This is a modern-day tragedy awaiting judgment! The male slave would be embarrassed to have the female slaves see him being treated like a boy. This was the norm for them, but he wished he could save his woman. If he fought, he would be killed or sold to another plantation, so the slave women would do all they could to make him feel belittled and less than a man. This became their culture.

Sometimes while a slave may not have been allowed to marry, they would love anyway and try to hide, because cause if the master had an inkling of them liking or loving each other, he would come to them in the night while they were sleeping as a family and call for the slave's wife and have sex with her.

Then, when the master was finished, she would return home, and the husband would pretend to have been sleeping the whole time, trying to maintain dignity and manhood. Imagine the pressure and shame. Because of the love the slave wife had for her slave husband, they would pretend it never happened.

This was a problem in the slaves' community because no matter how much the female slaves tried to protect the feelings and manhood of the males, the male slaves felt inferior and knew the females saw them this way. Much of this is still going on to this day. This issue is not resolved.

The black male is looked upon as lazy, making babies, not taking care of them, and having babies with multiple women. He's unstable, angry, and untrustworthy. The black female is given housing, money, and food.

The male is not allowed to live in the household legally; his name is not allowed on the lease. The children experience multiple males in and out of the house for greater chances of abuse. The master is still over the slave girl to this day in many facets of life.

The correctional facilities are run by black female officers again to degrade the black male and rob him of his manhood. The corporate jobs are given to the black female while the black male is selling drugs, using drugs, gang banging, or pimping.

The lyrical contents are destructive and shameful to the black community. No one degrades the black woman more than the black male. Listen to how the music has changed in the past 25 years. I do not speak as a critic but as an oracle concerned for this nation's future.

Who's giving these lyrics? We can most certainly agree that it's not God Almighty. How can these artists give thanks to God and Jesus Christ, for winning an award that's sending a message of damnation and destruction to their people—God's people?

Satan is using you, and if you don't turn from your evil, then your sins will remain, and your blood will be on your own hands! How can Dr. Martin Luther King Jr honor God Almighty for his ability to lead non-violent demonstrations and protests in such a hostile and violent setting to save a people?

How dare the children of this generation disrespect God with such blasphemy? Children have too much access to knowledge. Read Revelations 18 and hope to God that we are not the people and generation declaring war on God and the Holy Angels, who shall pour out the vials of destruction from heaven!

Be sure to be on the right side of God, because if you are not Right, then you will be left! How could Dr. King be so victorious if God was not with him? With the recorded hate crimes committed by his opposition, adversaries, haters, and non-believers of peace, these things had to be on record for judgment. They thought they were fighting Dr. King and the people, but they were fighting God.

They were seeking to do the will of their father, the devil. Dr. King is home with God, living the life of a king—the kingdom life.

Where do you think his enemies are? Not sitting at God's Table, that's for sure? I speak these things by authority; again, Dr. King served God. These things were not of his own doing, but they were all by the will of God! The Bible records this:

"The day will come when men kill you and think they do God a service." That's why understanding fruit is essential and not being blinded by titles and positions.

"You will know them by their fruit; if you don't believe in me, then believe in my works. An evil tree cannot produce good fruit, and neither can a good tree produce evil fruit. You will know the tree by its fruit!"

When you look at history, recognize the tree by its fruit; don't be deceived by titles and positions. Dr. King was not moving away from what his Heavenly Father had instructed him to do. Even though he did not understand what was happening then, he followed God's call. He was meeting a need, and God was establishing His word.

This was one of the things Lucifer was hiding in his heart while serving God in heaven. Dr. King and God's people represented Michael, Gabriel, and the Holy Angels, while the oppressors of the movement were Satan and the fallen angels.

They were vessels to express and expose the secrets of treason plotted by Lucifer, who was the master in heaven. Do you know that given the right circumstances, you will be surprised at what's in the heart of the people you fellowship with almost daily?

The circumstances allow you to know the truth about someone you have or something you are willing to dedicate your life to. If you are a child of God, He will reveal His enemies and yours. Reality check: God's enemies are your enemies!

Without this atmosphere, the world would never have known that America was hiding this kind of evil, hate, and prejudice in its heart. What makes this so real is that Dr. King knew he was just a man, but when God put His hands on his life, he became justified and glorified.

Though we try to find faults and flaws, God has proven that no matter what the enemies of God manipulate to discredit the person and their works, they speak for themselves. Jesus had many enemies: "If you don't believe in me, then believe in the works that I do!" So, what can we say about this man and all of those who have preceded us, when it comes to their works?

People are hypocritical and do not support confident leaders, but they are the first to receive the fruits of their sacrifices and labor. Many churches did not support Dr. King, but were the first to benefit from equal rights, equal housing, equal credit, affirmative action, and all the benefits of desegregation.

You should check the records and see how many preachers bought Cadillacs after his assignment, as if this was in honor of him. I hope that before they left this planet, they repented and asked God to forgive them, because if not, they are not sitting with God and Dr. King to this day!

I'm already there because now we are a people who are so rebellious, we don't think anybody can say a thing to us! We will see many changes by 2020, which means perfect vision. We all will see what God sees! In the Pentecostal church I attended, they believed God didn't want us to enjoy anything except eating! We didn't know any better, following leaders who didn't know enough about God's word.

They may have had good intentions, but at some point, somebody should have put the brakes on and stopped this madness, because they were taught by unlearned pastors and leaders who manipulated them at the time.

No harm intended, but the church owes many people an apology and reformation, just as the Slave Master does. I don't know why pastors cannot say they were wrong and ask for forgiveness, except for pride! Look out, Lucifer; they are working for the Master Cherub!

Read Jeremiah 23. How can we simultaneously be the world's most talented and so messed up? Here's the analysis: We have people who were on a plantation and were set free in 1865 by the government. Then the preachers picked it up and enslaved us with a doctrine to keep the people enslaved mentally.

If reading was outlawed for slaves, then who gave the preachers the word that they were giving the people? What the slave master told them became the word "in the good book," and the rest through praying and fasting. I'm no enemy of the true Church of Jesus Christ, but we must, *"Study to show ourselves approved unto God, a workman that needs not to be ashamed, rightly dividing the word of truth" (2 Timothy 2:15).*

I'm not saying they need a college degree; that would be ridiculous However, they need to read the Bible not just carry it, I'm not saying they weren't called, but I do believe at some point there was a gap pride stepped in by way of our true enemy Lucifer and deceived many.

Then we had people believing in what was taught as the word of God and misquoting the Bible because of rehearsed and memorized quotes from their pastor. Here we are, 150 years after the

The Emancipation Proclamation and the 13th Amendment tried to abolish a different kind of slavery in the United States of America. With a free people who cannot read or write and are afraid, and they have no home, no land, no people of freedom they can call their own, they have only God.

I am not saying the church as a whole; of course, we have churches birthed from that era, and they were the free people who could read and rightly divide and teach the word. I'm sure that some masters were convicted and eventually helped some of the preachers along the way. God will always touch somebody. I am a spirit-filled person, and believe me, I would never go against God.

Someone who puts God's name to this mess of a doctrine needs to address this. I'm sure many leaders did their best under the circumstances, but by now, with all this education and media, we are still not dealing with the truth; God forbid.

The church carried the spirit of God, and He did lead them, but somewhere along the journey, Lucifer mixed himself in the middle of fearful and desperate people looking for God. Confused and desperate, they chanted, sang, danced, and shouted, compensating for the lack of words they could not read and understand.

Therefore, the black church services were so long, because we were led in the spirit if we did not know how to move the service with the word of God. Abraham didn't do it, Moses didn't do it, even Jesus

Himself and the Apostles didn't, and He established the church on his blood.

He is the Living Word of God. It's not recorded that He did hours of singing and so-called dancing and was lost for words. These men preached and taught the word of God. "Man shall not live by bread alone, but by every word that proceeds out of the mouth of God." Do we see this? I'm not against praise and worship. I grew up with it and still do, so please understand me.

But know this truth, we cannot out-worship angels in song and dance because they don't get tired or sleepy and are not juggling thoughts, fighting the devil, trying to pay bills, and dealing with work and family.

Our worship that the angels cannot do is help somebody, save somebody, feed somebody, clothe somebody, visit the sick, help some prisoners, or love somebody; all of this is in the word, these are works out of the angels' jurisdiction! This is where we truly worship God, and the angels become our assistants. We hide in the church on Sundays and can't find a Christian all week.

If a Christian breaks down on the road on Monday morning, you will hardly find help from a Christian among the tens of thousands passing by who praise God all day. Now, this Christian is praying to God. He or she has no money because they gave all they had left to the church on Sunday, but no one hears God saying, "Help that person." God is not cruel like that.

He is not selfish like that. He is not blind, so tell me, who were we worshipping on Sunday? It just might have been Lucifer because he doesn't care about anybody but himself. We had better do a spiritual checkup because I don't think God is where we think He is.

These are the same people who will pass by people in the churches and neighborhoods, and not even speak to the people they pass by going into the church! Man, I've seen it, and I'm telling you, they are deceived into believing they are the Apple of God's eye! Lucifer thought so, too!

We see what happens to him! The Church needs to repent! I, too, thought I was doing God a service by attending all these church services, but honestly, what is God getting out of it?

Cities, states, and nations are going down. What have we done to ourselves? As a Christian nation, we can't even get the Republicans and Democrats to work together long enough for God to get the Glory by giving us a noticeable turnaround blessing for the world to see. "A kingdom divided cannot stand!"

These are Jesus' words, and I think it is wise to consider what he says since we claim to be a Christian nation! We do call on Him when trouble comes! God forbid if we don't make some adjustments and changes ASAP! I'm focused on the mess created by ignorance and how so many people are scattered all over the place, confused by what they were taught growing up, and now, as adults, it's not adding up.

We were given so many rules and laws that it's hard to keep up with them all. What happened to Grace? Maybe it ran out because they didn't give us any; they gave us the blues! Going to a secular school helps with all these rules in the first place. Why aren't Christians in our schools?

Then you have pastors who are ruling the people with the spirit of Jezebel, and if they are questioned concerning any practices, the pastor and leaders will tell the people that they are cursed, and God is going to get them for going against the pastor.

These people are witches and warlocks, not of God. Educate yourselves concerning the word and things of God. Compare Jesus' ministry and that of the disciples, and then do a Pharisees comparison check, read in Matthew, Mark, Luke, and John in the New Testament Bible, and ask yourself if they are of the church of Christ or a false Christ. Even Jesus warned us of the future of these wolves in sheep's clothing! If nothing else, know this: God loves and cares for His people.

If you lack wisdom, ask God and He will give it to you. He will lead you, so don't be intimidated or afraid to go to God for yourself and ask Him to lead you to a place or house of worship preaching the kingdom of God! Many cannot read or understand, so they make up words and put God's name on them!

This is understandable because of the circumstances of a slave, but now we need some leaders and pastors to take some responsibility and fix this mess among the people.

We need some reformation concerning the injustices and losses of ignorant people because we were forbidden to read. We did not have the luxury of being indentured servants, but abused and degraded human beings, and God instructs in that same Bible in which I believe about how to deal with and treat slaves.

They need to be regarded as people of misfortune and given a portion after serving their time so that they can take care of their families and move on. Then God promises to bless and protect that land. We all need to repent before God and start over as a nation and people, haters, just love, and peace of God.

We must take responsibility, and then we can move onto a road of restoration and healing. I've been through some things, from growing up in church, to strip clubs, and broken marriages, to finding God for myself and building a real and solid relationship with Him.

It doesn't matter if any organizations accept or reject me. I'm tired of the foolishness. All I want is to do God's will! Dr. King and many others paid a price with their lives and left their families behind to live a life of customized uncertainties.

However, because of those who did not share in the suffering, sacrifice, and labor, they were not good stewards and managers of the prosperity God had given. By doing so, they set the wrong example for the children by seeking God's hand, more than God's face! These are cowards behind doors praising God, serving themselves instead of God's people. The people need the leaders to come forth from the grave. They are calling it "Church!" Church is a community, not a building! Jesus had no building with His name on it; I'm not opposing the worship experience, but challenging it.

"You're Worshipping, but you know not what of," is a quote from the most excellent Teacher ever to walk this earth, and He gave his blood for his church (people). We have leaders who won't give even a portion of God's tithes to the people in the streets in helping to restore the cities that are in ruins, but we have pastors riding past all the real work, instead choosing to go to a beautiful building to have church as if they do God a service!

Christ told us to preach the kingdom and make disciples of all people, not members, because membership has privileges, but discipleship has an inheritance! We are then joint heirs with Christ; now, which one would you want to be? *"Seek ye first the kingdom and all these things will be added to you!"*

This fight is about kingdoms, not religions, and there are only two! Christ says, "There will be a separation of sheep from goats, the tares from the wheat." The two look alike when they are young in growth, but when they grow up and mature, there is a distinct and noticeable difference between them. God is separating, not the devil—the True Church (people) versus the False Church (people).

How will you know the difference between the two? The True Church is established on the truth of God's Word and God's Love, which gives. The false church and prophets can do everything the true church can do, except for love. They cannot and do not have.

No matter what, they will not love you. They are in it for the money and do nothing for free; they are takers, not givers! Anyone who is not willing to do anything for free for you or help you, no matter how long you have been giving to them, is a prostitute.

God, with Christ and the Holy Angels, is on a mission to restore His Church! Jesus said, "I AM THE WAY, THE TRUTH, AND THE LIFE; NO MAN COMES TO THE FATHER, EXCEPT THROUGH ME."

He was not endorsing a religion here. He was saying that if you don't have the love that He has for His Father, you will not make it in His Father's House.

The love Jesus demonstrated in this world is the love passed to heaven. It doesn't matter how much we attend religious services. If we don't have love, we don't have anything! This is about the haves and the have-nots.

If we do not have love, then we have nothing! The war in heaven was over the absence of love for God, not religious ceremonies or attendance to God's temple, but rebellion and hate against God, for the lack of love for Him!

Do we honestly think after all that God has gone through with the deceptions of fake worship and praise in heaven, that He is hard up for praise and worship in our world; He's only concerned with whether we can love Him like His Son demonstrated His love the love of God right here on earth!

This is the righteousness He seeks after. Jesus also said, "Love one another as I have loved you. This is how the world will know you are mine or my followers." We are so lost right now and far away from God and His truth! Do we understand how many lives have been taken because of hate?

Do we know and understand how many innocent people have died in the name of all religions and those who want to be gods? Do we know that every person on this planet did not have religious experiences but dealt with the same adversaries, devils, demons, and enemies of God? Still, different generations came up with different ways to worship God and methods of serving him.

For example, how fair would God be to favor my religion over yours, when we all are seeking the same thing (hypothetically speaking)? Stay with me for a minute because I know I'm hitting some pressure points and soft spots with religious folks. It's ok!

But what about all the people who walked this planet and have never heard of the belief systems we have in place? The purpose of all the prophets and Jesus was to show us the way back to God, and that way is LOVE! Everyone on this planet has not heard my religious arguments for why my religion is the right one.

Still, every human being has fought with the same "Devil of Hate" and felt something in their hearts, which is the love of God. They demonstrated that love with families, children, friends, and communities! They all had to choose between love and hate, good and evil, and right and wrong!

This is the war that took place in heaven because there were no religions, only love, until someone envisioned praising God and worshipping Him, but did not love God!

So, you tell me, do we think for a minute that God cares about our religious beliefs, or does He care if we truly love Him for Him? How can we say, "We love God, whom we've never seen, and hate our brother, whom we see every day!"

I will not defend or argue this point with any devil, but if you don't believe that LOVE is the key to eternal life God, then continue in your dissection, hate, vain services, and offerings to a God, who is not receiving them in the first place, go on, but let this go on record, I have done what I was commanded to do!

The religious leaders attempted to kill Love in hopes of not having a witness on the day of judgment to testify against them, but Love can't die, not as long as God lives; you will have to die to know this, and you will!

Those who have the love of God, when you kill them, are still living with that same love in eternity because love can't die! We are supposed to love everybody and not hate! We have no control over our being born or our race, color, and nationality, but we do control this.

Do we love God or hate him and love the things of the world? Do we love God or hate him and love money? Do we love mankind or hate them for whatever reason?

We were all sent here on Earth to be tested. Will we love God and show Him by loving one another, or are we the devil's children and haters? We will be given a series of tests while here on earth and will be rewarded if we pass the test of love!

We must know this is the truth because every religion has failed the test of love, so its evaluation is an individual test...it's personal. When we leave this world, every person will be tested to see if they have love in their veins.

Love came and showed us the way, and we still missed it! Because we found another way to be divided rather than united! Don't look for the pastor or music the next time you attend church or any religious service.

Don't look to be entertained or even for a Word, but first look and see if love and compassion exist, because if love is not in the house, then neither is God and Jesus! You just may have been seduced by Lucifer, and he will get you high, but you won't get delivered and set free, so check for shackles and chains of bondage!

Hate killed Jesus and all the Prophets; they all died at the hands of hate crimes, but love resurrected them all! When it is all said and done, it will be love that will lift us! As if they are blind...wait...maybe they are!

But Jesus can heal your blindness, if you humble yourselves, but you probably start kicking and fighting like your forefathers, the Pharisees. They won't represent Him outside in the real world...Great is your reward (Revelation 22:12).

WHO'S WHO

Chapter 8

The Day of Reckoning

Imagine the day when our Heavenly Father gathers all His children to Himself, and you find yourself standing before the very enemies you had no earthly power over, simply because God ordained it that way. Their power was merely temporary. It was part of a greater plan. Satan was set up from the beginning. He is an opportunist, a thief, and a liar — it is in his nature to exploit the helpless. That's why he is called:

The Molester. The Rapist. The Thief. The Murderer. The Cruel Slave Master. The Abuser of the Righteous. The Oppressor of the Fatherless and Widows.

Throughout history, many women have stood up for what was right, even when it seemed they had lost the battle. Yet God sees everything. As Dr. Martin Luther King Jr. declared: "Injustice anywhere is a threat to justice everywhere." Countless wrongs have been committed, but a day is coming—a day when God Himself will make everything right. On that day, your enemies will stand before you, trembling like leaves in a violent storm, terrified not of you alone, but of your standing with Almighty God as your Father and Judge.

God has always had His vessels of righteousness—many women —who used their influence for good, even when it meant standing against powerful husbands or worldly systems. They were not moved by rebellion but by a deep, divine compulsion to do what was right, believing that God had placed them in those moments for a greater purpose. This is not a question of whether God lacks power—He never does. It is about the revealing of hearts.

"The heart is deceitful above all things, and desperately wicked; who can know it?" (Jeremiah 17:9) The hurts and betrayals we suffer offer glimpses — small samples — of what God Himself endured. God was betrayed even in Heaven, where He should have found only peace and loyalty. From beginning to end, He experienced treachery at the hands of His creation. There is nothing we can suffer that God Himself has not first endured. He is not distant from our pain; He shares it.

In this life, God separates those who truly belong to Him from those who do not.
Those who cause pain, betray trust, and murder without repentance—without a broken and remorseful heart—do not belong to Him. It is not just about the sins we commit but about how we respond afterward. A repentant heart shows the marks of God's hand. An unrepentant one reveals its true master. When a wife betrays her husband, or any act of betrayal occurs, she is not the originator of that sin—Lucifer is.

The spirit of rebellion and betrayal was first conceived in Lucifer's heart, hidden in Heaven itself, as an act against God. What was once hidden will be revealed. What was once tolerated will be judged. And the faithful—the ones who endured injustice, pain, and betrayal—will stand vindicated in the presence of God.

Only God could see it and feel the pain from it. It is like you seeing your husband living a whole other life outside your marriage with another woman, having children, and all. Then you hear the plot of how he hates you and only wants you for your money and power. How he wishes he could get rid of you and your children to live this life with his new woman.

Well, imagine you have this information, and no one else knows it but you. What will you do? How will you handle this information? Do you approach him? If you do, what would you say, and how much would you want him to know that you know? He is too deep to deny it, but what will happen afterward? Well, I'm giving you, for the first time, a peek into God's private life and secrets that the earth has not known. Have you ever held on to something for the sake of someone you love, not to hurt them because they were too young to understand or because you didn't want to appear as the hater or the evil one?

Well, here goes... we are big enough to give God our behinds to kiss, put Him out of schools, government, our marriages, relationships, and even churches. We don't want God to tell us anything because most of His children think they are so grown that they don't need Him like that anymore! We are prosperous and have education, our homes, and bling, iced down and living the life, but we have a little more to go through before we are spiritually grown. Tribulation is next, such as the world has not seen, and then we will cry to the Lord, but will He answer?

Read the book of Revelation! Our Father wants us to know the truth now that we are grown. We are mature enough to handle it. Everything that is happening, God knew in advance. Lucifer did these things to God in heaven, but behind His back. Lucifer planned to turn heaven into a democracy, but God was not and is not having it. Would responsible parents have their 7-, 9-, and 10-year-old children voting on whether to pay the mortgage, car payment, and utilities, or to go to Disney World? Now, which choice do you think the children would make? Exactly! Well, Lucifer thought he had grown because of the privileges, teachings, and exposure to the wisdom that God afforded him.

Yes, in essence, Lucifer was a "Spoiled Brat!" Because of his royal position and power as God's greatest display of Himself, Lucifer knew he was it! He was full of pride and arrogance! He had unsettled feelings in his heart. Have you ever had a boss or supervisor dismiss an idea you may have had, whether they were right or wrong, and felt disrespected? It takes maturity to accept that they are your superior at work and have the final say. Let it go! Well, Lucifer didn't let it go! He held it in his heart and began to plot and scheme against the will of God.

Therefore, the Lord's Prayer addresses, "Holy be thy Name, thy kingdom come and will be done!" This war began like most do, over disagreements where someone becomes selfish, self-centered, greedy, and prideful. From this, they start moving blindly with a plan of action, causing a misappropriation of power and authority. Iniquity in Lucifer's heart was like a nuclear bomb. He, in turn, betrayed God and the angels' trust by influencing other angels to be like himself. One out of three angels followed him. He had the power and glory of God; God created him personally. God trained him; he was educated, intelligent, and anointed to lead.

This seems like everything. However, they missed the most crucial ingredient: "God's Approval and Blessing!" The angels were deceived; God was not informed of their intent to move forward with a plan that had not been approved by Him. Now, understand this: you can have a supervisor, captain, general, law enforcement officer, CEO, CFO, manager, teacher, principal, pastor, bishop, mayor, governor, president, king, or any other leader in a position of authority.

This is why we have laws and rules in place. When a person in authority takes it upon themselves to bend or break the rules, they are violating and disrespecting all those who took the time and effort to establish these governance rules, which ultimately exist for our good.

The person in that position only deals with their current circumstances and what they want for the future. Most of the time, they work with limited vision because of the present situation. However, the laws in place have longevity and have proven themselves for generations, benefiting all with due consideration.

Lucifer believed his plan was superior to God's. He felt as if God was restraining him, and he would not accept that. This marked heaven's first and last rebellion because God does not tolerate it! God understands what is in Lucifer's heart, much like a parent can perceive the impending destruction of a disobedient child. God possesses the experience, whereas Lucifer has the zeal.

Lucifer is motivated by a desire for shiny things that bring pleasure without restrictions, while God is driven by love and aims to secure everything good with protection. Not only is Lucifer arrogant and self-centered, but he is also secretly devising a hostile takeover that involves removing God, His rules, and His throne. Lucifer is dreaming of becoming King,

The Ruler of Heaven, The Most High God. And Lucifer said in his heart, "I will set my throne above the throne of the Most High God!" Now, imagine how limited we are when betrayed by those we trust. The feeling of betrayal is like no other. Betrayal by a best friend, a partner, a husband or wife, a father or mother, a brother or sister, a leader… just betrayal, period! This pain is what God experienced first! God had no one He could talk to… no one! Who could God trust with

His feelings... He's God?

Now, what do we do with that? What do you do when someone to whom you gave your life, in return, betrays you? Don't get stuck in your pain! Though tempting, don't harbor hate in your heart. Push through your pain! We know it's not easy, but it is doable and very necessary! God gave birth to His most significant work to date out of His pain! You will be surprised at what you can accomplish if you don't quit. Please do not give that kind of power to your past; you will need that energy for your future and destiny!

With God, you will discover that your better days are always ahead of you because God is never through with us...even throughout eternity! He's always ahead of us, preparing everything better. Think about every luxury we seek and enjoy in life; it comes from Him, and this is His mind. Understand this little fact about Lucifer: he's obsessed with being God and always stealing God's ideas. He is the first to use a sample without paying or giving credit to the original writer and the publication's owner! Lucifer is overrated! He is a thief! He is a liar! Listen to this God of wisdom.

He saw what was in Lucifer's heart and cast him out of heaven before he could act on any of this. God was hurt, of course! Did God stop? No! We are here because God had a vision that He believed in. We are part of God's new plan. Because of the pain God endured, His sentiment was,

"If I'm going to hurt like this, then let it be for my children." God could have replaced the angels with more angels, but why? God wanted His own family. But here's the deal: My children will identify with me through my hurts and pains. They will feel what I feel and endure what I had to endure. This makes us family, and this is how I can trust them—I'm in you and you in me.

Every war we have faced was in Lucifer's heart, and he did not have the chance to activate in heaven. Every betrayal and act of treason existed in his heart while he served God, appearing loyal and faithful to Him. He was an adulterer in his heart while grinning at God's face. How do you think he is capable of these horrific acts in this world?

As God filters through generation after generation, He gathers His true children to spend eternity with Him without reluctance or concerns about another betrayal or outbreak. Don't you get it? If Lucifer had committed all these horrific acts and crimes in heaven, we would not exist and would have no hope. Lucifer intended it for God's demise and his benefit, but it backfired.

God is greater and better than this. He did not destroy Him but showed mercy, giving Him space to repent, and we have His nature and ability to do the same. God is our Father; we will endure persecution for the cause of righteousness. If you have suffered from hate for no reason except to help someone, if you are hated for doing the right thing and have not used your power to eliminate your enemies, welcome to the Kingdom of Righteousness Club!

Let your critics criticize; they do you a service because on the Day of the White Throne Judgment, no one can hide their dirt! Every word we speak will be used to justify us or condemn us! Not God's Word, not Jesus's Word, or any other prophet or god's, but our own words. Watch what you say; watch whom you're lying to because it just may be God! While people in positions of power may think they are wise, intelligent, and getting over, here's the deal: you are taking the place of Lucifer and are under the radar to see if you are God's followers or Lucifer's, and it's okay; it was designed this way. "The Father knows them that are His." No one gets away!

 Every murder has a motive, whether you know it or not. It is larger than the reasons for which they were killed; they were sacrificed! Why do you think the death of Jesus was so barbaric and brutal? God, with His brilliance and infinite wisdom, humbled Himself and submitted to His enemy. Lucifer harbored this in his heart while he was in heaven.

These were the secrets of his heart. How can the heavens perceive what lies in my partner's heart, who was trusted throughout eternity? Every hatred, every scheme, rape, war, and betrayal. Satan offers Jesus the glory of the world for a price: worship! Lucifer desires to be worshipped by God!

Imagine the Devil tripping... the thought of the Greatest now under your power and authority… even if only for a little while. He desperately desires that; he wants to be God of Gods, King of Kings— this is his fantasy! He bargains for power without sacrifice, hatred, and persecution if others will bow down to him and worship him instead of God. You should know that a true king will never bow down to anything beneath him.

No matter what, Lucifer will always be beneath Him. God had a meeting in heaven back in the day with all parties involved, just as we would if we could be diplomatic about it. If you are going to break up over fidelity, you talk to your children and maybe keep the details from them for the moment because you don't want to hurt them any more than they are already hurting.

Lucifer is now thrown down to the earth along with his followers. He is seething! He is full of madness and fury! This separation is necessary because all of heaven will witness the truth during the time apart. The things Lucifer will do daily will shock all who thought they knew him. They will find out who Lucifer is.

The lifestyle Lucifer was leading was bestowed by God, who is not arrogant but rather humble. His works express Him; God knows who He is, and if He revealed nothing of His essence, His presence conveys it all. Lucifer, on the other hand, possesses nothing, is nothing, and remains nothing without God's resources. Yet, he is filled with pride and vanity; he's a showoff and a perpetrator, using everything he possesses to impress those easily swayed.

He uses God's resources as bargaining tools for mankind because men and women were earthly creations at the time of his fall. He will find it easy to impress them since they are naive. Jesus, on the other hand, knows him and what he's all about, but the Son is responsible for exposing this devil through His presence and not betraying His heavenly Father.

No matter the sacrifice and pain, Jesus must remain focused on being our example of how love is meant to operate in a world without love and demonstrate how love is genuinely expressed. Never love the gifts more than the giver. If God had come in His glory and riches, those who hated Him would have pretended to love Him, just as Lucifer did in heaven. God chooses to go to the earth in humility rather than glory; now we will see who's who.

The priests in the temple, you would think, are the faithful servants of the Most High God, but this is not the case. They couldn't stand God; they only sought enough of Him to profit from the poor who needed Him. These were Lucifer's partners in crime. The king and the priests worked together to eliminate the Son of God. The Son, who was doing the Father's will, was exposing their hypocrisy.

Have you noticed that most religious organizations are often the most prominent critics when someone helps people whom they neglect? They will find fault in almost everything you do because they are not doing anything themselves. This is how Lucifer's partners are revealed.

The priest and king asked Him to prove Himself if He was the Son of God. Jesus did not entertain them by proving Himself to them. He used His power to save those in need and desired to be there for them rather than show His power to His enemies. We can learn much from this: anyone seeking you to prove to them, for selfish reasons, how much of anything you are and have is nothing more than a club, the children of the devil.

When someone dies, you will find that the club will not save you but will desire to take your place. If you are significant enough, they will put someone in your place. You have no value outside of money. The reality is this: the True and Living God always puts life before things and money. While living life, your value will not be based on how much you love yourself, but on how much you have given of yourself to others.

Some people will spend every waking moment of their lives on themselves; most of the time, they are simply consumers. You need to engage with people who have old money, particularly those who understand the real deal. Money spent on yourself daily is not a godly satisfaction, but using your position or platform to help others will bring true fulfillment.

This is one of the most significant rewards you can achieve because this is what God will evaluate in eternity. Yes, live your kingdom life, but don't forget who and where it comes from. When you see the chaos in this world, remember this.

If God had not stepped in and cast Lucifer and his vision down from heaven, this mess would be in eternity, not just time. We may not like it, but the incentive and comfort are this: no matter what we go through down here, it's only temporary!

When you think of the killing at Calvary Hill, God is showing us something: He was brutally beaten. The Sanhedrin was the religious organization behind the horrific death of Christ. They were Lucifer's agents, the vessels of submission to the will of Satan. This is left on record for us to take notes. This was the greatest "Hate Crime" ever committed!

These so-called men of God express and demonstrate a hidden hatred for God and what He loves. When someone can organize a murder against you solely out of hatred, these are the devil's children; it doesn't matter the cause or what name they use. Don't be deceived; God sends rain on the wicked just as He does on His children, meaning He still sustains His known enemies.

Why? Every secret must be exposed and expressed to be judged. Their day is coming... This is a brief period to deal with the wicked. God remains hopeful for their change of heart. We have been taught, or at least heard of, the devil, but not much about Lucifer.

That's why I provide his origin, the place of beginnings. We get caught up in titles and positions, but we should recognize the spirit in operation! This is how we will know who's who; consequently, there are crooks in every genre. While we're looking for the "horns, forks, and red suit," he's walking among us every day. Many times, we are sleeping with that Devil regularly because he knows how to make you climax in everything! Not just Sex? Lucifer has people staged everywhere.

It's not difficult—find anyone who wants to rise in life and doesn't care about whom they step on to get there; then you are a prime candidate. This is why we have so many sell-outs talking about their houses, cars, money, clothes—it's all vanity! Do you know why Satan doesn't care about this kind of person? Because he knows that you're not going to keep any of it!

You will have millions and die broke. You will have nothing to leave to your family, and, as a matter of fact, the so-called blessings you thought you had destroyed your family! Satan is laughing his behind off, saying, "Another One Bites the Dust!" He's cruel like that! These guys are doing all this bragging and are not faithful to anybody, not even the devil; they will end up in his house, and they will have no home of their own—Satan owns you!

When Jesus endured the pain of shame and humiliation for things he did not do, he did it for us too. They lied to him, created scenarios to support their lies, mocked him, laughed at him, called him names, spat on him, beat him, arrested him on false charges, convicted him, and then hung him! Does this sound familiar?

"Cursed is the man that hangs on a tree!" This is in God's Word! This is bigger than just a religious story; it exposes unrevealed secrets in heaven. Lucifer strategically turned this into a religion to downplay its global impact. This is not a religion; this is life! He knew what some of his children would endure in the future because the devil has great wrath!

Look at how many people of all races have suffered from hate crimes; these are all God's children. Satan is furious at God and His children! He is being exposed, and the purpose of the Son of God coming is to unveil the devil's works.

Until Jesus arrived, the devil had never been exposed and placed under subjection because no one understood how he operated. You can see how desperate the enemy is in all his actions. When Jesus visited John the Apostle on the Island of Patmos, He revealed things and instructed him to write them down. This included the account of slavery; He said they would come into the ports of Africa and Ethiopia.

He showed him the ships and mentioned that they would cast many overboard. He spoke about Judgement Day, when the sea would give up its dead to stand with the captains and crew; the small and significant would stand together to be judged. He suggested that the events done as a cover-up would be revealed.

God will allow us to see the footage; isn't that cool? Well, maybe not for those who were the perpetrators. All those court cases, all those false reports, all those falsely plotted convictions, all of those late nights and wee hours of the morning, all of those creepy nights cheating. Nothing about heaven is going to be boring. We should focus on the inevitable! What side of God will we be on? Now, doesn't it sound ridiculous for people to think that those who killed and mistreated others without an apology or repentance are in heaven?

People who were cruel and wicked to human beings and children —would they be in heaven? If they were, what would they be doing? Raping an angel, lying to the archangel, or God? Stealing from the street…what? The only purpose of time is to build a case for the haters and the guilty to execute judgment! To separate those who would have revolted against God with Lucifer and his followers from those who would not sell God out. After this, we will have everlasting peace. We will see our enemies and haters no more…forever!

Your actual family members will do the Father's will, not Satan's! Hiding in church will not save us, but doing the will of the Father will. On that day, He will not ask, "How many church services did you attend?" No one is good enough—let's get this straight: the holiest person you think you know is still short of God's glory. Most of the time, they believe they are more sacred than God and His Son. We are not entering in based on our goodness but on His righteousness! Repent every day. Ask God what His will is for us each day.

The church should be the spiritual hospital. When someone is hurt or sick and goes to the hospital, they know they do not have to worry about being judged because they are ill. A person can get shot by a gun while trying to rob someone; the first thought they have is, "I need to go to the hospital to get some help." They are not thinking about being judged. They know that doctors and staff are professionals and are depending on them to save their lives. Do the doctors and staff condone what he's done? Of course not! Will they do everything to save his life?

Absolutely! The doctor, nurses, and staff will do their jobs, and the proper authorities must do theirs. The hospital operates solely within its jurisdiction of saving lives. The church needs to learn from Jesus and these professionals! When people can visit the church as a hospital without worrying about being judged before saving a life, perhaps more individuals will come instead of feeling threatened. Most people say, "I'm going when I get myself together."

What would happen if a person who was shot went home first, took a shower, changed clothes, and said, "I think they will accept me now?" God is the Saving Station, and we are supposed to be working for Him. Let God do the judging; these are His sheep. I believe we should be working to save them, no matter what. If we are called to save, we must understand that God gave His best gift to a messed-up world needing saving. "For God so loved the world, that He gave His only begotten Son, whosoever believes shall not perish but have everlasting life." (John 3:16)

God is rebuilding His kingdom, a righteous kingdom. Whether you realize it or not, we are all kingdom builders. The question is: whose kingdom are you building? At 12, you experience a new level of awareness and responsibility. Your enemy intensifies his efforts, pressuring you through life's circumstances, friends, family, and peer influence. This is your identity stage. The kingdom of God is built on light, truth, and love...the right hand.

On the other hand, the kingdom of Satan is built on lies and lust, and lust doesn't love anyone. At the age of 15 and 16, he pressures the young woman to have sex and give him a baby. Your enemy cannot put a seed in a woman to produce life; it's unlawful by God's order. So he's an adamant recruiter searching for candidates for his kingdom.

His next step is to conceive a child out of lust so he can become the stepdad. He pressures the relationship to instigate a breakup. Breakups cause pain. Satan then uses that pain in hopes of having you and your baby in his kingdom. He established a support system if you vow not to allow the biological father to reside in the house as a family. Satan is serious about raising your baby. Satan endorsed the system to ensure a generation. What kingdom are you building, and who's your boss? Whose name is on your paycheck in this world?

The Choice That Changed Everything

The decision she made—to keep her child—would shape every part of her future.
From that moment on, there was no turning back. She had to become a woman overnight—and ultimately, a mother.

Expecting a baby girl, she quickly realized the weight of her new reality.
With only a high school diploma, she faced the brutal challenge of finding work that could support them.
She was young, naive, and unaware that her struggle wasn't new—it was an old tragedy replaying itself through yet another life. Her dreams of going to college?

They had to be set aside for a little while, perhaps forever. The baby's father had no room for her in his life. He was married, desperately trying to protect the life he already had. She was on her own, fighting to build a future for herself and her daughter.

Later, hope flickered once more. She met a man who appeared to be a good prospect — someone who could provide stability, a family, and perhaps even love.
Eventually, they married, and for a while, it seemed she had succeeded. Maybe — just maybe — she could break the cycle of fatherless children.

She could give her daughter a real chance. But like every marriage, challenges began to creep in. As a wife and mother, she had to work even longer hours, often late into the night, to keep the household afloat. Meanwhile, her husband fell into dangerous habits: hours of TV, endless drinking, a little weed... and something far darker.

While she was out working to keep them alive, he crossed a line that should never, ever be crossed.
He touched her child in ways that shattered innocence and trust. The thought of someone you trust violating your baby is almost too much to comprehend.

The worst part? Many mothers don't find out. Not for years. Sometimes... never. This sick betrayal became the child's "normal." It stretched across years, hidden behind closed doors and silent cries. The little girl grew up confused and broken inside, believing this must be what life is like. After all, doesn't everyone have problems?

Even when she sensed something was wrong, she couldn't find the words to explain it. Was it her fault? Could she even tell anyone?

And so, the cycle of silent suffering continued. Meanwhile, her mother—exhausted, overworked, and barely surviving—was trying to hold everything together. Her dream was simple: to take care of her family, find peace, and maybe get a little rest.

But while she worked herself to the bone, the monster inside her home went unchecked.
And a little girl's world slowly crumbled.

The day when our Heavenly Father gathers all His children to Himself. You stand, not in fear, but in the calm assurance of divine justice, before those who once held sway over your life. You had no earthly power to resist them, which was also by design. Their dominion was permitted for a season, as part of a plan far beyond human grasp.

But their power was temporary. Their arrogance was borrowed. From the very beginning, Satan was never sovereign—only permitted. A thief. A liar. An opportunist. And on that great Day, he too will be judged.

As it is written: *"Vengeance is Mine; I will repay," says the Lord* (Romans 12:19). The Book will be opened, and every injustice, every secret cruelty, and every act done in the shadows will be brought to light (Revelation 20:12).

On that day, it will be clear that the righteous were never forsaken; they were simply being prepared.

In short, it's the who's who of life.

GOODS

Chapter 9

Why Is the Woman So Hated?

Where does the hatred toward women come from? What is its origin?

Picture a young woman — beautiful, full of life, and freshly graduated from high school. She lives with her single mother and steps outside on a warm, sunny afternoon for fresh air. Her future feels wide open, full of unknown possibilities.

As she enjoys the day, she notices a handsome, slightly older man — confident, driving a nice car. She's intrigued. Curious. She makes herself visible, hoping he'll notice. He does.
He approaches her and starts a conversation.
"Would you like a ride?" he asks.

She plays it cool — she doesn't want to seem desperate — but inside, she's thrilled. They spend time together, grabbing something to eat, laughing and talking. For the first time, she feels seen, noticed — like a woman.

Soon, he comes around again. This time, the excitement is real, and the guard is down. She feels ready — a moment every woman understands, though it's hard to explain. He's ready, too. And in that moment, she gives him her trust, her body, her heart.

But he left out one crucial detail: he was already married.

She was giving love; he was fulfilling lust.
She, too young and inexperienced, believed what she felt was real love. How could she know otherwise? Her father wasn't there to teach her what a man's love should look like.

This tragic mismatch — love versus lust, innocence versus experience — is where devastation begins.
Two people, two different perspectives.
But at that moment, who cares? The damage is done.

Not long after, she discovers she's pregnant at just eighteen years old. The dreams she had for herself now collide with the harsh reality she never saw coming.

She tells him the news.
His response? Cold and crushing.
"I'm married. I already have a child. I can't be with you."

Her heart shatters.
How could something that felt so good turn into something so painful?

Suddenly, the man who once brought her joy becomes her deepest regret — her greatest distress.
The dream has become a nightmare.
It's an old story, but it feels brand new to her.

We don't talk about these stories enough. We hide them out of shame. We think if we expose our past — our falls, our flaws — we'll lose the love, respect, or acceptance we crave. Fear drives us into silence.
We bury the pain deep because we fear the past will ruin our future, especially once we've built families of our own.

The guilt.

The shame.

The fear.

We silently beg our past to "just go away."

But it doesn't.

Many women live daily with these invisible wounds — trapped in prisons of their own minds, tormented by what they cannot undo. Some become overprotective mothers, raising their children in fear. Some wrestle with anger and trust issues, and their children don't understand why.

Meanwhile, seeing the freedoms their friends enjoy, these children feel confused, resentful, and isolated. They don't know the battles fought in silence.

We're all different — and yet, in many ways, we are the same. Our scars unite us more than we realize.

This is spiritual.

It crosses every boundary, every race, every generation.

Without knowledge, without healing, we leave the next generation vulnerable, wide open to the same foul play. In this young woman's story, she tries to move forward with her mother's help. She faces the impossible choice: Should she terminate the pregnancy?

The man doesn't want the child.

The world says it's her "choice."

After much soul-searching, pain, and tears, she makes the most selfless decision:
to keep the baby.

Not for herself, but for the life growing inside her — a life that deserves a chance.

This decision she makes will be the decision of decisions that will follow her for the rest of her life. Now she must become a woman and, ultimately, a mother! She must find work to support her child, and she's having a girl. Working now as a single mom, she faces the challenges of not being able to earn the necessary money with a high school diploma. She's naive and has no clue that this is an old problem happening to a new victim.

The young new mom must let go of her dreams of attending college, at least for now. But who knows? The baby's father cannot afford to deal with her because he's trying to maintain his marriage. While working to provide, the young mom faces challenges creating a life for herself and her baby.

Later, she meets a guy who appears to be a viable prospect for her and her child's future. Eventually, she marries and seems able to give her child a fair chance at having an everyday life. Perhaps she can break the vicious cycle of single moms with fatherless children… She is giving her child a chance.

Like any marriage, some challenges began to develop. The woman who has become the mother and wife is challenged by working long hours, and eventually at night. The husband has an appetite for TV, alcohol, a little weed, and something else, but his wife is not home.

He decides to touch her baby inappropriately. The thought of someone whom you trust violating your baby is appalling. It's hard enough trying to make ends meet and making countless sacrifices. To top it off, the mother often does not find out for years, sometimes… never!

Violating this poor baby will become a newly formed habit and a part of his or her normal. This goes on for years, and the child is growing up confused and dysfunctional, but thinks this is normal, everyone has problems… right? From the child's perspective, even if they suspect some wrongdoing, they can't quite put their finger on it. This has been her life from when she had memory to the present school-age years.

As she grows older, this is more difficult to live with, but who does she tell, and is it her fault? So, the saga continues. The mother works so hard that she wants to care for her family, survive, have peace, and rest. In the meantime, the husband is not trying to contribute to the household, but is at home drinking and watching television as a daily routine.

When the daughter comes home from school, she needs to find a way to spend less and less time in the house with her stepdad. Maybe out of sight, out of mind, but little does she know, this thing is way bigger than him wanting her or having a fetish. What's driving him, or what is his goal here? Surely, he can't see me as his woman, or can he? Now he's showing signs of obsession and even jealousy. I'm a child, aren't I? This is too much for me at my age.

Now I can't even be with my friends without him calling me into the house or finding reasons to get me away from them. He wants me all to himself, especially while my mom is away at work, seizing any opportunity he can find. I'm afraid to bathe or use the bathroom because of the fear that he might be peeping on me.

Man, this is making me sick. I can't help but wonder, would this be happening to me if I were his biological daughter, or if my dad were living with me, or in my life?

This man is sick! I find myself more mature than the average person, even though I have issues! I feel resentful, angry, and filled with mixed emotions because I just want to have a normal life; I don't know if that's even possible. I'm surrounded by chaos and abuse—both physical and verbal; it's my normal. Will I ever have peace? Now, I'm facing a new fear: I have my period! I'm entering womanhood now, and this monster is still trying to do me!

We are fighting now because I don't want to go home or be in the house without my mother there. It seems I am the problem because he describes me as a grown-up and disrespectful. To my mom, it appears that I am the issue. I'm even angrier and standing my ground, but I don't know the outcome. All I know is that I don't want to get pregnant; I'm too young for all of this! What can I do—maybe if I get a boyfriend? That might protect me, but I'm too young for a boyfriend.

Wait a minute, I'm really confused! This is too much for me at my age; I shouldn't be thinking about things like this, but what can I do? I need to do something, but what? I think I'm too young to have a boyfriend, but this man doesn't see anything wrong with touching me regularly; this is not right! I want to get out of here, but where can I go and whom can I trust? I need my own life; can I just have a life?

As I grow older, I'm having confused thoughts and unanswered questions in my mind. When did all this start, and how did I get trapped in this mess? Why do I feel as if I've done or am doing something wrong? I am so disturbed! This situation I'm in has caused me to grow up much too fast; I had to because this is the only way I know to survive. All I want is some rest and peace. I'm twelve and feel like I've never had a good night's rest since I've been on this planet.

All I want is to be normal and have a good life. I wish he would leave me alone. I hate him, and somehow I know he hates me! Why won't he just leave me alone? How long do I have to go through this? I pleaded with my mom to let me stay at a friend's house or my cousin's—anywhere but here. He treats me as if he were my man instead of my father. Now I'm feeling manipulated and controlled, and I'm not going for it! My mom and I are going through this because I don't want to do this anymore, but how can I put an end to it?

At the age of twelve, I must try to consider how I played a part in this. Am I at fault here? It's just not right. Imagine growing up and coming of age without remembering or knowing when your virginity was lost or taken. Was I ever a virgin?

What is that? Since my memory began, I've been touched! How could a man do this to an innocent child? All the child wanted was to be loved the right way. What's sad is how this damaged soul can know what love is and whether she will recognize it when it comes. What does love look like anyway?

Surely she can't pick it out from a lineup, or maybe it will never come? The hate that the enemy has for the woman is real; it's spiritual and will continue to manifest in and through something as long as the earth and life remain, until the day of Judgment.

From the beginning, this war was initiated by the one whom she replaced. She did not know anything about the previous arrangements of the position she was called to fill. She just opened her eyes one day, enjoyed life, and then was suddenly interrupted by hate and war.

Just as all of us who are born, we have no control over what race or country we are born into or whether we are what God envisioned us to be. Therefore, we should accept the destiny that comes along with birth and calling.

We are all born with a calling—divinely placed, irrevocable, and untouched by the labels of race, nationality, class, or religion. Whether we realize it or not, every soul contributes to this life—for good or for evil. And, woman, you are no exception. In fact, you are the reason the war began.

The enemy doesn't hate you because of what you've done. He hates you because of who you are—**the one who took his place**.

When he sees you, he sees God's favorite. He sees the one chosen to carry life, to birth destiny, and to reflect the glory he forfeited. And though he rages against you, make no mistake: **he studies you,** learning while he hates—because you still hold what he lost.

Woman, you are crowned with the glory of Almighty God. And if you dare to surrender your life—not to the lies, wounds, or whispers of the enemy—but to the One who created you on purpose, for a purpose, then you will rise. You will no longer be the victim; you will be the victor.

Your journey may look different—shaped by struggle, colored by culture, scarred by betrayal—but your design is divine. You were born into the life you have, not by accident, but by intentional strategy. Each woman carries within her something that the next one needs. We are not meant to compete—we are meant to complete.

Life may not always seem fair, but God is still just. Because his most treasured creation has become the prime target of hell's fury, justice is coming. Your day of reckoning is near. One day, you will stand before the throne and see every scheme exposed—every whisper, every betrayal, and every person who wore a friend's face but carried the heart of your enemy.

You will understand how Satan used familiar faces—yes, even blood—to try and crush your purpose.

But take heart: just because you share a womb does not mean you share a spirit. Sometimes, your greatest adversaries will be born in the same house. Still, you are called to love, even when you must leave.

If they stand against what God has placed inside you, then they are not for you. And if they are not for your calling, **they are not from God**—no matter what name they go by.

Like the woman with the alabaster box—broken, scorned, misunderstood—yet still determined to worship, you too are called to press through the noise. CeCe Winans gave voice to her story, but it is **also our story.**

It is the story of every woman who chose worship over shame and poured out her past to receive the forgiveness of the Savior.

Let the world judge. Let the enemy rage. Let the pain run deep. But **run deeper into Jesus**. He alone knows the full weight of your calling and will avenge every wound. Until that day—walk boldly, love fiercely, and never forget:

You are not what you've been through.
You are who God called you to be.
You are the glory that hell cannot silence.

DAMAGED

Chapter 10

It was strict. So strict, in fact, that we couldn't listen to secular music, go to parties, or express interest in anyone from the opposite sex—because almost everything outside of church was considered a sin. Anything that felt good, joyful, or freeing—if it wasn't wrapped in scripture or soaked in church tradition—was treated as rebellion.

So we kept secrets.

If you liked someone, you said nothing. It was safer that way. Over time, we became more comfortable hiding than confessing, more conditioned to relate to the same sex than to navigate our natural feelings toward the opposite. As children, it was confusing. But as teenagers—coming into ourselves and our questions—it became unbearable. We had no one to talk to without fear of judgment. So, we turned to each other, broken teens trying to counsel other broken teens, none of us having the wisdom or tools to help.

Sex education originated in schools, but never in churches. It was a forbidden subject—off-limits. And when someone became pregnant, especially a girl, she was publicly shamed. Not counseled. Not helped. **Shamed.**

She'd be forced to stand before the church and be reprimanded. Once her belly showed, she was told not to return until the baby was born. The rejection was profound, the silence deafening, leading many never to return. And the few who did? They were never seen in the same light again. Imagine the devastation. The church wasn't just our community—it was *our entire world.* To be cut off meant spiritual exile.

I believe our elders did the best they could with what they knew. But here's the problem: as we tried to grow and learn in school, our leaders warned us not to get *too educated*—as if gaining knowledge would offend God. How can we ever rise as a people, a church, or a nation if no one is willing to admit what is broken?

We suffer under two evils: **ignorance and arrogance**.

Ignorance binds us because we refuse to use the gifts God gave us to break free. Arrogance blinds us because we refuse to admit the system is flawed. We keep sweeping things under the rug—but the rug can't hold any more dirt. Yet, we pretend as if nothing is wrong.

By seventeen, I was losing respect for the church—and especially its leaders. Everything felt like a cover-up. The answer to every crisis was more church, more singing, more preaching—but never the why. No one dared to address the root. While the adults were busy hiding, the youth were falling—over and over again. My friends were disappearing, one by one, caught in sex scandals or pregnancies, as everyone around them whispered and gossiped.

It was surreal. People would just vanish. And if you dared to ask where they went, the only response you'd get was:

"Just pray for them."

But it wasn't said with love—it was said with judgment. It was code for: *They sinned. The devil got them. Stay away.* The truth is, we inherited something that slavery birthed—two monsters: a people who hate *a people* and a people who hate *their own people.*

Both monsters inhabit the church and the government. Both need to be confronted, not hidden. If we want healing, we must stop pretending. We must start telling the truth. There is no longer room under the rug. The damage is real—and it's time we address it.

The Awakening

We need each other to fix this. We must work together—not out of ego, not out of fear, but in humility. We need God on our side, and that begins with forgiveness. If we can truly forgive one another, we can move forward and show the world what divine love looks like. Then we will become the most powerful people on earth—not because of might, but because God is with us. **"20/20 Vision"** will no longer be a dream—it will be our reality.

I've always been inquisitive. I asked questions because I wanted to understand—not to rebel, not to defy—but to know. That curiosity became a problem in church. I remember irritating my leaders because I kept asking why God seemed so angry. Why was He portrayed as so unforgiving towards people who made mistakes or simply wanted to enjoy life?

I loved God just as much as anyone else. But when I asked these things, I was rebuked.
"You don't question God—just obey Him."
That never sat right with me.

If I didn't understand something in school, I could ask my teacher. If I was confused at home, I could talk to my parents. But now I'm told I can't even ask *God* questions? That makes no sense. It feels like a contradiction to everything I read in the Bible about Jesus—the same Jesus who welcomed questions and spoke in parables to make people think.

Suddenly, I was labeled a troublemaker. Rebellious. A threat to the "order."

I began to sense that something was seriously wrong. If the church continued to expel individuals for making mistakes, soon there would be no one left. Then, one Sunday, while I was playing the organ during a high point in the service, something within me shifted. My eyes were opened.

I realized that as long as you obeyed, followed the rules, and didn't mess up, you were the star. But if you made one mistake, you were condemned, stripped of your role, privileges taken away, and people would look down on you as if you were nothing. I was ten years old when I decided to fast and pray on my own. I had no guidance—just a hunger to know God and understand my purpose. I woke up, read Psalm 23, washed up, and went to school. When lunch came, I gave mine away. My teacher asked why, and I told her I wasn't hungry. Then I asked to use the restroom—but I didn't go to the restroom for that. I went to pray.

I remembered how Jesus taught His disciples to fast:
"Don't look miserable, don't announce it—wash your face, anoint your head, and your Father who sees in secret will reward you openly."
I took that seriously.

The more I read the Word, the more I felt confident that God was truly *my* Heavenly Father. I spoke to Him like I would speak to my earthly dad. That night, after finishing my chores and schoolwork, I went into seclusion and prayed again. That's when something happened.

I had an out-of-body experience.

I descended into a place of mourning and sorrow. It wasn't physical—it was spiritual, like pressure in the atmosphere. People were enclosed in something resembling transparent cocoons. I was drawn to one in particular. A voice—presumably the Lord's—asked me, **"Do you know this man?"**
I replied, "No Lord, I do not."
Then the man inside spoke:

"Go back and tell your mother what she told me is true. And tell my family—they do not want to come to this place."

I was disturbed. What did he mean? What had my mother said to him? Then, I was taken to another place. I couldn't control any of it. Suddenly, I found myself inside a building, at the entrance of an aisle with a casket at the end. I was pulled forward as if gliding—exactly like a Spike Lee film effect. I stopped in front of the casket. Again, I was asked, **"Do you know this man?"**

I said, "No Lord." He replied, **"This is your family—your cousin."** Even then, I didn't recognize him. The next thing I remember is waking up to the sound of my father asking my mother, "What did you do to him?" I was drenched in tears. My mother replied, "I didn't do anything to him!" I felt embarrassed and afraid. My father asked if I was okay. I replied, "Yes sir." Then I cleaned up and tried to process what I had just experienced.

Whatever it was, it was real.

Later, my mother called me to eat. I told her I wasn't hungry. She insisted, telling me this was my last chance to eat before she cleaned the kitchen. When I still refused, she said more firmly, **"Get down here now and eat your dinner!"** Up to that point, I hadn't told anyone I was fasting. I hadn't eaten or drunk anything for over 24 hours. I wasn't trying to be disrespectful—I just knew I wasn't supposed to break the fast without a release from God. I felt His presence. I felt something bigger than me. I felt...Heaven.

But I also knew I needed to explain. So I told my mother what I had been doing—how I felt led to pray and fast, to seek God for my life and purpose. I was ten. Ten years old. I just wanted to know my Heavenly Father. You could see her reaction shift when I said that.

Crossing Worlds

My mother was a church-going woman who understood fasting. However, hearing it from her ten-year-old child—I think that rattled her. Still, she didn't force me to eat, and for that, I was grateful. She excused me, and I returned upstairs to pray and read. I felt light, as if I didn't belong here anymore—like I had discovered my true self. After I was spiritually released to break the fast, I felt compelled to share everything with my mother—my out-of-body experience, the voices, the visions.

At first, she listened while multitasking. Then she stopped— still. Something I said struck her. Some part of what I described resonated with her spirit, even if neither of us fully understood how or why I undertook such a journey.

Who was this man telling me to warn my mother? What did it mean to be speaking between two different worlds?

Two weeks later, the phone rang. My mother screamed. "I don't want to answer it!" she cried. I didn't understand. She looked shaken, panicked in a way I had never seen before. She turned to me and said, "Answer it." It was my father. He was calling from a pay phone.

He asked, "Where's your mother?" I turned to her. She asked, "Who is it?"—both terrified and desperate to know. "Please," she whispered, "don't let it be about my mother or my husband." Again: "Who's on the phone?" "It's Dad," I said. Relief washed over me. A momentary breath of peace.

Later, I discovered that she had been fearing bad news about her mother, who had severe asthma. But when she answered the phone, she immediately asked, "Is my mother okay?" My father reassured her, "She's fine. But I have news… about your cousin." Then came the wailing. My mother screamed and wept as my father described the tragedy. Her first cousin—a man with whom she had shared the Gospel—had been shot in the face at close range with a sawed-off shotgun. He was killed by a so-called friend over a car race bet. The man had lured him outside under the pretense of paying up. When he turned to get the money, he pulled the trigger instead.

It was all so senseless. Brutal. The betrayal... unimaginable.

This wasn't just anyone; he had survived the Vietnam War. Presumed dead after his dog tags were found without his body, the family mourned him, held ceremonies, and grieved his loss. Then, miraculously, he came home to a wife and a child he had never met—a new lease on life.

I remember his return—it was one of the happiest days I had ever known. Celebration filled the air: food, family, music, joy. It was as if God had handed back a lost treasure. But then—this? To survive the horrors of war only to be murdered in his own community... by someone he knew?

That was hatred at its deepest level. A hate crime of the spirit. Brother against brother.

At ten years old, I didn't fully grasp it—but something within me shifted. It left a mark on me. When the time came for the funeral, I didn't want to go. But we all had to. I stayed outside with my cousins. That felt safer. Less real. But then I heard it again—that same inner voice:

"Go and see."

I hesitated. My heart pounded. But the voice continued, calm and sure:
"Go. I Am with you. You must see." I walked inside. It was exactly the place I had seen in my vision during the fast: the doors, the aisle, the casket at the end. It felt surreal—like time stood still. I knew I wasn't alone. The presence of God was with me. As I approached the casket, fear rose, and my steps slowed.

And then... I saw him.

This was the man I had seen. No wonder I hadn't recognized him before—his face had been destroyed. The morticians had reconstructed one side with clay and makeup, allowing for an open-casket viewing. In my vision, I had only seen the reconstructed side. I was too short to see the full face.

But now I saw both—the recognizable side turned away from me, and the damaged side closest to me. It was horrifying, real. And I knew—I had *seen* this before it happened.

After that, I was never the same. My mother knew it too. She remembered what I had told her weeks earlier. It was real. All of it. I had nightmares afterward. I couldn't sleep. I started going to my parents' room at night. I was scared, confused, and overwhelmed.

Why me?

What did it mean?

Some nights, I would see things—shadows and figures in my room. They would say,

"Don't be afraid. We are here, watching and protecting you."

My prayers and fasting opened a door to another world—a world of spirits, where warnings precede tragedy and where a child can perceive what no one else can explain.

And that door… had been opened inside me.

From this time on, I had encounters I dared not share because my mom grew frustrated with me, and I didn't understand why. We were Pentecostal and Apostolic, and it was said that I had the Holy Ghost. However, when I started having real experiences—like those preached about and recorded in the Bible—I was treated as if something was wrong with me or as if I were a troublemaker. What I didn't understand was this: we went to church all the time, talked about God and Jesus constantly, and everyone claimed to experience the Holy Spirit. Heaven was a real place we all were supposed to go to after we die—this was normal for us. Yet when I talked about my experiences, I was frowned upon, as if I were speaking of fantasy! I was so confused.

At 11 years old, our church didn't have any musicians because the musical family had left to start their own ministry. The pastor told me, "Don't you want to play? Come up here and play the organ." I had shown interest in it. I used to sit with my sister, the church organist, who was very kind to me. She could sing and play, but I didn't know how to play music. Every Sunday, I would go up and sit at the organ, banging on the keys. I remember praying, "Lord, please help me. Don't let me embarrass myself with all this noise I'm making."

Then, one Sunday, as I was banging on the keys with my eyes closed, something incredible happened. I heard beautiful music, and for a moment, I thought someone from another church had come to help us out. But when I opened my eyes, to my surprise, it was me playing the organ. I was playing a Hammond organ—upper and lower keyboards, bass pedals, and a volume-controlled pedal—all at once. The church was going crazy because they were witnessing a miracle. I can't explain it, but from that day on, I understood music and how to play it. I also taught myself to play bass guitar, without any lessons. I became the head musician for our church. Strange things kept happening to me, and I knew it was a result of my faith and prayers.

My father was a concrete contractor, and I prayed for him to spend more time with me—like taking me to ball games or Boy Scouts. I wanted him to take a break from work to be with me, but we had a large family, and he was the sole provider. He worked incredibly hard to build his new business, which had been in operation for just over two years at the time. I was fasting and praying again, asking God to answer my prayers. I received an answer. In the stillness of prayer, I heard these words: "Instead of asking Me to make your father stop working to be with you, if you love him and want to be with him, why don't you start doing what he's doing, instead of trying to get him to do what you want him to do for you?"

I jumped up because I knew I had heard from heaven! My prayers changed. I began praying for an understanding of my father's work and how I could help him. I started waking up extra early to load his tools onto his truck and ask if I could go with him. He was impressed with my initiative but still said, "It's dangerous on the job. You're too young to be out there." But I didn't stop because I knew I had heard from God. I kept praying and loading his tools.

After a while, I began to feel discouraged. It seemed hopeless, and I didn't load the truck one day. My father called out to me, "Where are you? You're not going to load the truck today?" I was shocked. He had recognized what I'd been doing, and it felt like he needed me—not just as his child, but as his son. I stood before him and asked, "What do you need me to do?" He said, "Load the truck. Did you quit on me?"

This was like music to my ears. I was so excited! While loading the truck, my father came outside and asked, "Do you want to go to work with me today?" I couldn't believe it. "Yes! Are you serious?" I screamed.

Not long after, I learned to keep his tools organized and clean. Wanting to take it to the next level, I prayed again, asking the Lord to help me learn more so I could better assist him. That summer, my dad poured concrete on several houses at once. He had many workers, and I offered to help wherever I could.

One day, he left me at a job site where he was pouring a garage foundation. The concrete was starting to set, and I was getting bored. I felt compelled to check the concrete and realized it was hardening. In the concrete business, you need to work with it before it becomes too hard to finish. I prayed again, asking God for help, and pulled out the tools I remembered my dad using to finish the concrete. I worked on it, hoping my dad wouldn't get mad at me or think I was overstepping. After all, I was only 10 years old.

My dad came back hours later and asked, "Which one of the guys came up here to finish the concrete?" I replied, "No one. I finished it." He was upset and asked again, "Who finished this?" I said, "I did. I saw that it was getting hard, and I started working on it." He stared at me, clearly frustrated, and then said, "If you finished this, show me what you did."

I nervously took out the tools and began showing him how I had finished the concrete. Suddenly, everything was quiet except for the sound of the tools. I looked up at my dad, and to my surprise, he had tears in his eyes. I asked, "What's wrong?"

He knelt beside me and asked, "How do you know how to do this? Who taught you, and when did you learn?" He took my hands in his and demonstrated the techniques. I told him I had watched him and prayed for guidance.

That moment meant the world to me. I had never seen my dad

cry before, and to hear him say he was proud of me was one of the greatest moments of my childhood. My dad went to get his crew and showed them my work. He said, "Look at this job." The guys were shocked and asked me to demonstrate. When they saw how I finished the concrete, they were amazed.

But the attention I received for my music and work started to create tension in my family. I noticed that my mother seemed distant, and no matter how much I tried to please her, it didn't seem enough. I began to realize that when I shone, it bothered her. I was becoming popular through my music and my father's work, but at the age of sixteen, I played at the Baltimore Civic Center—and none of my family came to see me. When I told my mom I had played for the "Mighty Clouds of Joy" as a fill-in bassist, she didn't believe me.

Despite the recognition, I felt a disconnect. I could see that my success was driving a wedge between me and my family. My mother's growing distance was something I couldn't understand, no matter how hard I tried to bridge the gap.

I bought my first car at 16 and was so excited although it would sit in the driveway...lol. By the age of 17, I saw things differently and made up my mind that when I turned 18, I would give myself a present, I was leaving the church for good and I went to work in the medical field, I needed to get out of this. Anytime any of us would want to talk about a situation that involved someone, especially in the religious circle, we would be shut down or rebuked In this place, you have no voice, except for your gifts and talents and you were gaged or governed in that as well, so in essence, you had no real voice. If you were bold enough to bring up a topic no one wanted to discuss, then you were made to look disrespectful or put to shame in such a way, you would know, not to ever try that again. So as a teen, I watched so many good people made out to be bad because they just wanted answers, they wanted to live and not just have a good time in church, having no resolve. I was surprised at how many adults from our church would talk to me and explain why they were leaving the church as if they needed someone to know the truth.

If anyone left the church for any reason, their names would become mud and the preachers would take the time and talk bad about them mixed with their sermons. We were instructed to stay away from them, do not call them and the most popular one was, "They got the devil in them, pray for them!" It's so sad and for the most part, nobody would talk to them and if they did, it would be in secret. I used to wonder, "How are these grown people so intimidated by so-called men and women of God?" While playing the organ again on another service, I looked around and the faces were changing, the old were gone (not age) those who had been there so long, our family had been replaced. I started wondering, where are all those sisters who were put out of the church because they made mistakes? Why are these people so angry with them, how can people of represent Jesus be so unforgiving of a person who messed up or made a mistake?

I witnessed people pouring out their hearts for prayer and forgiveness and was told they had to sit in the back of the church for one year and prove themselves. They could not praise God, they could not participate in any of the church activities and the members of the church were instructed to have nothing to do with them because they sinned! By this time, I was an avocet reader, because I wanted to do a comparison between them, the religious folks who killed Jesus and who the devil was supposed to be. One thing stuck out to me in particular. We were taught, that paying Tithes and Offerings was a part of worship, then why is the church accepting Tithes and Offerings from these, "So-called sinners, who could not participate in any other part of the church or service, except for giving money?" My feelings were this, If God does not want your praise, then surely, He should not want your money. This didn't sit well with me at all. Why are they so mean-spirited and cold-hearted? This is not the church of Jesus Christ, and this is not the ministry I read about in my self-taught studies.

According to the Bible, John the Baptist and Jesus of Nazareth did their Father's will. I'm reading like crazy now, because I need answers, and nobody is telling me anything.

I am reading for myself where Jesus rebukes one of his disciples concerning forgiveness. Peter asked sarcastically about forgiveness "Am I supposed to forgive my brother 7 times in one day?" Jesus replied," If anyone asks for forgiveness, then you should forgive them 7 & times 70 a day!" I am in school reading this on my lunch break, I need to know what is going on, my world is starting to fall apart, everything I believed in, is starting to feel like a lie! In my church, if you made a mistake and wanted to fix it, they would dog you out and make you a slave to prove yourself! They made it hard to stay and worst to leave! If you did stay and make it through the year of torment and shame, they still would never forgive you. They would never see you the same again as there would be a noticeable difference. I call it the birthing of a hypocrite! It seemed better to hide your sins rather than to confess them. This is not what the Bible says but it is surely the way of this church! This is abuse, and If God is like this, I don't want anything to do with it.

On my eighteenth birthday, I got up like I was going to church on a Sunday morning, and I went to the movies and stayed all day, eating popcorn, hot dogs, candy, and soda. I had the time of my life. This may not sound like a big deal to most, but we were taught if you went to the movies, Jesus would get and you would go to hell. Sounds silly right, but we believed it! What is so sad concerning all of this is that there are pastors now who were young men and women then and they are guilty of doing some of the same things and they are educated, so what's the problem? This can only mean; that they are master manipulators! No one has apologized for these lies and misleading of God's people but continuing this for another generation. I started to understand that this religion is as sick as it was in the days of Jesus dealing with the Pharisees! When we can take what Jesus taught and the clear blueprint he left on record for us to follow and still promote, hurt and pain, we have no excuse. God has given all of us a lifetime to make choices and one day we will give an account to Him for those choices, good or evil, life or death.

Don't give up your right to choose those who will stand before God one day for their own choices. You will feel crazy standing before

God and seeing how they will be handled when you thought they were so powerful. To support anyone who destroys lives and talks about it in private but continues to carry out the orders, don't we know God has every word and deed recorded? When anybody can manipulate you and a group of followers for years to pay them for destroying lives including your own...This is a Cult and the Occult! God is love and the church where I came from did not have it. They had religious services but did not serve God, you cannot serve God without serving people...this is impossible! Just because they say yes to God does not mean they are doing His will. God loves people and is concerned with their well-being. I did everything to disqualify myself from even being used by God because I do not want to be one of them, but Heaven will not leave me alone. My first gig outside of church was a strip club, how likely would that be?

When I met these girls and heard their stories I was in shock; 9 out of 10 had been, raped, molested, brutally beaten, raped by family members or their mother's boyfriends and some, even their fathers. We were taught to frown on these people and judge them, when in fact most were victims of these circumstances even worse! I used to look at these in a judgmental way out that out of ignorance, prejudices are taught. Now here am I, this, "Pentecostal Church boy gone bad!" I didn't know it at the time, but for a guy of my background, this was the worst and best thing that could ever happen to me! How many of these girls have tried to go to church and were looked down on? This is not the ministry of Jesus Christ! I was angry with God because I was naive enough to believe the lies that I was taught, and thought God was some old and bitter Supreme Being getting His rocks off by screwing with humanity!

I started to have compassion on these souls, behind the scenes they seemed a little callous, but deep within, they were like little children, lost sheep, scared, but trying to be brave and make it in this cruel world. Truth be told, I learned more about the love of God in the streets than I did in church. I loved music and eventually would find myself in the drug life and hustling and became a cocaine addict. God delivered me in one day and I never did drugs or got high ever again. I know for myself that He is more than real to me! I can't speak for all, but I'm like Paul, I can speak for the churches that represented the churches, who believed to be the Holy of Holies. No, you are not but are "Mean and hateful birds" and need reform! They do not speak for our God!

There's a prophecy from the olden days concerning showing up in the last days to deceive God's people by using His name and a description of your works and nature and you fit it to the letter! Jesus warned them to watch their works and they will not have love but will be religious killers and think they do God a service. I Am free now, by the truth! The Lord is looking for a church (people) without spots and wrinkles meaning; we represent a garment in need of cleansing and ironing, we all need to be, washed and pressed! Somehow, the deception of doing these rituals will get us into heaven...not by Christ's example of ministry and messages! We have a lot of damaged goods out here, who love the Lord and are his children...many have never even heard the gospel preached. Those who have suffered this spiritual abuse, need a true word, an apology with some understanding to get their healing, to know that God did not treat them this way, but false prophets...as pastors did!

The church has become the most Segregated Institution on the planet! They are not the "House of Prayer" for all people. They are selective in who they worship with, but everyone is supposed to be welcomed in your God's House, the healing house for life, and drink freely from His Fountains of Love and Life! They do not represent God who is love! I had my former Bishop and Pastor who taught us kingdom to personally say to me on a movie set in 2009. "You cannot hide out in my church or anyone else's church. God has called you to speak to His people, but you must go back home first. I do not know what it is you must do, but when you are finished, God is going to take your ministry global!" I was upset at this word because I knew those who hated me! I heard someone say, "When God calls you, He comes in a whisper, and He'll call you again a little louder, then He will hit you upside the head with a brick, and lastly if you don't get it, the who brick wall will fall on you." I want to thank you.

I wish I would have heard you instead of these others. Well, the wall came down, I came back to my hometown, and I cried as I looked at, "a city in ruins." How can leaders pretend to be serving God without first serving His people? The state and condition of the city are a representation and display the secrets of the leaders' minds. This is the evidence of poor leadership!

I will not apologize for the truth. I must reach out to all of those who are wounded and hurt, who got off track thinking these people were servants of the Lord but are not!

CAN'T HIDE

Chapter 11

Throughout history, many remarkable women have been abused, and many have been killed for bringing goodness into this world.

We have no control over whom God chooses to reveal His glory through. In the face of wickedness and evil, only God demonstrates His presence through weakness and helplessness, enabling them to triumph!

In judgment, those who were persecuted for righteousness will stand before their persecutors and realize they were persecuting God! Do we honestly believe that those who lied to people, leading to their abuse and death, will receive a reward of good on that day? Many women were exploited to accuse innocent men falsely and were sometimes imprisoned or even killed!

The women sometimes wanted to speak up but felt voiceless because of the powers that be. The enemy's weapon against us is his mouth…his words. Our weapon against the enemy is our mouth… God's Word! The enemy will use people to speak falsely against you in hopes of destroying you.

You must use your faith and speak to yourself, proclaiming the Word of God against anything that contradicts what God has declared; God will prevail! For those who can rap and use spoken word as a form of expression, utilize your gifts to the glory of God. Use your God-given talents to set someone free, not to bind them with greater chains than they already bear.

Then what will be your reward? "Many are the afflictions of the Righteous, but God will deliver them from all" as so many have been before you, including prophets and the children of God. "Blessed are the Peace Makers, for they will be called, the children of God." The words of (Yeshua) Jesus are Spoken Word.

Dr. King, for example, is "Spoken Word." He was inspired from above. It was his Heavenly Father speaking through him. This serves as a promise to us when we allow God to use us for His will and what's right. We become vessels for Him to communicate through us for the building up of a torn-down people or person; for the healing of a broken heart; to set free those who have been bound; to heal those who have been abused; and to restore those who have suffered losses.

This is the will of Almighty God, as dealing with ordinary people in extraordinary circumstances sounds familiar! This is not about religion; this is about life! The kingdom life is the life God has planned for His children everywhere! We are part of His kingdom, which is our kingdom to come, as His will is being done on earth as it is in heaven.

We must uphold the standards of the kingdom of righteousness. Heaven is not boring; it's a variety of everything without the drama!

Wouldn't life be dull if we ate only one type of food or lived in just one style of house? What if everyone drove the same kind of car in the same color?

What if everyone wore the same clothes, had the same haircut, or followed the same style? With the same perfume, everyone would smell alike; we wouldn't like it at all. So, aren't we hypocrites for wanting all these varieties while being racist or prejudiced and having issues with the diversity of people?

Every race is either guilty or justified in this. I have a taste for what? Regarding food, why do we have so many restaurants to choose from? Because we want variety. Who provided us with all these choices? God did! How can I enjoy Italian food but dislike the Italians who created it? This is their culture. What if I enjoy Chinese food but harbor hatred for the Chinese?

I could go on and on! From the studio creating music to furnishings and vehicles, everything around us reflects the creativity of God! Then why do we love the gifts of a people but despise the individuals from whom those gifts came? Come on!

These things must unfold in our lifetimes, for this is what Lucifer and the angels did in heaven behind God's back. God had no physical evidence, only his knowledge; thus, from heaven hidden to earth revealed, this is the evidence to bring judgment forever.

We may think we are doing these things to people, but we are being exposed to whose side we would be on if we were with the angels in heaven before the split. God is building His case because He's just. He could do whatever He wants, but He is letting the remaining angels see the revealing of their peers, and God is showing them the evil that was hidden in their Boy's Heart, Lucifer!

Understand this: evil is not a race; it's a family. There is evil in every race, sex, religion, government, and family. It is scattered across time and generations, but the Holy Angels of God will gather them together, and they will not have to worry.

For those born into a good family, they will be joined to their rightful family for eternity! God intends for that family to stay together forever because He is just! I know that sometimes we may struggle to understand how some people can be so cold-hearted and cruel; they're simply emulating what they've seen their father Satan do… he's their teacher!

Do you even know why we have a Devil (Satan) in the first place? Because when Lucifer was in heaven, he was a good angel who went bad. He had a lot of evil in his heart that was concealed. Only God could see what remained in his heart, and he thought it was somehow hidden from God.

If God had acted based on what He knew, it might seem unjust to eliminate this wickedness within him along with him; it would have been fair. However, God cast him out and provided him with space and time to amend his wrongs and rectify his evil ways, perhaps hoping for a change of heart.

Surely when Satan sees the damage he has caused, he will change, but he didn't, and things got worse. He acts through those who submit their lives to him for his use. Thus, he fulfills his fantasy of being God and destroying God's plan, family, and vision. Here it is, all in our face.

A good relationship gone bad started in Heaven and made its

way here to be exposed and judged. God recorded everything!

Everything is being recorded! No one gets away unless they can repent. If Satan is your Daddy, no matter how wrong you are, you will not feel remorse for anything wicked or wrong that you've done, because it's not in you or your father's nature to repent or change.

"Wicked and Evil" forever are your new names! We have the greatest enemy besides death hiding out, and only one can draw him out of hiding…guess who? The case is nearly ready for trial and judgment! The time approaches for the revealing of the Anti-Christ; this will be the Grand Finale!

THE MOTHER'S SON

Chapter 12

Dr. King was destined for his role in the civil rights movement long before he actually stepped into it. God Himself ordained his purpose. Even before he was conceived, God assigned him a mission and equipped him with an anointing. He was selected from the very start.

The prophecy has existed since the beginning. God informed Eve that her offspring and Satan's offspring would be in conflict throughout her life. What does this signify? There are children of God, as well as children of Satan.

Those aligned with Satan are incapable of love and righteousness, and they will fiercely oppose truth and goodness for as long as we exist on this earth. They will not feel remorse for their actions. They will always find ways to justify their wrongdoing; ultimately, their offenses are against God, not humanity.

They believe they are fighting against humanity, but humanity is merely a vessel used by God. This is precisely why humans have imperfections; they are human. However, their actions are influenced by their Creator.

This underscores the importance of seeking God's guidance when it comes to decisions about giving life or ending it, as each generation's support and answers come through a woman's womb. Consequently, there is animosity towards women.

The woman is God's lifelong partner in creating life. She collaborates with Him to bring forth Rulers of Righteousness, Kings,

Leaders, and Deliverers into the world.

The animosity that Satan holds towards the woman fuels his evil actions. He is reminded of God's love for her whenever he sees her. This drives him to target her, her children, and even those yet to be born. Your child could be significant, and you can't know who you bring into the world.

In ancient Egypt, the Pharaoh ordered the death of every Hebrew male at birth, a task meant to be executed by the midwives. Yet, the midwives refused to comply, guided by their conscience. He became alarmed when Pharaoh noticed the Hebrew population was growing despite his decree.

The Egyptians worried about being outnumbered and overpowered by the Hebrews. Pharaoh's solution was to eliminate them quietly, starting with Lucifer's deceptive spirit. Lucifer embodies hypocrisy and deceit, presenting a friendly facade while harboring sinister intentions. He feigns support while scheming against you, aiming to eradicate a people.

Insecurities arise from weak spirits influenced by the devil. When he acted covertly against the Hebrews, he grew bold and used his forces to carry out the king's order, resulting in the death of every firstborn male among them. However, one child escaped this fate because a woman was willing to risk her life for what she believed was God's will. This woman was Moses's mother. She crafted an ark, a waterproof basket, and followed the inner voice guiding her to send her son down the Nile River, placing his destiny in the hands of her God and his.

When Jesus was born, King Herod issued a decree to kill all male infants among the Israelites up to two years old. His motivation stemmed from a desperate attempt to maintain his power. In his quest for authority, he resorted to the murder of innocent children.

Although he held the title of king, he could never secure his rightful position on the throne, which belongs to God and, by extension, to His Son. He slaughtered those children yet failed to establish his authority in the kingdom.

The genuine kingdom is rooted in God and transcends a physical realm. God reigns as King wherever He may be, independent of location. All is under His dominion as the King of kings. Can you envision the woman in the heavens giving birth to a son who ascends to God?

The dragon was filled with rage against the woman and sought to destroy her child at birth. This illustrates a deeper truth about Lucifer, who pretended to love God while masquerading as His most devoted angel. We must understand the true essence of love.

Love begets love but also reveals hidden animosity. Any love can be compromised if it is not diligently protected against hate. History is filled with individuals who believed they loved until circumstances arose that unleashed uncontrolled emotions, leading them to act on hatred and harm those they once cherished.

Many are deceived into believing they love or are loved; yet, how can one truly know if that love has never been tested? Without love confronting the challenge of hate, one cannot fully comprehend what love is. Who teaches us about love? What serves as our standard for love? What does love genuinely look like? Who personifies love?

Love is about giving, whereas hate is about taking. "For God so loved the world, that He gave his only begotten Son, that whosoever believes in him will not perish, but have everlasting life." I encourage you to temporarily set aside traditional perceptions of the Son of God and view him as the very embodiment of love rather than merely a religious figure. Love exists across every race, color, religion, culture, and community; yet alongside it, hate also thrives.

We often remain unaware of the depth of our hatred until faced with specific situations. Many have encountered uncontrollable anger, and some have even committed acts of violence without realizing they were capable of such actions. When love is distorted, it can become destructive, manifesting through evil and hatred.

Hate crimes are precisely that—actions driven by hate. How many lives have been irreversibly altered or lost due to hate? How many groups have clashed against one another solely because of hatred? This, too, represents a form of ignorance, yet even ignorance plays a role in our journey toward salvation.

The truth about all of us must emerge, and we have only one lifetime to gather evidence for love or for hate. God aligns with love, not with religion, while hate aligns with Satan. "The man has become as one of us, knowing good and evil."

We have so misunderstood the message God sent to all of us; his Son was not designed to give birth to another religion, but the exact opposite. Religion brings about segregation on all possible levels of misunderstanding God. God wants unity and harmony.

God gave us a living example of what love looks like and how love can be so hated and misunderstood; not only that, but how love starts as a seed and has to grow. Love is pure and innocent, but to some who understand its potential, love is an enemy, a threat, when hate is the fuel and primary focus for the destruction of people.

Sometimes love can be plotted in its state of innocence, especially when it is defenseless; it's a mystery how cruelty can surround love, seeking to annihilate it. Even in the days of Jesus, King Herod desperately sought after the child's death, even at birth.

This is parallel to the woman in the 12th chapter of Revelation: "And the dragon stood before the woman, for to devour her child as soon as it was born." Her battle to protect her children has been since before time, even now as we know it. Remember that in the Garden of Eden, God said to the woman, "Your seed and the serpent's seed shall be at war all the days of your life."

This matter involves the woman and the serpent, not the man and the serpent. Consider the concept of the woman's seed versus the serpent's seed. Scientifically, we understand that a woman does not produce seed; that role belongs to the man. The woman and the serpent represent two distinct species—one human and the other reptilian. Thus, using the term "seed" implies a spiritual connection.

The conflict they face has a common origin. When faced with opposition, the woman and the serpent exhibit similarities, which reflect the essence of the "Strip Club." When not in conflict, they work together to lead men into inappropriate worship.

This is harmful to her, as she is intended to achieve triumph over Satan's domain. The woman is meant to dismantle his kingdom, not to support it! Therefore, she needs to recognize her true identity. Together, the woman and the serpent pose a serious threat to humanity.

She, the giver of life, and Satan, the taker of life, create a dangerous mix, like fire and gasoline! The woman embodies fire and moves with its fervor, while the serpent navigates through water, avoiding desolate areas.

The serpent entices the woman to harness her fire, making her target fervent. The serpent utilizes water to drench them. This spirit merges with the woman when she allows it, guiding her in a seductive dance. How else can she captivate so many?

She begins to move like a serpent, entrancing her victims. The more they unite, the greater her gains, both in wealth and influence. He serves as her mentor and guide. When the music begins, it summons worship and submission.

Music is a powerful tool designed to attract and soothe the victims, organize those who will partake, and show no mercy once ensnared by the venom, allowing the serpent to claim everything. From this realm, there is nothing constructive for nurturing marriage, family, or community.

The serpent entices the woman, using her to draw in the man or woman, ultimately ensnaring the children and robbing them of hope for a secure and bright future. If men and women shared their experiences, the truth of how it concludes would be far from beautiful. The serpent employs allure to seek out its victims, fully aware of their desires.

As he incites the woman, building her desire, he makes her receptive, both physically and emotionally; this drives her target wild with longing. At this moment, she demands her tribute...Baal (money) becomes her deity! You must present her with wealth! The serpent unleashes a spirit, and the DJ calls out to those who yearn for more, urging them to pay or offer generously!

Remember, no one has received anything real, only a promise wrapped in illusion! Then the serpent instructs one of his followers to ignite the celebration with offerings, commanding, "Make it rain, MONEY!" When the cash flows, so does the fire.

A spirit has been unleashed, elevating worship and desire to a new level. SEX has entered the scene and become this space's dominant force. A diverse crowd is present, some calling it "The Devil's Den!" Here, you'll find everyone from Hustlers and Rappers to Singers and Producers, Athletes and Agents, as well as Murderers and Politicians, Bankers and Bank Robbers, Drug Dealers and Drug Addicts, Students and Teachers, Lawyers and Judges, Police Officers and Correctional Officers, Pimps and Players, Preachers and Parishioners, Singles and Married couples, Straight and Gay individuals, Molesters and Rapists, Government officials and Corporations.

It's essential to recognize that sex is a divine gift; anything good does not and cannot originate from the Devil—let's get that clear! The Devil is a deceiver and a thief! We must understand our God; every gift is meant to bring us pleasure and joy, accompanied by the responsibility to uplift humanity and establish God's kingdom on earth. When sex is used to manipulate and control, it becomes "Witchcraft!" This seductive spirit of witchcraft is prevalent worldwide, and the music is spreading across social media. Satan has his followers tirelessly crafting beats to fuel the serpent's worship.

The serpent unknowingly sways many people. You create and produce music for him. She offers him gifts, yet the serpent deceives her into believing she is giving them to a man. If she could free herself from this deception and reclaim her true self, she would turn away from everything tied to this lifestyle.

Instead of squandering your talents, why not direct them toward your marriage and committed relationships? Preserve your gift, but use it for God's intended purpose. God delights in our happiness, just as we enjoy seeing our children thrive; please understand this!

Causing harm is never part of God's plan for humanity, clearly differentiating those who serve God from those who serve Lucifer. This message is not meant to insult or condemn, but to reveal the truth. I am not a politician or public figure, so I do not adhere to political correctness.

It's troubling to see so many young people unknowingly serving Lucifer or the serpent, remaining oblivious to it. Often, they believe they are pursuing their own desires, while they are being manipulated by their greatest enemy, a Master of Disguise. You are in bondage, and your master is Lucifer!

He is serious about this war of destruction and control. His mindset is clear: the woman has usurped my position, and I want it back. She stands in the way of the serpent's schemes. He is astute enough to stay close to her, recognizing her power, authority, and God-given gifts and talents.

However, she likely remains unaware of this. If he could eliminate her, he would be perfectly content, watching men destroy each other over power. The serpent realizes that the woman holds true power, ruling the earth. God has appointed her as an Executive Producer, yet the serpent has her functioning like an artist, devoid of proper management over her career or finances. However, for the woman who understands her role, the man may hold a position, but she is the one who orchestrates everything, wielding her influence through humility rather than arrogance.

This is the woman who rises to power. It is God's will for her to embrace her glory, a gift bestowed upon her from the beginning, which entails righteousness in aiding and saving others. She consistently works behind the scenes to make things happen. Aware that she is despised and hated, she feels this every day yet perseveres, for God created her to fulfill the purpose of restoring all that was lost in Heaven.

The life we seek is eternally linked to the woman.

She faces violence, suffering, and death every single day...why? Because Satan despises women. He harbors an eternal hatred for her! This hatred spans generations...it is relentless! Regardless of race, color, nationality, or beliefs...the enemy's disdain remains!

All women who seek the common good should stand in solidarity with each other. No one is exempt. Look back through history, from European and Egyptian queens to Geishas and women in harems, from masters to slaves, from virgins to those labeled as immoral; it doesn't matter.

Simply being a woman invites his hatred! She is manipulated due to her lack of awareness of her true identity.

The wife is at home, focused on securing and caring for her

family, while the other woman, often seen as a seductress, might be out on the streets or trying to lure married men. The truth is that both women face the same adversary.

While facing challenges, one has a marriage that is fundamentally happy, yet temptation arrives in the form of a man who seems to fill the gaps in her life. For those with experience, the choice is clear, but for the naïve and sheltered woman, an allure leads her to take risks.

If she could hear the voices of women who have come before her, they would urge her to resist temptation. She must realize that her adversary can wield her body as a weapon, but with the wisdom granted by her Creator, her mind is the true power she can use to overcome her foes.

It's ironic that while God designed women, others often seek to manipulate and control them, and even the enemy exploits them towards self-destruction.

The serpent aims to lead her towards destruction by undermining relationships, while God intended her to foster and enrich both life and connections. The woman has the potential to bring immense joy to Aman and fill his heart with love, but if she acts independently of God, she can inadvertently harm him for a lifetime.

She becomes a natural healer and nurturer when she submits to her Creator and embraces her true purpose. She needs to recognize the damage caused by heeding the wrong influences. A woman was not designed to raise a son single-handedly, guiding him from boyhood to manhood.

God's plan does not include a father's absence. While a mother may sometimes fulfill both roles when necessary, that was not her original purpose.

Many fathers have been pushed out of their children's lives, while other men enter, potentially causing further harm, especially if the mother is dealing with abuse or unresolved trauma. Seeking love from someone new out of desperation isn't true love; it's an opening for negativity to take hold again. We all have our flaws and have made mistakes, some more severe than others.

I've faced challenges from both perspectives and don't claim to be an expert from formal education, but rather from the lessons life has taught me. I share the truth as it comes to me, shaped by my failures in running from God and my true purpose instead of embracing them.

Family members often pay the price when this occurs because it extends beyond one person's aspirations. It reflects God's desire for a better life for all. Despite the many available opportunities, I hope and pray that children receive a fair chance at life. A woman claiming to be both mother and father may sound appealing, but it isn't a reality and strays far from the truth. The transition from boyhood to manhood can be devastating if young men harbor anger and resentment toward their mothers, feeling that something essential is missing and blaming their mothers for it.

He might never express it, but society suffers tremendously because of his unjust grievances. The woman influences the mood within the relationship and marriage. Men can display negative traits on various levels, yet the right woman has the power to uplift or undermine them consistently. We must acknowledge the blessing that God has given us in women and strive to be accountable and responsible.

I often chuckle while writing, anticipating the comments and reactions I might receive for certain statements. Believe me, there are many things I could say about men, but I will do my best to remain focused on the woman, her child, and the serpent.

How about, *"Why I Satan HATE THE MAN?"* A woman should write it...don't you think?

The woman occupies the place that the serpent once held in heaven, which is why he refuses to leave her side on earth. He harbors hatred for her, yet simultaneously feels a need and envy towards her. He cannot fulfill his mission without her, leading him to battle against her and her aspirations continually.

This reflects women's struggles when they struggle to articulate what they are experiencing. A woman must maintain her relationship with God, her Father and Creator, not merely for religious reasons but because her eternal existence hinges on it. Only He can shield you from adversaries and lead you and your children towards your purpose and destiny. Deception surrounds us; "These things must come to pass, so don't let your heart faint because of it."

Mothers and wives who love and support their children endure significant challenges when God chooses their child. This can create divisions within the household. Frequently, the father and mother clash over how to raise the child. The father may have strong feelings about the situation, while the mother may have various instinctual responses.

She plays a crucial role in the child's future. Mothers unaware of their child's calling can unintentionally become obstacles, aligning with negative influences to undermine the child's dreams and purpose. Despite this, the chosen child often finds support from unexpected sources, such as teachers, community organizations, or spiritual leaders.

At times, the enemy can manipulate the mother to control the child and their gifts for her benefit, hindering the child's ability to fulfill their destiny. Out of love, the child may feel obligated to stay close to their mother, unaware of the manipulation at play, and for many, it may be too late to realize the truth.

Some may grow bitter and struggle to rebuild their lives after such experiences, while others may escape into destructive behaviors, seeking solace in drugs or unhealthy relationships.

To her surprise, the runaway child is being managed by the same adversary, albeit through different means. God will send someone to recognize the abilities and gifts within this child. When God is ready to instigate change, He typically calls one individual and has others follow that vision.

The chosen one will be apparent, and everything will align for their benefit when the time comes. Opposition will always arise, but this should not be misinterpreted as a sign that the individual is not called. They must grasp the calling and safeguard the child, avoiding competition or destructive behavior in the child's life.

You have been selected to guide the child toward their purpose, which requires significant sacrifice and hardship. The mother holds great influence during childhood, but as they mature, having the right partner or spouse becomes essential.

In our generation, we have a remarkable example in Coretta Scott King. She stands as one of the greatest, if not the greatest, representations of what a wife and mother should embody in times of success and deep struggle. Mrs. King has exemplified what it means to be a true woman of God, not by the standards of religion but by the divine standards set by God Himself.

Only God could sustain her through the trials faced by her husband, who sought to fulfill God's will.

At that time, Dr. King did not fully grasp why he was pursuing righteousness, yet he recognized its necessity. This reflects the reality of those whom God places in significant roles in the world. Many may try to replicate their actions, but can only imitate them.

History reveals individuals who had the opportunity to instigate change; they were human yet possessed an inexplicable drive, almost supernatural, to foster transformation and support others. They understood how to be the support and foundation for someone called to fulfill their divine purpose.

Despite the challenges, she remained undeterred by opposition and maintained her focus on the mission. It was certainly not easy; anything valuable is rarely attained without difficulty.

According to her husband, she selflessly exemplified dedication, loyalty, faithfulness, and devotion. He held her in high regard, not only as a wife and mother but also as an individual.

Many marriages today struggle because we tend to be self-absorbed, selfish, break our commitments, prioritize ourselves, and act vainly, often neglecting the welfare and purpose of future generations. How much longer can this continue? Mrs. Coretta King embodies a moral compass and strengths unparalleled in her sphere. She persevered steadfastly. She was an exemplary wife and mother.

She never betrayed her husband or succumbed to the pressures that might have led her to do so. When a man publicly and privately honors his wife, it signifies genuine respect. Dr. King acknowledged his wife's unwavering devotion, dedication, loyalty, and love.

In his moments of vulnerability, he could rely on her strength derived from her passion. She stands as one of our unsung heroes. I cannot help but recognize the ongoing struggle between the seed of the woman and the serpent.

With a woman like Mrs. King, how can we allow children to grow up witnessing the degrading lifestyles and disrespectful lyrics directed at black women and women in general? The music industry is one issue, but the responsibility of the writers and artists is another.

Do we genuinely believe this is merely an accountability problem? The world has been watching us for long, and we must get this right! Our democracy has faltered not only in its policies but also in its messaging. We do not speak for God, as He does not express Himself that way!

While Mrs. Coretta King may be overlooked on this earth, we can be assured she is celebrated eternally in Heaven. She exemplifies what it means to be a faithful wife, demonstrating integrity by steering clear of temptation.

We cannot fathom how many individuals sought to exploit her weaknesses, perhaps hoping to lead her to failure. Let's be honest; how many detractors attempted to drag this remarkable young woman into scandals? They raised allegations of infidelity, hoping to provoke her into seeking revenge.

How many influential men would have given anything to be with this beautiful, educated, loyal, and devoted woman? She was truly a treasure! She upheld her husband's dream and raised their children, becoming Martin's voice until she reunited with him.

I envision her presenting him with the report on freedom. I picture Dr. King inquiring about her feelings and thoughts regarding the people's progress. He has received many reports from those who passed away before her. Knowing her loyalty and commitment, he can trust her insights.

Imagine delivering a report to heaven about youth in black communities who are not voting, engaging in violence, or selling and using drugs. What about the failure to take advantage of available education? Could we play the current top 40 R&B songs and let him hear their lyrical messages? "Desegregated African Americans?"

What is the message conveyed through the music? Would we take pride in the voices that have replaced his, the voices of the people for whom he sacrificed everything? If we believe this would upset Dr. King, how much more would it concern God, who sent Dr. King to liberate a people?

We need to eliminate this wrongdoing, beginning with ourselves. It's time to stop blaming others and to take accountability as a nation and community. If God guided us through and beyond slavery, He will support us as we stand for what is right. We have to stop compromising our values for money.

To the women who value life over material possessions, you are our beacon of hope. It's difficult to strive for a fulfilling life and desire nice things without compromising your integrity, especially when so many examples of success are depicted as strippers, gold diggers, or those seeking wealth through superficial means.

I've heard someone say she wasn't just a gold digger but a platinum digger. This woman is in her 40s and has children. Men and women abandon their commitments and marriages for illusions or false narratives.

None of this will last. Love and family are what truly matter. God demonstrated His love by being willing to sacrifice everything for His family.

Calvary symbolizes a love story of someone who chose to sacrifice himself for the sake of life rather than for material wealth. Our children have been led astray, sacrificing their lives for possessions instead of valuing life; some even take lives for these things.

They overlook the significance of life while still wanting to live. This is the devil's deception, and many refuse to recognize his presence. The devil's clever trick is making you believe he doesn't exist. What else could this be, if not the ongoing struggle between the woman and the serpent, a conflict that started in heaven?

We belong to one side or the other, the kingdom of righteousness or unrighteousness; we cannot represent both. Serving two masters is impossible. Even a drug dealer wouldn't allow you to work for him while also working for his competitor. In the NFL, you can't play for two teams; you must choose one and dedicate yourself to it.

In government, you cannot serve two different administrations; your loyalty must lie with your nation. So why do we think it's acceptable to serve evil and ruin lives, only to hear some preachers at funerals claim that the deceased is now in a better place, implying heaven?

How can we reconcile the idea that someone who sacrificed their life for a cause ends up in the same afterlife as those who lived for evil and took innocent lives? This notion is a deception from the depths of Hell!

Do we genuinely believe that a person who murdered someone and then died in a violent encounter is in heaven alongside their victim, sitting together as if nothing happened? They would not coexist peacefully; they would be in conflict over the crime committed.

Heaven is not about hiding the truth; rather, it is about uncovering it. Our purpose on earth is to clarify this once and for all. We have the choice to align ourselves with good or evil, life or death, to nurture or harm. Take, for instance, the religious leaders during Jesus' time.

Despite claiming to represent God and regularly preaching in the temple, they opposed everything he stood for. They were regarded as holy men and priests. When Jesus began his ministry, they took issue with him and his teachings. They had not trained and did not know him, which meant they could not control or take credit for his approach.

Despite his positive impact on many lives and the large following he garnered, they continued to oppose him. They held positions of power alongside the government, whereas Jesus held authority with God.

They were swayed while Jesus held divine authority. It was clear to anyone that this man focused on helping others, not harming them. His critics consistently intended to find faults and undermine his ministry and mission. Jesus prioritized the salvation of individuals and championed their right to a dignified life.

He provided them with teachings and hope that extended beyond their earthly existence. The religious leaders opposed everything he did. Why? Because Jesus spoke of love, freedom, and liberty. The liberation of a people often threatens those who gain from their oppression or subjugation. Economically disadvantaged individuals who seek false hopes are usually vulnerable to deception.

When the rich man asked Jesus how he could attain eternal life, Jesus replied that he should follow the Torah. The rich man claimed he had adhered to these laws since his youth. Jesus then told him that if he wished to be perfect, he needed to sell all his possessions, give to the poor, and follow him, promising that he would have treasure in heaven. The rich man, shocked, asked, "Everything?" and Jesus confirmed, "Everything!"

Ultimately, the rich man left in sorrow. The lesson here is that while one can possess wealth, how it is acquired matters greatly. This man had gained his riches through the oppression of the poor and the shedding of innocent blood. His true god was money. Jesus offered him a chance for redemption and a new life.

When our wealth comes at the cost of others' lives, God will hold us accountable. In eternity, no amount of wealth can save us. It's akin to a wealthy individual whose riches stem from illegal activities, ultimately facing imprisonment. Such a life leads to memories of past choices that only torment, as one cannot reclaim or enjoy what they once had, while others benefit from it.

Thus, one becomes trapped in one's past, with no future ahead.

When we depart from this life, our past existence will be a memory, and if we haven't contributed anything meaningful to God, we will have no reward or real life. Those who live extravagantly without regard will face eternal consequences. Everything in this life has its beginnings.

If we can conceive a question, the answer must already exist. It is impossible to formulate a question without the answer being present first. The truth precedes falsehood; a lie is derived from the truth, not vice versa. Thus, the visible aspects of this world originate from eternity.

They arise from thoughts, ideas, plans, dreams, hopes, or schemes. This world represents the realization of something that remains hidden. Our time here serves to reveal who our true father is. There is a distinction between being weak and being wicked.

If you are weak, you can recover through repentance, forgiveness, and making amends. However, being wicked means you are aware of wrongdoing, choose not to correct it, and are willing to defend that evil for future generations. In that case, Satan becomes your father, and you will go to great lengths to satisfy him.

When God is your father, you'll choose to do good, even sacrificing your life for those who wrong you. Others may not share your perspective and perceive you as weak, but you are actually strong. You have chosen humility for the greater good, and your reward will be great. It will all be worth it when you transition to the other side, and we will all make that journey.

What motivated the Pharisees to kill Jesus? They acted in the name of God, using religion to attack what God cherishes. This is the deception of Satan, the fallen angel who insists on manipulating God's purpose for his ends. Why does he do this? Because he is a thief and a liar, unable to change his nature, which is evident in his offspring. The traditional church leaders wanted to prevent the people from truly finding God; they aimed to make them believe they could only see God through them.

They oppressed God's people, but Jesus offered them freedom. This was unacceptable to them. Jesus is the Son of the Great Wonder in heaven, born of the Woman clothed with the sun. The religious leaders serve the dragon, resenting the Woman and seeking to destroy her Son. What better way to undermine God's Son than to secure a position within God's house?

Lucifer is a leadership expert and understands both the kingdom and religious protocols. He utilizes everything he learned from God for his purposes and against God. Have you ever experienced teaching someone who takes those skills and uses them against you? Because of this, treason is considered a serious offense that is not accepted in this world or the next. There are consequences for those who violate this.

This is what occurred in heaven, leading God to cast them out! While we may have differing opinions on various matters, we can agree on this. A peaceful individual would not wish to partner with someone violent, just as a caregiver would never want to collaborate with a predator or abuser.

He will never let anyone take his position. Anyone who opposes his rise to prominence is considered an enemy and must be dealt with. Jesus poses a threat, and he feels the need to eliminate him. It wasn't the Romans who brought about Jesus' death; it was Religion that caused it.

Religion competes for a place alongside God, while God seeks a relationship. God is focused on His sons and daughters ruling His kingdom with Him. Religion is about striving for power with God and acting on its agenda, whereas a relationship is about being born of God with a purpose and fulfilling His will.

Do we genuinely believe that if we destroy what God cherishes because we think they are unqualified or belong to the wrong race, religion, or gender, that God will reward us for harming His children? That's madness! What would we say? I killed them to help you? In God's realm, this would spark another heavenly conflict.

We must understand better and think more clearly. We know that penalties deter crime; life would be far more chaotic and dangerous without them. The absence of security and order would render hope for a safe environment impossible. Despite our flaws, if we desire a good life and a safe place for our children, how much more will God prepare a place for His children in eternity? Consider the level of crime, even with penalties in place. God is not foolish; He is merciful!

Forgiveness is already granted for every sin. There is a pardon available for each wrongdoing. God intends to address the underlying issues. However, we must demonstrate true repentance, a genuine shift in heart and mind regarding our offenses against life.

A day will come when we must account for our wrongdoings to life and the Earth. The Earth is alive and sustains life, as ordained by its Creator. Some exploit her just as a man might violate a woman. Her resources are continuously ravaged. Toxins are released into her as a sick man might interact with a woman, fully aware of his condition, driven by hatred and selfishness.

We were not meant to harm or be harmed. Life is the most valuable gift, yet some show no respect for it or its Creator. Conversely, the woman holds a unique and cherished position with God. True worship occurs when one is deeply connected to God's heart.

When you genuinely connect with what God feels, you enter into genuine worship. You are on the right path when you are prepared to do whatever it takes to please Him. Make no mistake, God has integrity and stands by His promises. He is a savior, not a destroyer.

To all the cults out there, you are inadvertently working for me. I misused God's name to tarnish His reputation. When you follow God's guidance, you become united with Him. No matter your challenges, don't allow yourself to remain trapped in your suffering; instead, rise up, transforming "From pain to power."

Avoid getting stuck in your pain. You might face trials, but don't dwell on the hardships; push forward toward resurrection! This is your liberation! God pursues those who are marginalized and despised. You should pay attention to those who are rejected.

Those who are unjustly hated embody God's heart and love. God is love, and His adversaries despise Him and all of His children.

Every race and color embodies God through His righteousness, not merely by deeds but by their love for Him. Regardless of language, belief, or any other distinction, those who love God will experience His eternal love. You will recognize His followers by their commitment to truth and their efforts to act righteously, rather than hiding their wrongdoing behind authority and influence.

God does not discriminate; He created all races to reveal the hidden evils in humanity apart from Him. It is not our words spoken in God's name that reflect His true nature and character, but our actions, which should embody love. We are not aligned with Him when we harbor hate for any reason.

Many of us may have valid reasons to justify our animosity

toward those who have wronged us, yet the essence of our Father shines through, sometimes making us seem foolish. However, no one escapes accountability. Ultimately, we will all answer for our actions. God does not show favoritism, but He honors faith.

Without faith, we cannot please God. We must first acknowledge His existence and recognize that He rewards those who earnestly seek Him. We should be mindful of how we treat others because God records our actions, noting that the righteous care for the poor and the marginalized.

Their situations often stem from larger spiritual battles of greed and hatred, which ultimately oppress the vulnerable. Many are victims of poor decisions made by leaders throughout their lives.

While we may search for God in powerful places, He is present among those who suffer: the abused, the unjustly persecuted, the broken-hearted, the imprisoned, the children who go hungry, the faithful widow, the discarded elderly, the meek, the thieves, and the impoverished.

He states, "When you care for them, you care for Him." God is not concerned with the mortgage payments of a church building if His people are suffering from hunger, homelessness, lack of clothing, unemployment, anxiety, and oppression. Isn't life worth more than structures, attire, and material possessions?

How can we face God knowing we have turned His flock into mere commodities? Jesus was sent as our model of righteousness to reveal God's compassion for His people. He nourished the flock, while the priests exploited God's people for their gain. If Jesus (Yeshua) is not the Son of God, then why did we reset time in his honor? Who was He? A humble carpenter or the divine Son of God?

Why would the entire world agree to restart time because of this one individual? He was not an earthly ruler, lacked financial riches, was branded a criminal, and executed by His foes, yet He received the highest honor...B.C. and A.D.!

Every nation, language, race, government, and religion has bowed to this Man and honored Him; in accepting this change in time, they all recognized that "Jesus is Lord!"

Each time we schedule an appointment and set our clocks, we are, in essence, affirming that He is the Son of God, as Heaven has proclaimed it. This renders humanity powerless and prompts the entire earth to embrace a new beginning, a New Age for all time.

Additionally, a ten-month calendar constituted a year when God's Son walked among us. However, following His profound influence, with twelve disciples who became Apostles, He established a kingdom order of divine governance, twelve plus one.

The Romans later added two months to the calendar, resulting in the current twelve-month year, a practice that has persisted ever since. This illustrates the incredible power of a woman and her son.

To all the mothers who have faced the heartbreaking loss of a son or child to hatred, remember that God truly understands your feelings and the depths of your grief. Jesus knows what it means to die, surrounded by lies and animosity. You are never alone in this journey.

For this reason, no one can enter heaven without recognizing the incredible gift God has given to the world—His Son (John 3:16).

Jesus advocates pursuing justice for your child's case beyond this life. His unwavering commitment is to justice! You will be reunited... Take heart, Mom... "Behind every great man, there is a great woman!"

WITHOUT THE WOMAN'S CONTRIBUTIONS TO LIFE AND HER STORY, WE WOULD NOT HAVE HISTORY...

LOVE IS?

Chapter 13

Love is

We must exercise caution in our interactions with others, as we may unknowingly be touching the heart of God. Life revolves around purpose and the realization of that purpose. God's love is evident all around us, and life reveals His heart, present in every moment, including our newborns. God is inherently good, but something went awry. Lucifer, once God's greatest creation, chose to pursue his path, desiring to surpass God, not merely in thought, but in reality.

God serves as the catalyst, using life to bring about transformation. Betrayal arose in Lucifer's heart in heaven, and one-third of the holy angels shared the same treasonous sentiment with him. These hidden secrets are poised to be acted upon at the right moment. God sees all, yet has chosen not to disclose His knowledge of these matters.

God observes and monitors every heart, even without the awareness of heaven. Purity and innocence have been tainted. However, God has a plan, and soon, it will be revealed. Prophecies speak of "A Weaker but wiser generation," and this is that generation!

Technology is advancing at an unprecedented rate, surpassing any previous period in human history. A "New Heaven" and a "New Earth" await us, but first, humanity must transform before kingdoms can change.

Love represents the most authentic essence of an unblemished heart. It embodies the innocence of a newborn, untouched by experience, simply yearning for affection. God's love for humanity reveals to us the nature of love itself.

Through His actions, He illustrates what love truly means. God shows that light is most impactful in shadowed places by sending His Son into a darkness-filled world. Some individuals twist situations to portray themselves as virtuous, casting others as more sinful than they truly are, allowing them to position themselves as the good in the narrative while obscuring the truth and distorting history.

Every individual, race, nation, religion, and gender has a purpose. Purity must be restored, and heaven must be returned to its former glory, free from evil. God has a plan.

He perceives the darkness within hearts that have yet to be revealed. It is time for every heart to undergo testing. God possesses the purest heart and is eager to demonstrate it. He has fashioned the earth as a testing ground for all life considered throughout eternity.

God's plan for salvation is complex but essential for achieving eternal peace. He establishes a space where every hidden aspect can be uncovered, addressed, healed, and restored to its original state without corruption. Everything created through love will ultimately pass the love test. If love remains untainted, it will return to its original purity; this is God's infallible system.

Earth serves as the proving ground, while human beings are miniature representations of God, composed of body, soul, and spirit. The body is temporary, as the spirit belongs to God and the soul belongs to humanity, with the body housing both. They function together and rely on one another for life. Jesus asked Peter, "Do you love me?" Peter replied, "Yes, Lord, you know that I love you!"

Jesus then instructed him, "Feed my sheep!" He repeated this question three times, referring to his followers as "Lambs," indicating that part of a person is gentle, reliant, and non-threatening. This part often suffers the most.

Every human being has three parts: Body, Soul, and Spirit. A person is not whole or complete unless all three are taken care of and content, becoming "Triune," three coming together as one. The church mostly continues to deal with the spirit and part of a person's soul on Sundays and leaves the person to deal with the other part of his/her soul and body for the rest of the week.

Therefore, this leaves a person incomplete and often confused because they can't get a complete resolution. So many go back to what they are familiar with, making them believe that something may be wrong with them after looking at examples in the church where people seem to have it all together.

The "Church," born out of Christ's very nature and personality, sets an example of God's will for all His people. How is the Church so off base? How is the Church reflecting the very Religious Leaders who did not believe in Christ in the first place and had Him killed?

He told his disciples not to be like the Pharisees! These Luciferians have infiltrated the true Church. Denial is a terrible thing...the Church needs Reform!

We have no excuse for not following His pattern, except if we are wicked! Jesus served people and esteemed them higher than himself, calling himself the Son of Man. He humbled himself to serve God by serving God's people.

As in all things, there are some exceptions when it comes to churches helping people, but for the most part, it is a "smoke screen" to enslave people and paralyze them, causing them to be counterproductive. In the meantime, the leaders are doing "The come up!"

With so many gifts and talents, what is the problem? For the last 40 years, we have been wandering in a wilderness, but it is time to cross over into something Real! We need a "Deuteronomy" generation!

We have innumerable churches across the country, but our cities are in ruins. What is the purpose of the Non-profit status if it is not used to assist the government with the people?

Religious leaders compete with each other, and it's about their kingdom, not God's kingdom. I pray the Lord opens the eyes of all who read this. Do we not see the parallels here? Don't we see a repeat of what Lucifer did or plotted to do in heaven?

Then what would make us think that we will go to heaven and be rewarded for destroying God's (people's) sheep? Everyone wants to justify their actions, but "The tree is known by its fruit!" We hear the message and the leaders' words, but judge the results.

Lost sheep don't have to speak, their being lost is their voice to

God of poor Shepherding and Leadership. I'm tired of going to funerals and watching mothers cry over their young children being buried.

How can we who say we are of God, have no compassion for the lost, and be content living lavish lives, with the evidence of being so cut off from the people who provided our lifestyles? How can the love of God be in us if we don't have compassion for the hurting mothers crying out for their dying children?

If a doctor prescribes medication for a patient, the doctor expects the medicine to improve the patient's health. Still, if the medicine is not working for the patient's good or does not see improvement, then the doctor, as a professional, will change treatments until something works.

Then tell us why we are getting the same word, message, and delivery of something that is not working. Shouldn't we revise a plan and renew an action to help God's people get restored, so that they, too, may live? Too many, way too young, are dying single deaths! This is not what Love is!

Love gives and hate takes, love gives life and hate takes that same life. Christ did not give his life for us to be divided or go to church to have a good time. It's ok as a part of the worship experience, but accurate and complete worship is doing God's will, not having a seductive and counterproductive service that is not meeting the needs of God's people! The "True Church of Christ" was a Movement called "The Way" to establish God's kingdom, with and for His people, and order and morality during corruption.

The leaders were corrupted in all positions of power in the days of Jesus walking this earth, in and out of the Temple. We should not go to church to get high or drugged up. What's the difference between people getting high in the streets and high in the church...both are High! The roads are high on drugs, and the church is high on religion! I speak this by authority, the Church and the World need deliverance from bondage. This is truly about love and hate, good and evil, the kingdom of God, and the kingdom of Satan. The purpose of this life is to expose what is in all of us. Life puts pressure on us to reveal what's in us. It cannot come out of you if it is not in you.

Therefore, repentance is necessary! Whatever is in me that is contrary to God is my sin unforgiven, but repentance eradicates all my sins and trespasses. Every religion has some of God and some of the Devil in it...some good and evil, but the kingdom of God cannot be divided and will not be divided again.

In God's kingdom, there is no Devil, and in Satan's kingdom, you will not find God, unless He's there to turn it out (Jesus is proof of that). It takes a free man to free a man, and if the church is in bondage, how can it set anyone free? Moses was a free man when he went back to set the Hebrews free.

Most of our leaders are still slaves in their minds and trying so hard to be masters, while using God's stuff, including His anointing and people to do it. One thing is missing: the Glory of God.... Anointed but have no glory. Many of our leaders from the past were anointed but also had the glory, because they respected God and their women; therefore, having her support gave them Anointing and Glory!

Until we as leaders submit to God, we cannot tell this generation anything; they have lost respect for leadership, in and out of the church!

Jesus said, "There will be many who will claim to be of Christ, but do not follow them if they do not do the works of Christ!" Read and study! Look into the Word and see what the living Word of God looks like in Jesus Christ.

You will be surprised at what you find! After Jesus's death and resurrection, witnesses and Mary Magdalene entered the tomb where Jesus' body had been laid. They found the grave clothes that his body was wrapped in, which were laid on the grave's table.

The garment wrapped around his body was now lying on the table, unraveled and in disarray, but the cloth wrapped around his head was folded neatly and placed at the head of the table. What was this about? Who would take the time to do such a thing?

God has so much personality and is intentional! The Lord left a message to his faithful and dedicated followers: The head is in order, but the body needs to get it together. The head represents God, the Creator, the Son, Heaven, and the Universe, and the body represents us as a people on earth.

We must be unified in working together, so we, too, may be able to fold our grave garments and place them neatly on the grave table. We must know our place and role in this world. We have not done this yet, because we are too divided over foolish things that don't matter and have not resurrected as a people, but are in limbo as the "living dead! "

Until we stop manipulating for the love of money and start serving, truly loving one another, we shall remain dead people. It was hate that killed Christ, but Love raised him from the dead. If we don't believe in the resurrection, then there is no better place after we die. "So, no matter what the haters do, love will not and cannot die!"

When the enemies of Jesus said, "Don't you know that I have the power to release you or crucify you!" Jesus replied, "You would have no power over me if it were not given to you from above." So don't ever think for a minute that Heaven is not in control and monitoring all of us.

Leaders have failed a generation, so we have a generation who chose to lead themselves, called "Hip-hop." Yes, Hip-hop is the new leader of the younger generation, and seeing the results, this is not working either, but they did try; Because something needed to be done and our leaders would not hear their voice, they created a language and voice of their own...this was genius on their part. They used it to shut out the parents, adults, leaders, and those who exercise authority.

Satan is in hot pursuit of this generation.

We need to swallow our pride, repent, and apologize to God and this generation for playing games with their lives. We should pray to God that heaven will have mercy on all of us as a people and nation. We must show respect, humble ourselves, and turn from this glamorous road of destruction.

"Woe unto you, Pharisees, hypocrites, for you appear as righteous before people, but your hearts are far from God. You seem to uphold the law and be law-abiding citizens, but violate the heart of that very same law!

You shall know the truth and the truth will make you free!"

Where is the truth? What is the truth? Every potential eternal being must prove themselves in time before being transferred to eternity for evaluation and judgment.

Everyone must die to leave time. "After death is the judgment." God is looking for love because He is love and created all things with His love. Everything starts with love; every new birth represents the innocence of new life.

As we go through life and find ourselves on the wrong side of God, He has made it possible to fix anything and everything we may have done. Repentance to God is how we can get a new, pure, and clean heart. Don't discount the power of a new birth in the spirit.

This is important because the spirit is our eternal Being. We can always get a new house for the soul and spirit. This is the moral code and fabric of a person. Every human being was born and came alive by God's love.

Even the most notorious person of death had a pure, fresh, and innocent start, no matter the environment or conditions of birth. All life comes from God, and God is love! When God gave His son, God gave His love and heart to mankind. Divinity came just as we did and submitted to His law.

The Creator is putting His heart on trial just like the rest of us. What if iniquity was found in His heart? We would have a problem. When a disease breaks out, everyone needs to be tested. If God were infected, then He, too, would require treatment.

God ran to heaven with His mind (Head), while His heart was on earth. God submitted Himself and entrusted His heart to a woman. The woman carried His heart, nurtured His heart, watched His heart grow, and admired its work ethic.

The heart was born in trying surroundings, but could not take a chance to be born in the Temple, because murderers were there disguised as priests and pastors. No matter the person, position, or title, all will be tested (sin was heaven's COVID-19 outbreak). God's Son would be in danger there because they were undercover for Lucifer. They have all the likeness of him, by way of loving money and material things.

These men appeared to be holy, blessed, and prosperous to the average person. What's sad is that they believed themselves to be holy, Godly. When judged by the law and other people, like the Romans who were openly murdering at the time, they were looked upon as righteous. We use other people who are worse off than us to make us appear righteous.

This is an old device of self-righteousness and justification. Therefore, he's referred to as the old devil and serpent. At 12, Jesus goes to the temple, and the leaders, teachers, and scholars are impressed with his doctrine and knowledge of the scriptures. When his mother lost track of him and sought to find him, they finally go to the temple, where Jesus teaches the teachers.

In a voice of rebuke, Mary says, "Son, we have been looking for you everywhere?" and Jesus responds, "Why would you be looking for me everywhere, you should know, you would have found me in my Father's house!" All of those who heard this were astonished at this saying.

Jesus is called to start his work and ministry when he becomes an adult. The timing couldn't have been worse. His natural father, Joseph, is dead, and according to the Law of Moses, he is responsible for taking care of the family in his father's stead as the firstborn.

When he leaves home, everything changes; he's going as Joseph's son, the carpenter, but is walking into his Heavenly Father's calling now, the son of God. Ministry will be very different from the life he's been living.

He was rejected by those who thought they knew him: family, neighbors, and friends. Even when he went to the Synagogue in his hometown, after he read the scriptures:

"The spirit of the Lord is upon me because he hath anointed me to preach the gospel to the poor; he hath sent me to heal the brokenhearted, to preach deliverance to the captives, and recovering of sight to the blind, to set at liberty them that are bruised, to preach the acceptable year of the Lord."

After this, he was rejected, and they were very angry with him, because he commented, "That this word is fulfilled in your hearing." He was put out of the Synagogue for speaking these words, and they wanted to kill him for it. He couldn't get much done there because of their disbelief. Amazingly, they did not recognize the God they'd been teaching about all those years.

They put God out of His church. He went to the next town and was received, and he helped many people because they took him as a prophet. Jesus preached a message of hope and restoration to people. He preached and taught them concerning the kingdom of heaven.

The message about the kingdom had never been preached before. How could this man know about God and heaven? It was recorded that he performed many mighty works and miracles for and among the people. He told them, "The kingdom of God was at hand," meaning within reach, not far away...has arrived!

As great as Jesus was and is, like most people in all generations, he was not seen as great while alive or walking among the people. All generations have been guilty of the same thing: giving greater honor to the dead than to those alive. Jesus touched many lives and performed many miracles in his 3 1/2 recorded years of ministry.

He had so many followers and testimonies of the good things he had done; still, he had haters. Haters must understand that they are working for somebody, and it's certainly not God! God is not the author of confusion.

He will not confuse anyone by being double-minded or having a double standard. While Jesus was working on feeding the lost sheep, which means the folk no one seemed to care about, when he helped them, the church of yesterday became his greatest critics.

Why would religious people, or anyone for that matter, have a problem with anyone willing to help those whom they had no interest in at all? No matter what Jesus did, they had a problem with him; they made up stories and lies to deter his followers.

But Jesus told his critics, "If you don't believe in me, then believe in the works that I do." Jesus is our best example of this. When people do nothing to help others, they have a problem with you helping them; they are working for God's enemy, making them the enemy of good works.

Who are critics and haters, anyway? Do we seriously believe

they will have a job in heaven? Who will they hate and criticize? Remember this: God is the solution to the problem, and Satan is the problem. Satan always finds something wrong to report, and God always resolves any situation.

God came to uproot this devil; don't be his fruit. These are two total opposites of the spectrum. Listen to those who always find the negative in everything. No matter how good, they will find something wrong or deficient.

Later in ministry, Jesus was set up, betrayed, lied to, falsely accused, sold for the price of a slave, judged, tried, condemned, beaten, made a mockery of, spat on, rejected, executed, hung on a tree (cross), and died.

Even the Roman Procurator said, "He could find no fault in the man." But for political reasons, he carried out the Capital Punishment. Jesus was totally and undisputedly innocent and still was found guilty in a court of law. The reasoning behind this?

God is love, and He sent his son to represent all humanity and die for us, with us. God knows from the beginning of time that so many are falsely accused and punished for crimes they never committed. Therefore, he encourages us who can to visit those who are in prison. He said, "You are visiting me." Two thieves executed Jesus that same day, which was no coincidence.

Why is this so important? The two thieves represent all humanity. No matter what race, religion, sex, or culture, there are only two types of people born and will die in this world: we are Love or Hate, Good or Evil, Weak or Wicked, Sheep or Goats. The Sheep are on God's right hand, and the goats are on the left; this is kingdom protocol. All of those who will be condemned and taken away will be on the left side of the throne, and all who are God's children will be on the right side of God.

When you leave this life and appear before the Judge, if you find yourself on the left side, you will spend eternity with Satan and his followers. "To the left...to the left, everything you own in the box to the left." Beyoncé and Neo are songwriters who speak about heavenly revelations, and even if they are unaware, the message has been released on earth.

This generation will be surprised by how God is at the top of the minds of so many young people. So, where are these messages coming from? Jesus at one time told the Priests and Religious leaders,

"I'm striving to get these people into the kingdom, and you are hindering them and trying to keep them out. God will be your Judge, you will be cast into outer darkness, there will be wailing and gnashing of teeth, and they will enter the kingdom before you do!"

During Jesus' ministry, he taught about his Father's kingdom and mentioned a very important fact. He spoke of the Throne of God and how the Sheep would be on His right hand and the Goats on His left. This fact was so important that the heavens arranged the unique circumstances surrounding the order of executions on that day.

Jesus was placed between two thieves, one on the right and the other on the left. When they hung Jesus up there, while he was bleeding and in pain, he said, "Father, forgive them because they don't know what they are doing."

First, he forgives everybody--the religious folks, the Government, the world, and the Church! God knows, sometimes we are victims of following the wrong gods. Also, while he was up there in pain, he relieved his mother of the ties she had with him as her mortal son.

She struggled with what God was doing with her family's lives; she didn't understand, just as many of us do today. We often think that because these people did extraordinary things, they had to be exceptional, but the truth is, they were human; ordinary people chose to do extraordinary things.

He tells his disciple John to take care of Mary as his mother, and to tell his mother to accept John as her son. Jesus has transitioned from her son to God's son through revelation and destiny. One of the two thieves says to Jesus, "If you are who you say you are, then why don't you save yourself and then save us!"

The other thief rebukes him, saying, "Have you no fear of God even while dying? This man has done nothing wrong, but we are receiving the just punishment for the crimes we have committed." Then he said to Jesus, "Jesus, will you remember me when you enter your kingdom?" Jesus told him, "Today you will be with me in paradise!"

The records do not bother with the details of whether these men were Jews or Gentiles, Romans or Greeks; all we see is that the thief acknowledged his wrongdoings, asked for forgiveness, and believed he was saved!

My point is this: There's no record of him going to church, paying tithes, serving on the deacon or usher board, being baptized, tarrying at the altar, or any of the religious things or rituals over which we, as spiritual people, become so divided.

He repented for his wrong, he believed, and he is saved! Listen, we need to wake up because our enemy is getting the upper hand on us as a people worldwide.

We need each other for more reasons than we can even imagine. I am a Christian by faith, but I know there are so many things we are wrong about concerning misinterpretations of God's word and the purpose of Christ coming here for us, the entire world.

Salvation is a gift and a work of the heart. God is the only one who can change the heart. When the thief repented and believed, his heart was instantly changed. Why do we labor for something that is a gift to us from God? God paid the price for us.

We could never afford it; it is beyond our mortal budget! Please hear this. After reading this book, you should know that this is bigger than us. The Religious leaders thought they were lying to a man, but in reality, they were doing God all of this injustice. God sent his love and heart to be on trial here. God is testing everyone's heart, including His own.

There will be no more disease outbreaks in heaven ever again. God is so just that He, too, had His heart tested for "Spiritual COVID-19" for any malice, hate, unforgiveness, pride, deceit, or anything other than righteousness.

They were beating on God's love! Everything they did was to God's heart; Jesus was God's heart and passion. So, after it was all said and done, Jesus said, "It is finished!" He passed the test and completed His assignment.

Everything hate did to us on the outside, where everyone could see, can't get to the inside of us unless we grant access. Love is not contaminated, so rejoice. Love has overcome the world! God is too vast and intelligent to have reduced His work from glory to just one race or religion.

This is a trick to divide all of us who love God; it was Love, the Heart of God, who was on trial. When Jesus said, "I AM, the Way, the Truth, and the Life, no man can come to the Father except by Me," He is saying that He is LOVE, and that love is the Way, Love is the Truth, and Love is the Life.

No man can come to the Father except through (Him) Love. If people had never heard of Jesus by name, they would have known Him by love. It was Love that was lost in heaven, not a religion! God created everybody and race!

Every heart will operate in love or hate, and there's no way around it. It's a test for all of us, and we get one lifetime to reveal it! How dare we be so arrogant as to think that the entire world doesn't matter to its Creator? How can we understand God without love or a relationship with Him?

Look at the Universe, it is a display of how infinite God's mind is; it is so vast that it cannot be measured.

None of us is in control of choosing our race or parents to get here, so how can we judge people because of race or our religious beliefs after God gave us such an incomparable performance and lesson on how to handle Hate and our haters?

By the time Jesus was crucified, He was a Slave legally. He was sold and bought for 30 pieces of silver, and then they came to arrest him, to claim their property. His life, according to them, had no value or worth! He did not come wrapped in royalty, prosperity, or wealth, but in humility.

We must learn from his example and not judge based on the outer appearance so much because many of us "have entertained angels... unaware." So throughout history, we see the experience of injustice everywhere! Love will expose hate! Jesus did nothing to deserve to die such a barbaric and horrific end, but the grave could not hold him because Love can never die if it is pure and not infected with hate.

Everyone who has suffered an injustice, remember, when they do it to you, Jesus says, they are doing it to God, they are hating God Himself! They are not hating you, but they are hating the God in you, meaning, His love and heart!

Christ has redeemed us from the law's curse, being made a curse for us: for it is written, "Cursed is every one that hangs on a tree." God knows all things, and He knew the day would come when people would think they could curse a people by hanging them on trees, but it is the most incredible honor because they died like their Lord, and if you suffer with Him, then you will also reign with Him!

Love is the access code to entering through the gates of Heaven, so let the haters hate and stay in love with your God. Great is your reward in heaven. This gift is for all nations and peoples to the glory of God! Whatever your haters do, don't allow them to penetrate and enter your heart, causing you to hate!

God did not send his Son into the world to start a new religion or change anyone's religion, nor did he come to persuade anyone to abandon or deny their race or culture. Still, he came to rid our ways of hate and evil, turning to Love and God, to change our Hearts!

For God so loved the world, that He gave his only begotten Son, that whosoever believes in him should not perish, but have everlasting life. (John 3:16) He came to show us life and how we should love one another and do whatever it takes to help people with the assistance of God to make someone's day a good day, turn from evil to good, and commit to doing those deeds for the rest of our days.

God is not dull. He's not boring at all. Therefore, we have so many races, cultures, foods, talents, gifts, animals, places, and beautiful scenery! Heaven is in the Universe. Imagine what fun that is. We can hardly explore the world, so what about the Universe? One planet is said to take a jet 1100 years to circle it once! This is massive! Imagine the galaxies, who is all of that for
God's Family!

"The heart is deceitful above all things and desperately wicked: who can know it? I the Lord search the heart, I try the reins, even to give every man according to his ways, and according to the fruit of his

doings." (Jeremiah 17: 9-10)

The woman is the chosen gift to bring forth innocence, nurtured to maturity, and then used to expose deep secret places, deep down and hidden in the heart, whether they are good or evil. While God was hurting and in pain, He created the Woman with all the love He had to give and gave her His heart, in which she conceived a Son that was God's heart and love..

God gave us that begotten love, and it dwelt among us, and God's enemies hated that same love called His Son and tried to kill that Love, and God sacrificed that love for all of us, and that love would not die, could not die, but was transformed.

If we do not allow our enemies--God's enemies--to kill our love and turn us into haters, we too will be transformed into a new body and place, where only love can live. We will have victory together forever—this is God's plan for a New Heaven and a New Earth. Life can have many uncertainties, and we all have questions seemingly no one can answer.

These are just a few of the most impactful songs to be written as a divine revelation of the soul crying out for consolation: "The Greatest Love of All."

Linda Creed wrote the lyrics to this song during her struggle with breast cancer. The words describe her feelings about coping with significant challenges, being strong during them, and passing that strength on to children to carry with them into their adult lives. Creed eventually succumbed to the disease in April 1986 at the age of 37; at the time, her song was an international hit by Whitney Houston.

We don't know what it takes sometimes to bring the world hope and joy through the arts. Death is our greatest and last enemy. We need to respect God's gifts! Imagine God saying this even about Himself when He had to reform heaven and thought about having children of His own instead of more or replacement Angels, thinking of all of us, His children.

"I Want To Know What Love Is"

Initially, it was written by Mick Jones and performed by Foreigner, and later, it was performed by Mariah Carey, who has a unique and majestic talent

. We have another gift of God in the form of Lionel Richie.

By divine revelation, there can be no other explanation for giving us the answer in his composition and delivery of "Jesus Is Love." The message and feel of these songs are samples of how heaven gives us gifts in life that are so influential and impactful.

Everyone should be able to hear the dialogue between the creature and its Creator, asking for an answer, with reverence, much respect, and expressions of love.

When a life is submitted to God, that life can hear and feel Him. Though it has many challenges of its own, this is what makes it so impactful and inspiring to so many. Where divinity and humanity meet, we can feel Him inside of us!

Those who hear and obey the calling are servants of God; even still, we cannot and will not please everyone. He is the one who calls us in the first place, so as long as we please Him, we will be rewarded. Sometimes He wants to tell us something or express how He feels, and then that vessel becomes a conduit connecting Heaven and Earth.

Hero, written and performed by Mariah Carey, must be one of the most inspiring, encouraging, uplifting, and motivating messages through song ever. It has helped countless people not to give up on life and their dreams— Thank You! God chooses vessels of clay to show His glory through, and it takes a lot to house the glory of God because without Him, we're only human. It speaks to all generations, especially to this one.

If we know what love is, then and only then can we know what love is not! So, don't allow anyone or anything to kill your dreams, because it is love that establishes dreams, but hate that attempts to tear them down and kill them!

Love and faith have been partners for a long time and when they are present, they speak to strengthen the heart and soul, encouraging people everywhere to know, that we are not in this alone, because we all have a Hero... God is love and love is God—nothing can separate the two...Jesus is love!

If I speak with the tongues of men and angels but have no love, I become a sounding brass or a clanging cymbal. And if I have the gift of prophecy and know all mysteries and all knowledge; and if I have all faith, to remove mountains, but have not love, I am nothing. And if I bestow all my goods to feed the poor, and if I give my body to be burned, but have not love, it profits me nothing.

Love suffers long and is kind; love envies not; love vaunts not itself, is not puffed up, does not behave itself unseemly, seeks not its own, is not provoked, takes no account of evil; rejoices not in unrighteousness, but rejoices with the truth; bears all things, believes all things, hopes in all things, endures all things.

Love never fails, but whether there be prophecies, they shall be done away; whether there be tongues, they shall cease; whether there be knowledge, it shall be done away. For we know in part, and we prophesy in part; but when that which is perfect comes, that which is in part shall be done away.

When I was a child, I spoke as a child, I felt as a child, I thought as a child: now that I have become a man, I have put away childish things. For now, we see in a mirror, darkly; but then face to face: now I know in part; but then shall I know fully even as also I was fully known. But now abides faith, hope, love, these three; the greatest is love." (1 Corinthians chapter 13).

When God gives us life, it is His love as a gift, which can come through any race or any person, and can endure all the pains that hate has to give, though challenged and hurting.

It will not become hateful or give hate in return, but will continue to press through the pain, knowing that better is yet to come, while waiting on God for restitution. Then I must say, This is what LOVE IS; God is love, and love is God! "Greater Love has no man than this, than a man who will lay down his life for his friends." (John 3:

You can avoid God all of your life, but you can't prevent God at the end of your life.) The purpose of the universe, all creation, and every living creature is to bring God glory.

When God created the woman, He created and trusted her to give Him the greatest gift, without Him giving it to and through Himself...So, women, the next time you are being mistreated, misused, and abused, don't wonder anymore about your enemies—haters, because haters are just that, and they have their reasons!

Love is the greatest gift you could ever receive and give, but no matter how much love you give, you cannot make anyone love you back…love is a choice, not just a feeling.

Love is, "Why Satan Hates the Woman" because God loves her more than He ever loved him, and she has brought God through pain, the greatest gift and glory…which is God's Heart and Love…His Son!

NOTE FROM THE KINGDOM'S CORNER: If you don't know what love is during this time of your life? Know what love is not; it is not lustful, selfish, hateful, abusive,/or mean, nor inconsiderate, nor unnecessarily painful. Woman, it is your time and season! Do you see it? It's not revenge, but vindication! You must know who you are and don't allow the enemy to

INIQUITY 2

Chapter 14

Satan has but a short time to wild out!

How have you fallen from heaven, O Lucifer, morning star! How have you been brought low to the ground, you who weakened the nations! For you have said in your heart, I will rise to heaven,

I will elevate my throne above the stars of God; I will also sit on the mount of assembly, in the far reaches of the North; I will ascend above the heights of the clouds; I will be like the Most High.

Yet you will be brought down to the depths of the pit. Those who see you will gaze intently at you and ponder, Is this the man who made the earth tremble, shook kingdoms, turned the world into a desert, destroyed its cities, and did not let his prisoners go free?

All the kings of the nations, each in his glory, lie in their tombs. But you are cast out of your grave like a worthless branch, and like the clothing of those who have been slain, pierced by a sword, descending to the stones of the pit; like a carcass trampled underfoot.

You will not be united with them in burial, for you have devastated your land and killed your people; the offspring of the wicked will never be honored. Prepare destruction for his children due to the sins of their fathers, so that they do not rise, nor inherit the land, nor fill the earth with cities.

Lucifer was not always deceitful, evil, and rebellious. God made this cherub with unmatched intelligence and beauty. You were flawless in your ways from the moment you were created until sin was discovered in you.

Lucifer was the first being to test positive for sin, in the form of iniquity."But your iniquities have separated you from your God; your sins have hidden his face from you so that he will not hear. (Isaiah 59:2

NIV)

The parable of the outbreak: The Kingdom of Heaven can be compared to an outbreak, with iniquity representing heaven's version of COVID-19. In the initial outbreak, he chose to conceal his infection instead of confessing his sickness to God. He selfishly kept his condition hidden from everyone.

Yet God told him, "I see iniquity in your heart." My pressing question was: Where had Lucifer been to contract this disease? Due to his selfishness and defiance, one out of every three angels became infected. Embrace Jesus' teachings and words with an open heart and mind.

If this manifested in our world, its origins lie above. The angels were sent here to quarantine and find redemption, but they heeded Satan and rejected treatment.

If sin is akin to heaven's COVID-19, what makes anyone believe they can enter heaven without being healed? Heaven is a place free from sin and iniquity. Do not be misled. God did not go through all this effort for sin to re-enter heaven.

Solution: Get spiritually tested; if positive results are rendered, repent. Admit to being infected and get your treatment from the Lord Jesus. And for our duration on this planet, keep getting tested and as needed— treated.

Must we continue in sin? (Romans 6:1) Get treatment, mask up, get vaccinated, and be safe. When Adam and Eve ate from the Forbidden Tree, they were infected and hid themselves. "If I covered my transgressions as Adam, by hiding mine iniquity in my bosom: Where did the tree of knowledge, good and evil come from, in the first place?" (Job 31:33)

When Lucifer became tainted by iniquity, it marked the onset of a spiritual ailment. He experienced symptoms but concealed them from everyone.

The Lord awaited his confession of the pride he had been entertaining. This pride led to his infection with iniquity, marking the first betrayal in his relationship with righteousness. Scripture reveals that "iniquity was found in Lucifer's heart."

The heart serves as the source of spiritual life, where we determine whether to love or hate or embrace God or the world. Pride planted the seed of iniquity in Lucifer's heart while he was still pure, righteous, and innocent.

The troubling aspect was his attempt to conceal this condition from God; he was pregnant with iniquity. The seed of pride had taken root. The one who used to be a Holy Cherub was now afflicted, and everything changed forever. Lucifer tested positive for sin. "I confess my iniquity; I am troubled by my sin" (Psalms 38:18 NIV).

Iniquity is the deepest form of sin, firmly entrenched in the heart. It represents the spiritual heart disease that must be uprooted or aborted before it bears fruit. "Wash me thoroughly from my iniquity and cleanse me from my sin, for sin is the offspring of iniquity and is inherently tied to it" (Psalms 51:2).

Adam and Eve did not have iniquity; they sinned. This sin, when unrepentant and unyielding, matures into iniquity. "Deliver me from those who practice iniquity and protect me from violent people." (Psalms 59:2) "Hide me from the secret plots of the wicked; from the insurrection of those who commit iniquity." (Psalm 64:2) "If I hold iniquity in my heart, the Lord will not hear me." (Psalm 66:18)

The fallen angels are consumed by sin and are on the brink of destruction, a condition that cannot be tolerated in Heaven. They have never sought atonement for their transgressions. Unaddressed sin generates demons, the spiritual progeny of pride and wrongdoing.

These angels have given rise to these beings through pride, not in a physical manner like humans, but in the spiritual context Jesus referred to as being "born again" (John 3:5-8). Pride acts as the father of these demons and accompanies Lucifer and the fallen angels; it is their focus of worship. "And his tail swept a third of the stars from the sky and hurled them to the earth.

The dragon stood in front of the woman who was about to give birth, ready to devour her child as soon as it was born. Then war broke out in heaven: Michael and his angels fought against the dragon, and the dragon and his angels fought back, but they did not prevail; nor was there any place found for them in heaven any longer."

And the great dragon was cast out, that old serpent, called the Devil, and Satan, which deceived the whole world: he was cast out into the earth, and his angels were cast out with him." (Revelation 12:8-9) They never confessed, repented, or asked God for forgiveness, treatment, or a cure. "Add iniquity unto their iniquity: let them not come into thy righteousness" (Psalm 69:27). Iniquity was heaven's COVID-19 outbreak.

Believe it or not, God had to develop a vaccine/cure for Heaven's COVID-19 outbreak. One of the three angels was infected.

God, in His boundless wisdom, expelled them immediately. Heaven entered a state of protection, a phenomenon never witnessed before.

Lucifer and the tainted angels were cast down to Earth, burdened by the weight of this affliction. The Earth was designed to contain this disease, which gave rise to various beings and creatures. This era corresponds to the age of dinosaurs, the prehistoric period.

Lucifer's desire to become God was intense, but much remained secret despite all that God shared with him. Lucifer's attempts at creation were chaotic; his blend of creative ideas did not yield successful results. His endeavors placed the planet in jeopardy of destruction.

Iniquity surged in humanity and animals, creating a landscape of anger where it was a matter of hunting or being hunted. Picture living under such conditions today. Science has indicated that the world faced a sudden and drastic halt. Action was necessary.

When God restored order, the lion would lie down with the lamb, representing peace and harmony—until iniquity was unleashed. Adam undoubtedly surpassed the intelligence of all preceding humans. We are a species of mankind, made in God's image, and the Earth needed to be cleansed.

These issues arose from unaddressed iniquity. God devised a plan, with the Son of God (Jesus) integral to it; "And all that dwell upon the earth shall worship him, whose names are not written in the book of life of the Lamb slain from the foundation of the world."

(Revelation 13:8).

This intensifies his reasons to envy and resent God. How can God be so masterful in creation, making it seem effortless? Being God, He addressed the chaos caused by the fallen angel, which was laden with iniquities that led to brutal and selfish situations.

The Earth required a renewal and a fresh beginning. The earliest humans are not described as being created in God's image or possessing His likeness and wisdom. Adam is the first to be created in God's image. God made him and is considered His son, with Himself breathing life into him. Adam shares the intelligence of his Father, God, and embodies His nature.

He was free from iniquity and did not possess a sinful nature; he was pure. When God created Eve from Adam, she was pure and without sin. "And I will punish the world for their evil, and the wicked for their iniquity, and I will cause the arrogance of the proud to cease, and will lay low the haughtiness of the terrible (Isaiah 13:11).

Iniquity gave rise to the lethal venom of the serpent.

Without iniquity, snakes would lack poison, and roses would be thornless. Even heaven had to release the past to seek a new normal. This transformation requires significant effort, but the new heaven and earth will surpass any previous existence. I am running a few minutes late; my previous meeting is running a little overtime.

You may have faced loss and fear, yet there is so much to anticipate through our God. This world will never return to what it once was. The normal we experienced just three years ago is gone forever. "The enemy is filled with pride but is not just." "The just shall live by faith" (Habakkuk 2:4).

Be cautious not to support evildoers and liars in committing acts of violence. Ignoring the truth for the sake of a favored party or elected leader will not go unjudged by God, who will hold accountable those responsible for the harm and destruction of His children. "And I will punish the world for their evil, and the wicked for their iniquity; and I will cause the arrogance of the proud to cease and will lay low the haughtiness of the terrible." (Isaiah 13:11)

God is aware of everything. Do we believe these matters are

resolved by lying in court and swearing on the Bible, which is God's word? The truth is hidden beneath the innocent blood. "For behold, the LORD will come out of His dwelling to punish the people of the earth for their sins; the earth will reveal its bloodshed and no longer hide its slain." (Isaiah 26:21)

"For your hands are stained with blood, your fingers with wickedness; your lips have spoken falsehood, and your tongue has uttered deceit. No one calls for justice or pleads for truth; they rely on emptiness, speak lies; they plot evil, and bring forth wrongdoing." (Isaiah 59:3-4)

"And each person deceives his neighbor and does not speak the truth; they have trained their tongues to lie and wear themselves out to commit wrongdoing. Your dwelling is filled with deceit; through deceit, they refuse to acknowledge me, says the LORD." (Jeremiah 9:5-6)

"And if you find yourself asking, 'Why has this happened to me?'— it is because of your numerous sins that your skirts have been torn away and your body mistreated. Can an Ethiopian change his skin or a leopard its spots? Neither can you do good if you are accustomed to doing evil." (Jeremiah 13:22-23 NIV)

People of God, we need to confront the issue of iniquity, which is akin to a spiritual COVID-19, along with sin, which represents a spiritual Delta variant, and transgression, which is likened to a spiritual Omicron. Iniquity can be seen as Heaven's COVID-19, while sin and transgression are the variants that arise from iniquity in this spiritual battle.

If left unaddressed, iniquity and its variants lead only to death; it is just a matter of time. Jesus entered this world through 42 generations as a fulfillment of the prophecy given to Eve after she was infected with this spiritual illness. Throughout the Old Testament, various remedies were attempted over those 42 generations, but none were successful. Despite the sacrifices of lambs and bulls, along with numerous offerings and ceremonies, we continued to show symptoms of iniquity, as noted in Galatians 3:13.

The mission of Jesus was to obtain the final ingredient for the cure, which would be provided by God through Him. Our healing from this eternal affliction is found in the blood of Christ. The remedy had to come from both the source of the disease and something opposite—pure, holy, and filled with the light of life: God Himself. Recall when Jesus rose and said, "Touch me not; for I am not yet ascended to my Father: but go to my brethren, and say unto them, I ascend unto my Father, and your Father; and to my God and your God." (John 20:17)

He grasped the final element essential to cure Heaven's "CORONAVIRUS"... Iniquity. We need to recognize once and for all that "SIN" poses the greatest danger to life, to everything you cherish, and is creation's most devastating virus! Cease playing around with this VIRUS! Stop justifying the actions of the infected! We must do everything possible to encourage as many individuals as possible to accept this VACCINE! GOD HAS PROVIDED A PATH FOR US TO BE HEALED AND TO LIVE!

Jesus courageously absorbed the poison from that serpent and created the antidote. Look at how divided our nation is over trusting our government, scientists, pharmaceutical companies, and doctors. People might be dying needlessly... but it could be a matter of trust. When you place your life in the hands of someone you may not trust, you risk death; or you can take a chance and choose life. Should you trust God regarding the other virus known as "SIN?" Ironically, both viruses are invisible foes, posing a global threat to life.

Although the virus is invisible, its impact is clear. COVID-19 appears to be an indiscriminate collector, much like sin, which equally affects everyone. "For the wages of sin is death, but the gift of God is eternal life through Jesus Christ our Lord." (Romans 6:23)

We face significant choices ahead! We are compelled to place our trust in something. Our thoughts and prayers are with the families who have lost loved ones to this adversary. May the Lord support us in this ongoing battle for our lives and grant us the wisdom to secure a better future for the next generation.

Let's pray that God provides our leaders wisdom, guidance, and stability during these challenging and unprecedented times. We also pray for the mental well-being of our nation and the world… Peace! "

That at that time ye were without Christ, being aliens from the commonwealth of Israel, and strangers from the covenants of promise, having no hope, and without God in the world: but now in Christ Jesus ye who sometimes were far off are made nigh by the blood of Christ. For he is our peace, who hath made both one, and hath broken down the middle wall of partition between us;" (Ephesians 2:12-14).

After Jesus met with His Father in heaven, He achieved what would be impossible without the shedding of His blood, pure and holy blood combined with the sins of all humanity. "For it is impossible that the blood of bulls and goats should take away sins.

By which we are sanctified through the offering of the body of Jesus Christ once for all, but this man, after he had offered one sacrifice for sins forever, sat down on the right hand of God:" (Hebrews 10:12). Iniquity was like kryptonite to God. Jesus returns with all power, holding the cure.

He said, "I saw Satan fall like lightning from heaven. However, do not rejoice that the spirits submit to you, but rejoice that your names are written in heaven." (Luke 10:19-20). Jesus is our example; His work was and is too significant to be dismissed as another religion.

God did not send His Son to establish another religion but rather to provide what was necessary for our healing in heaven and on earth. This was the most challenging thing God ever did to demonstrate His love for us. While God and the holy angels in heaven were free from suffering, we were not.

Consider that God was not satisfied living in heaven without us. He endured shame and abuse to redeem us. He was willing to pay a tremendous price for our healing and restoration. His charge is to those who are converted, not just saved: "Go into all the world and give them the good news." "He said to them, "Go into all the world and preach the gospel to all creation." (Mark 16:15 NIV)

The Lord undertook incredible sacrifices to save humanity; why are we not treating this with the seriousness it deserves? Oh, my Lord and God, consider the price of our freedom—why allow your enemy to control you? "And hope does not disappoint us, because God's love has been poured into our hearts through the Holy Spirit, who has been given to us.

At just the right moment, when we were powerless, Christ died for the ungodly. Rarely does anyone die for a righteous person, though someone might dare to die for a good person. But God shows his love for us in this: while we were still sinners, Christ died for us. Now that we have been justified by his blood, how much more will we be saved from God's wrath through him!" (Romans 5:5-9 NIV).

God shows His love for us in this way: Christ died for us while we were still sinners, just as sin entered the world through one man, death through sin spread to all because all have sinned.

This conflict began in eternity, and the solution would be revealed and achieved on earth. Jesus faced immense spiritual pressure while praying in the Garden of Gethsemane.

He told her, "Do not cling to me, for I have not yet ascended to my Father. Go to my brothers and tell them, 'I am ascending to my Father and your Father, to my God and your God.'"

It astonishes me that Adam faced defeat in the Garden of Eden, while Jesus achieved victory in the Garden of Gethsemane. This is all part of a divine plan, not a mere coincidence. Don't let anyone diminish the significance of what the Lord has done for us, His true children.

The wicked may have their time, but if you can repent and acknowledge your sins and transgressions, then you belong to God, regardless of your age, race, or religion. Confessing sins instead of concealing them is the first step toward healing.

God will forgive us if we confess our sins, as stated in Deuteronomy 7:9 and James 5:16. We cannot manipulate the Lord; the devil has already tried that. There's no need to hide anymore. When we leave this world and face judgment, if we are found with iniquity, sin, and transgression, it simply indicates that we rejected the treatment God provided for us in this life.

No one will enter the kingdom without the cleansing power of Christ's sacrifice. "Surely, he has taken on our grief and carried our sorrows; yet we regarded him as stricken, smitten by God, and afflicted. He was wounded for our sins and bruised for our wrongdoings; the punishment that brought us peace was on him, and by his wounds, we are healed" (Isaiah 53:4-5).

"Jesus answered, Verily, verily, I say unto thee, except a man be born of water and the Spirit, he cannot enter into the kingdom of God."(John 3:5)

In life and death, acknowledge God, if he's your God? Love Him if He's your Father. He loves you, us. "Jesus said unto her, I am the resurrection, and the life: he that believes in me, though he were dead, yet shall he live:" (John 11:25)

Do not let anyone deceive you. God is not about political correctness; He is about righteousness. Do not sacrifice your relationship with God for politics; prioritize God over politics. If we find ourselves in a political role, we must reflect God's righteousness. On that final day, He will ask us to account for the gifts and positions He entrusted us with in this life. What did we do with the opportunities He provided? Trust in God's word and His plans for you.

No politician is willing to lay down their life for you.

Get your priorities straight! Everyone, including judges, will stand before God for judgment. Iniquity manifests in various forms and outcomes. The healing our nation and the world desperately need could be achieved if we follow God's commands.

Jesus said, "You shall love the Lord your God with all your heart, with all your soul, and with all your mind. This is the first and greatest commandment. The second is similar: You shall love your neighbor as yourself." All the law and the prophets depend on these two commandments

One of the most recognizable forms of wrongdoing is "HATE!" Hate embodies deliberate evil; it is inherent to the adversary. It is both a learned behavior and an inherited trait. Ultimately, it comes down to a choice. We can decide to love or to hate.

This is why Jesus addressed the priests of the temple, saying, "Woe to you, teachers of the law and Pharisees, you hypocrites! You construct tombs for the prophets and adorn the graves of the righteous. You claim, 'If we had lived in our ancestors' time, we would not have participated in the murder of the prophets.' Thus, you are acknowledging that you are the descendants of those who killed the prophets. Go ahead and finish what your ancestors began! You snakes!

You brood of vipers! How will you escape the condemnation of hell?" (Matthew 23:29-33 NIV). Another aspect of iniquity is our affection for pets. We care for them, provide for them, take them to the vet, and socialize with others through our pets, such as dogs.

We welcome them in various species, breeds, sizes, and colors. We do not mistreat them based on their appearance, whether it be color, size, or breed, including favorites like the American Bulldog, American Hairless Terrier, Alaskan Malamute, American Eskimo, Australian Shepherd, German Shepherd, Boston Terrier, Boykin Spaniel, Chesapeake Bay Retriever, Catahoula Leopard, Toy Fox Terrier, and Pit Bull.

If you understand dogs, you recognize that they come in various sizes, shades, and colors. We celebrate their diversity instead of judging it. We often remark on how adorable their colors are. We choose to love them! We offer them affection, and they give us love back (though there are always exceptions).

Now, let's address injustice: I despise human beings created in the image of the Most High God because of their race or color, as if they had the choice of their race upon entering this world. Love is a choice! Hate is a choice! Decide today whom you will serve: Love or Hate? In the end, we are choosing one or the other.

God embodies Love! Satan embodies Hate! No matter how we may disguise it. On that Day, there will be no cover for our hatred. Justice will prevail. We will be rewarded for our love. "And he saith unto me, Seal not the sayings of the prophecy of this book: for the time is at hand.

He that is unjust, let him be unjust still: and he which is filthy, let him be filthy still: and he that is righteous, let him be righteous still: and he that is holy, let him be holy still. And behold, I come quickly; and my reward is with me, to give every man according as his work shall be." (Revelation 22:10-12)

Time passes quickly, Hell is a place of suffering, Heaven is astonishingly beautiful, God is undeniably present, and Jesus still bears the five wounds on His glorified body—symbols of the hatred He endured, now preserved as reminders but no longer causing Him anguish. This demands justice! God is on His throne… He is SOVEREIGN! No matter the circumstances,

God has maintained control through all ages. God is sovereign! His authority is not up for debate and cannot be removed from His kingdom! Where are those who commit evil, engage in deceit, and even kill, thinking they can escape the repercussions?

They are in eternal confinement (HELL), awaiting judgment! This is the vital question to ponder. Disregard the deceit of the arrogant and self-serving, whether politicians or pastors. Explore God's word for yourself and seek His wisdom. Act with righteousness.

If you are under the guidance of someone who is racist, prejudiced, or fueled by hate, especially if they are a pastor… FLEE FOR YOUR LIFE! If you know God is your Father, why attend a church and risk missing Heaven? It is illogical from God's viewpoint or according to His Word! DO NOT BE FOOLED; God will not be mocked; whatever one sows, that is what they will also REAP!

If Satan is your father, then act as you please. Is it your right? Jesus said, "You are of your father the devil, and the desires of your father you will do. He was a murderer from the beginning and does not abide in the truth, because there is no truth in him.

When he speaks lies, he speaks from his nature; for he is a liar and the father of lies." (John 8:44) Some are children of the Wicked One who thought they had killed me and left me for dead, but God raised me! Jesus told His Sons and Daughters, "Those who believe in me will NEVER DIE!"

This section was not part of the original manuscript. I felt the need to pray and fast first, and then I was commanded by the Holy Spirit to write these warnings for God's people! "After seven days, the word of the Lord came to me: If I say to a wicked person, 'You will surely die,' and you do not warn them or try to turn them from their evil ways to save their life, that wicked person will die in their sin, and I will hold you responsible for their blood."

However, if you do warn the wicked and they do not turn from their wickedness or evil ways, they will die for their sin, but you will have saved yourself." (Ezekiel 3:16, 18-19 NIV)

This message is intended for everyone, yet it is not meant for all. America and the world urgently need a revival, but such a change will only occur when we truly repent. Repentance straightens the crooked paths, paving the way for the Lord's return. "

And he went throughout all the region around the Jordan, proclaiming a baptism of repentance for the forgiveness of sins; as it is written in the book of the words of the prophet Isaiah, 'The voice of one crying in the wilderness, prepare the way of the Lord, make his paths straight'" (Luke 3:3-4).

DON'T LET ANYONE LEAD YOU TO HELL WITH LIES, YOU CAN GET THERE ON YOUR OWN IF THAT'S WHAT YOU TRULY DESIRE...JUST BE WICKED AND DO EVIL...YOU'LL GET THERE!

***IF YOU ARE NOT SAVED...GET SAVED? REPENT FOR ALL OF YOUR SINS, ANY WRONGDOINGS, WE ALL WERE BORN IN SIN.**

***START HERE AND READ THE FOLLOWING:**

Sin entered the world through one individual, and as a result, death came through sin, affecting all humanity since everyone has sinned. Just as one man's disobedience led many to become sinners, one man's obedience will make many righteous.

The law was given to highlight offenses, but grace overflowed even more where sin increased. As sin ruled through death, grace will rule through righteousness, leading to eternal life through Jesus Christ our Lord. Romans 10 states: "What does it say?

'The message is very close to you; it is in your mouth and in your heart,' referring to the message of faith we share. If you confess with your mouth that 'Jesus is Lord' and believe that God raised him from the dead, you will be saved.

With your heart, you believe and are justified; with your mouth, you profess your faith and are saved. Scripture also says, 'Anyone who believes in him will never be put to shame.'

"And everyone who calls on the name of the Lord will be saved'" (Acts 2:21 NIV).

"Peter replied, "Repent and be baptized, every one of you, in the name of Jesus Christ for the forgiveness of your sins. And you will receive the gift of the Holy Spirit. The promise is for you, your children, and all who are far off—for all whom the Lord our God will call." Acts 2:38-39 NIV

If you seek salvation, read the Word of God above and believe in your heart. Pray this prayer: Lord Jesus, I acknowledge that I am a sinner and regret all the ways I have offended you knowingly and unknowingly. Please forgive me for all my sins.

I believe in my heart that you died on the cross for me and for my sins—past, present, and future. I think that God raised you from the dead and that you live forever. Come into my heart. I accept you as my Lord and Savior. Lord, please lead and guide me.

I dedicate my life to you from this moment on, in Jesus' name... Amen! If you have prayed this prayer, welcome to the Kingdom of God and His Christ; you are now part of the family. Get a Bible and read it daily to nourish your spirit.

Communicate with your Heavenly Father through prayer, build a relationship with Him, and find a church that believes in and teaches the Bible. God bless you, and we love you!

IF YOU ARE SAVED...STAY SAVED?

How to be saved and COVID-19 free---[the spiritual one] while God protects us from the natural one.

Now is not the time to give up, surrender, or regress! I understand you might be hurt and disappointed by losses, but continue to fight, believe, praise Him, and pray! The enemy attempts to substitute prayer with programs, but we need your prayers, woman of God!

Even in your pain, keep pushing forward; "God is collecting your tears and understanding all your fears. Yes, everyone, hold on just a little longer!

Remember, God is aware of your anxieties and concerns. The worst that can happen to God's children is death, which is merely our gateway to home, our Heavenly Father, Christ, and our true family in glory.

Please hold on and don't lose hope! Am I pleading with you to enter God's kingdom through your tears? If I never have the chance to meet you in this life, I will see you when we get home, my kingdom family. Woman of God, know who you are and remember whose you are; God is your Father!

You were created to be the solution, while Satan tried to make you the problem. Bless you! There is no one like you in all of God's creation. Don't let these insecure leaders tell you what you can't do for God and His kingdom at this crucial time. Claiming that God has not called a woman to preach, pastor, teach, or anything else is simply absurd."

"For ye are all the children of God by faith in Christ Jesus. There is neither Jew nor Greek, there is neither bond nor free, there is neither male nor female: for ye are all one in Christ Jesus."

"There is neither Jew nor Greek, there is neither bond nor free, there is neither male nor female: for ye are all one in Christ Jesus." Galatians 3:26-28

If you can worship God, sing for Him, fry chicken, sell dinners, feed the hungry, raise funds, contribute financially, support ministry, pray, clean, give birth, raise children, and serve, then why not truly follow Him as a disciple? God is wise and discerning!

Always remain humble, keep your humility intact, and never claim God's glory for yourself. Ensure your hands are clean, listen carefully, recognize your Lord's voice, obey Him, and do so as a woman.

Do not try to imitate a man; God wants to use you as a woman so that He receives the glory. We are living in the last and challenging days.

The Kingdom of Heaven embraces all assistance in glorifying God. Understand this truth: it was once unlawful for a Gentile to handle God's Word, and speaking His Word or using His holy name "Yahweh" was forbidden.

Yet, through faith and grace in our Lord and Savior Jesus Christ, we are adopted and welcomed into the Kingdom as family. How can a Gentile pastor, bishop, or anyone else prohibit a woman from preaching, teaching, or pastoring?

Under the law, a Gentile was viewed as being in the same lower status as a woman and was not allowed to preach because he was seen as unworthy, akin to a dog in their cultural context. Therefore, if women are barred from preaching the Gospel, then a Gentile man should also be prohibited from doing so.

Only an Israelite, specifically a Jew, would be permitted. We are all justified by faith! Who would rightfully deny anyone the opportunity to share "good news," especially in these times? We could all benefit from some positive news!

It would be like a man injured in a car crash, asking for help, and a woman responding, "I've called 911 and have good news; help is on the way." He replies, "You can't tell me help is on the way because it's not lawful for you to give me good news."

Now here's Jesus, saying, "Not only did I send a woman to make the call for you, but I'm also sending two female paramedics to save you! So, are you saying that if someone is dying and needs to be saved, and no man is present, a woman is not allowed to lead them to the Lord?"

These individuals share the same prejudiced and arrogant attitude as the Pharisees who condemned Jesus and remained unrepentant, even when they observed others repenting, being healed, and finding salvation.

They must have witnessed God's work. If God has appointed you as "daughters" to share the Gospel, then do so confidently! May the Lord Jesus Christ bless your endeavors and discern between us!

BE BLESSED ALWAYS AND LET NO MAN CURSE YOUR CALLING IN CHRIST JESUS! MAY THE LORD CONTINUE TO STRENGTHEN YOU FOR YOUR JOURNEY!

"WOMAN, YOU ARE GOD'S "SPECIAL EDITION"

"And the Lord answered me:
'Write down the vision clearly on tablets, so that whoever reads it may run

with it. For the vision awaits its appointed time; it will surely come to pass and will not fail. Though it lingers, wait for it — it will certainly come and will not delay.'

But your prideful Judas will not wait.
True faith requires the patience to wait for what has been promised."

"WOMAN, YOU ARE GOD'S "SPECIAL EDITION"

"And the Lord answered me and said, 'Write the vision and make it plain upon the tablets, that he may run that reads it. The vision is set for an appointed time, but at the end, it will speak, and not lie: Though it tarries, wait for it; because it will surely come, it will not tarry." Your (Pride) Judas will not wait!
Faith requires us to wait for certain things. (Habakkuk 2:2-3)

"RESURRECTION"

"BACK LIKE YOU NEVER LEFT!"

TO GOD BE THE GLORY!

SELAH....

www.kingdomrights2.org

NOTES

NOTES

TAKE A CLOSER LOOK!

Lucifer and the War on Womanhood

Lucifer was once the most beautiful of all created beings. He dwelt in Heaven and beheld mysteries and glory beyond human comprehension. But despite all he saw, all he possessed, and all he was, there was one gift God never gave him—*the power to create life.*

Of all the images in Heaven and on Earth, your enemy-the fallen one—chose the uterus as the symbol of the god he longs to be. Why? Because he sees your womb as the greatest treasure he was denied. He envies it. He hates it. And he fears it.

Lucifer fully understands the divine power and ability to produce life. He can never replicate this, as he lacks both the design and authority to do so. Every time a woman conceives and brings forth life, it is a direct reminder of his limitations—of what he can *never* be.

From the moment he first sets eyes on you, he has hated you. Not because of weakness, but because of your God-given power. He has repeatedly asked, "What makes *her* a woman?" He is obsessed with the answer. And until he can create life without you, which he never will, he remains dependent on what he despises.

He wonders: *Is it your anatomy? Your essence? Your divine calling?* In his twisted desire, he wishes he could steal your equipment, embed it within himself, and rival the Creator.

But he cannot.

What begins in the physical is deeply rooted in the spiritual. And this is why your enemy's greatest weapon is not physical—it's psychological. Above all, he seeks to conquer your mind. If he can convince you to hate your body, question your worth, suppress your power, or forfeit your purpose, then he wins without lifting a finger.

But never forget this: Your ability to bring life is not just biological—it is spiritual warfare. You carry a gift that the enemy can never obtain, and for that, he will always try to destroy you.

IT'S A WAR GOING ON...!

Forbes
100 Most Powerful Women

2021

Some Of The World's Greatest Women Achievers

U. S. Statistics of Domestic Violence and Abused Women

100 MOST POWERFUL WOMEN-1

Forbes

100 Most Powerful Women

World's Most Powerful Women

Rank	Name	Age	Country/ Territory	Category
#1	Ursula von der Leyen	65	Germany	Politics & Policy
#2	Christine Lagarde	68	France	Politics & Policy
#3	Kamala Harris	59	United States	Politics & Policy
#4	Giorgia Meloni	47	Italy	Politics & Policy
#5	Taylor Swift	34	United States	Media & Entertainment
#6	Karen Lynch	60	United States	Business
#7	Jane Fraser	57	United States	Finance

	#8	Abigail Johnson	62	United States	Finance
	#9	Mary Barra	62	United States	Business
	#10	Melinda French Gates	59	United States	Philanthropy
	#11	Julie Sweet	56	United States	Business
	#12	Kristalina Georgieva	70	Bulgaria	Politics & Policy
	#13	MacKenzie Scott	54	United States	Philanthropy
	#14	Gail Boudreaux	64	United States	Business
	#15	Emma Walmsley	55	United Kingdom	Business
	#16	Ruth Porat	66	United States	Technology
	#17	Safra Catz	62	United States	Technology
	#18	Ana Patricia Botín	63	Spain	Finance

	Name	Age	Country	Industry
#19	Carol Tomé	67	United States	Business
#20	Sandy Ran Xu	47	-	Business
#21	Kathryn McLay	50	-	Business
#22	Sarah London	44	-	Business
#23	Amy Hood	52	United States	Technology
#24	Tarciana Paula Gomes Medeiros	45	-	Finance
#25	Laurene Powell Jobs	60	United States	Philanthropy
#26	Catherine MacGregor	52	France	Business
#27	Janet Yellen	77	United States	Politics & Policy
#28	Gwynne Shotwell	60	United States	Technology
#29	Phebe Novakovic	66	United States	Business

#30	Tsai Ing-wen	67	Taiwan	Politics & Policy
#31	Oprah Winfrey	70	United States	Media & Entertainment
#32	Nirmala Sitharaman	65	India	Politics & Policy
#33	Ho Ching	71	Singapore	Finance
#34	Thasunda Brown Duckett	51	United States	Finance
#35	Marianne Lake, Jennifer Piepszak	-	United States	Finance
#36	Beyoncé Knowles	42	United States	Media & Entertainment
#37	Shari Redstone	70	United States	Media & Entertainment
#38	Kathy Warden	53	United States	Business
#39	Dana Walden	59	United States	Media & Entertainment

	#	Name	Age	Country	Field
	#40	Amanda Blanc	57	United Kingdom	Business
	#41	Susan Li	38	-	Technology
	#42	Margherita Della Valle	59	-	Business
	#43	Adena Friedman	55	United States	Finance
	#44	Mary Callahan Erdoes	56	United States	Finance
	#45	Lynn Martin	48	-	Finance
	#46	Sheikh Hasina Wajed	76	Bangladesh	Politics & Policy
	#47	Sri Mulyani Indrawati	61	Indonesia	Politics & Policy
	#48	Gina Rinehart	70	Australia	Business
	#49	Lisa Su	54	United States	Technology
	#50	Vicki Hollub	64	United States	Business

* * *

	#	Name	Age	Country	Industry
	#51	Nicke Widyawati	56	Indonesia	Business
	#52	Shemara Wikramanayake	62	Australia	Finance
	#53	Tricia Griffith	59	United States	Business
	#54	Jessica Tan	47	Singapore	Business
	#55	Judy Faulkner	81	United States	Technology
	#56	Tokiko Shimizu	59	Japan	Finance
	#57	Donna Langley	56	United Kingdom	Media & Entertainment
	#58	Jennifer Salke	60	United States	Media & Entertainment
	#59	Wang Laichun	57	Hong Kong	Technology
	#60	Roshni Nadar Malhotra	42	India	Technology

* * *

#61	Jenny Johnson	60	United States	Finance
#62	Yuriko Koike	72	Japan	Politics & Policy
#63	Hana Al Rostamani	-	-	Finance
#64	Suzanne Scott	58	United States	Media & Entertainment
#65	Lynn Good	65	United States	Business
#66	Sinead Gorman	47	United Kingdom	Business
#67	Bela Bajaria	53	-	Media & Entertainment
#68	Belén Garijo	64	-	Business
#69	Melanie Kreis	53	Germany	Business
#70	Soma Mondal	61	-	Business
#71	Paula Santilli	-	Mexico	Business

	#72	Mette Frederiksen	46	Denmark	Politics & Policy
	#73	Joey Wat	53	China	Business
	#74	Rihanna	36	Barbados	Media & Entertainment
	#75	Linda Thomas-Greenfield	71	-	Politics & Policy
	#76	Kiran Mazumdar-Shaw	71	India	Business
	#77	Güler Sabanci	69	Turkey	Business
	#78	Trudy Shan Dai	48	China	Business
	#79	Debra Crew	53	-	Business
	#80	Robyn Denholm	61	Australia	Business
	#81	Solina Chau	63	Hong Kong	Philanthropy
	#82	Lee Boo-jin	53	South Korea	Business

	Name	Age	Country	Category
	Robyn Grew	55	-	Finance
	Zuzana Caputova	51	Slovakia	Politics & Policy
	Mary Meeker	64	United States	Finance
	Makiko Ono	64	-	Business
	Ngozi Okonjo-Iweala	70	Nigeria	Politics & Policy
	Mpumi Madisa	44	-	Business
	Melanie Perkins	37	Australia	Business
	Dominique Senequier	70	France	Finance
	Raja Easa Al Gurg	-	United Arab Emirates	Business
	Julia Gillard	62	Australia	Philanthropy
	Samia Suluhu Hassan	64	Tanzania	Politics & Policy

#94	Xiomara Castro	65	-	Politics & Policy
#95	Kirsten Green	52	United States	Finance
#96	Choi Soo-yeon	42	-	Business
#97	Jenny Lee	52	Singapore	Finance
#98	Mo Abudu	59	Nigeria	Media & Entertainment
#99	Mia Mottley	59	-	Politics & Policy
#100	Barbie	65	United States	Media & Entertainment

SOME OF THE WORLD'S GREATEST WOMEN ACHIEVERS

Harriet Tubman: 1820-1913

Edited by Debra Michals, PHD

Known as the "Moses of her people," Harriet Tubman was enslaved, escaped, and helped others gain their freedom as a "conductor" of the Underground Railroad. Tubman also served as a scout, spy, guerrilla soldier, and nurse for the Union Army during the Civil War. She is considered the first African American woman to serve in the military.

Tubman's exact birth date is unknown, but estimates place it between 1820 and 1822 in Dorchester County, Maryland. Born Araminta Ross, the daughter of Harriet Green and Benjamin Ross, Tubman had eight siblings. By age five, Tubman's owners rented her out to neighbors as a domestic servant. Early signs of her resistance to slavery and its abuses came at age twelve when she intervened to keep her master from beating an enslaved man who tried to escape. She was hit in the head with a two-pound weight, leaving her with a lifetime of severe headaches and narcolepsy.

Although slaves were not legally allowed to marry, Tubman entered a marital union with John Tubman, a free black man, in 1844. She took his name and dubbed herself Harriet.

Contrary to legend, Tubman did not create the Underground Railroad; it was established in the late eighteenth century by black and white abolitionists. Tubman likely benefitted from this network of escape routes and safe houses in 1849, when she and two brothers escaped north. Her husband refused to join her, and by 1851 he had married a free black woman. Tubman returned to the South several times and helped dozens of people escape. Her success led slaveowners to post a $40,000 reward for her capture or death.

Tubman was never caught and never lost a "passenger." She participated in other antislavery efforts, including supporting John Brown in his failed 1859 raid on the Harpers Ferry, Virginia arsenal.

Through the Underground Railroad, Tubman learned the towns and transportation routes characterizing the South—information that made her important to Union military commanders during the Civil War. As a Union spy and scout, Tubman often transformed herself into an aging woman. She would wander the streets under Confederate control and learn from the enslaved population about Confederate troop placements and supply lines. Tubman helped many of these individuals find food, shelter, and even jobs in the North. She also became a respected guerrilla operative. As a **nurse**, Tubman dispensed herbal remedies to black and white soldiers dying from infection and disease.

<u>Susan B. Anthony</u>

by Emily and Lyndsay from Cincinnati

Susan B. Anthony is our hero because, she stood up for women's rights, she went against society's norm to show women they are equal to men, and she was the leader of the women's Suffrage movement. Susan B. Anthony overcame so many struggles throughout her life, that she is now an inspiration to women and everyone throughout the world. She was fined 100 dollars when she attempted to vote in 1872. 100 dollars in 1872 is equal to $1,740.60 today. But she refused to pay and opened many pathways to success for other women out there. She was also president of the Women's Suffrage Association.

Susan B. was born on February 15, 1820, as Susan Brownell Anthony in Adams, Massachusetts. She was born to Daniel Anthony and Lucy Read, who were activists at the time, so she grew up learning that everyone was equal, no matter what their race or gender was. Susan B. Anthony was raised in a family of 6. And her father and mother treated everyone in the family as equals. Seeing how her family treated women and how others did, she noticed a very different world outside of her home. She dedicated her life to fighting for other women and making everyone's lives equal.

Susan B. Anthony did things for people that others wouldn't dare to do. She went against the law just to prove women are just equal to men. She would not let men push her around. She would not be told what to do. And she would not stop until she changed the way women were treated. When she was a teacher she was paid less than what the men were paid. This drove her to fight for equal pay among men, women, and African Americans. Susan B. Anthony is a hero in our eyes for her amazing accomplishments in helping other people.

Susan B. Anthony was elected president of the Women's Suffrage Association. Their drive was to create equal rights for women. She traveled to lecture about what she believed in. In 1851 Susan was introduced to Elizabeth Cady Stanton.

Elizabeth was an organizer of the Seneca Falls Convention in upstate New York. This is where she was introduced to the controversial resolution in support of women's suffrage. (Women in 20s) They worked together and formed a fifty-year partnership. Together they fought to stop women's suffrage. Susan B. Anthony was not going to just say she wanted suffrage to end. She went against society's norm to fight for other women. Susan B. Anthony decided that just saying she wanted equal rights wasn't enough. In 1872 she decided to vote. Yes, she voted illegally to show everyone that women have a say in the decisions our country makes. She was fined $100, for voting illegally, which doesn't sound like a lot in today's standards, but in 1872 it could be worth up to $1,740.60 in current USD. She refused to pay the fine because it wasn't something someone should be fined for. After this many women saw that they were just as equal as men, and should be able to contribute to the decisions that their country made.

https://upload.wikimedia.org/wikipedia/commons/thu
(Wikimedia)

Susan B. Anthony went against society just to show women that they are just as equal to men. She wanted to show that women have a right to do things men can do. She changed the world. She, in our eyes, is a hero to ALL people. A hero is someone who changes the world in a good way. Anyone can be a hero if you do something good for someone else. Standing up for someone could make you a hero to that person.

Any little thing can be a big deed for people who need it. Susan B. Anthony is our hero because she left a great impact on the world. We know she was one of many to stand up for women's rights, but she did things other people were afraid to do. She voted illegally, petitioned on several causes, and did many other things to show she was not going to be unequal to men. Now women all have equal rights, and we know that she contributed to the fact very much.

Frida Kahlo: 1907-1954

This Mexican artist survived childhood polio and later a bus accident that led to seven operations. She began painting to escape her lifelong pain and is considered one of the greatest artists of the 20th century.

Helen Keller: 1880-1968

A childhood disease left her deaf, mute, and blind. Helen Keller became an expert author and lecturer, educating nationally on behalf of others with similar disabilities.

Margaret Mead: 1901-1978

This anthropologist who studied Samoan culture caused society to rethink how it looked at adolescence.

Mother Theresa: 1910-1997

Founder of a religious group of nuns in Calcutta, India, Mother Theresa devoted her life to aiding sick and poor people throughout the world.

Ellen Ochoa (born 1958)

As an astronaut and researcher of advanced optical information systems, Ochoa flew her first shuttle mission in 1993 as a Mission Specialist with the Discovery crew, conducting atmospheric and solar studies to better equal opportunity for American women.

Because of her work, working women have a legal right to equal pay, and food labels by law must now list exact amounts of ingredients and the nutritional content. She served four U.S. Presidents in various capacities, including Assistant Secretary of Labor, and Vice-Chair of the first Presidential Commission on the Status of Women.

Dr. Sally Ride: 1951-

The first American woman in space was also the youngest American astronaut ever to orbit Earth.

Eleanor Roosevelt: 1884-1962

As a champion of human rights, she strove to further women's causes as well as the causes of black people, poor people, and the unemployed.

Sacagawea: 1787-1812

She was the interpreter for Lewis and Clark during the U.S. government's first exploration of the Northwest. Sacagawea's role was to help negotiate safe and peaceful passages through tribal lands.

Sappho: (circa 625 B.C.)

This Greek poet is considered one of the most important in Western civilization. In addition to creating the "Sapphic stanza," which consists of three long lines of poetry coupled with one short line, she also invented an instrument-the 21-string lyre.

Muriel F. Siebert: 1938-

Her advanced understanding of banking and finance led Muriel Siebert to the first seat owned by a woman on the New York Stock Exchange. She created the Siebert Philanthropic Program, which lets investors help charities in their communities.

Lillian Smith: 1897-1966

Honored in 1956 by the women who organized the Montgomery Bus Boycott, Smith was one of the nation's strongest European-American voices to expose the vicious ways that racism destroys the human spirit. She used her stellar writing talent and class privilege to expose and challenge racism.

Smith co-published the literary magazine South Today to help give voice to progressive black and white southern writers.

Margaret Thatcher: 1925-

This politician was the first woman in European history to be elected prime minister. Known for her conservative views, Margaret Thatcher was also the first British prime minister to win three consecutive terms in the 20th century.

Victoria Woodhull: 1838–1927

The first woman to be nominated and campaign for the U.S. presidency. She was nominated by the Women's National Equal Rights Party. Woodhull and her sister were also the first two female stockbrokers on Wall Street.

Babe Didrikson Zaharias: 1914–1956

One of the greatest athletes of all time, Zaharias won track and field gold medals at the 1932 Olympics, played professional basketball, and was a founding member of the Ladies Professional Golf Association.

Rābi'a al-'Adawīyya (d. 801).

One of the most important mystics (or Sufis) in the Muslim tradition, Rābi'a al-'Adawīyya spent much of her early life as a slave in southern Iraq before attaining her freedom. She is considered to be one of the founders of the Sufi school of "Divine Love," which emphasizes the loving of God for His own sake, rather than out of fear of punishment or desire for reward.

She lays this out in one of her poems: "O God! If I worship You for fear of Hell, burn me in Hell, and if I worship You in hope of Paradise, exclude me from Paradise. But if I worship You for Your Own sake, grudge me, not Your everlasting Beauty.

Lubna of Cordoba (d. 984).

Originally a slave-girl of Spanish origin, Lubna rose to become one of the most important figures in the Umayyad palace in Cordoba. She was the palace secretary of the caliph 'Abd al-Rahmān III (d. 961) and his son al-Hakam b. 'Abd al-Rahmān (d. 976).

She was also a skilled mathematician and presided over the royal library, which consisted of over 500,000 books. According to the famous Andalusi scholar Ibn Bashkuwāl: "She excelled in writing, grammar, and poetry. Her knowledge of mathematics was also immense and she was proficient in other sciences as well. There were none in the Umayyad palace as noble as her." [Ibn Bashkuwal, Kitab al- Silla (Cairo, 2008), Vol. 2: 324].

Khadīja b. Khuwaylid (d. 620).

Even before her famous marriage to the Prophet Muhammad, she was an important figure in her own right, being a successful merchant and one of the elite figures of Mecca. She played a central role in supporting and propagating the new faith of Islam and has the distinction of being the first Muslim. As the Prophet Muhammad himself is believed to have said in a hadith preserved in Sahih Muslim: "God Almighty never granted me anyone better in this life than her. She accepted me when people rejected me; she believed in me when people doubted me; she shared her wealth with me when people deprived me; and God granted me children only through her." Indeed, another of the most important women of early Islam, Fāṭima al-Zahrā', was the daughter of the Prophet by Khadīja and it is only through Fāṭima (especially through her two sons, al-Hasan and al- Husayn) that the lineage of the Prophet Muhammad is preserved. These facts make Fāṭima and her mother Khadīja among the most revered female personages in Islamic history.

Nusayba b. Ka'b al-Anṣārīyya (d. 634).

Also known as Umm 'Ammara, she was a member of the Banū Najjār tribe and one of the earliest converts to Islam in Medina. As a Companion of the Prophet Muhammad, there were many virtues attributed to her. She is most remembered, however, for taking part in the Battle of Uhud (625), in which she carried a sword and shield and fought against the Meccans. She shielded the Prophet Muhammad from enemies during the battle and even sustained several lance wounds and arrows as she cast herself in front of him to protect him. It is said that after she sustained her twelfth wound, she fell unconscious and the first question she asked when she awoke (a day later in Medina) was "Did the Prophet survive?"

Zaynab b. 'Alī (d. 681).

She was the grand-daughter of the Prophet Muhammad through his daughterFāṭima (d. 633) and her husband 'Alī ibn Abī Ṭālib (d. 661). She was among the most illustrious and admirable figures of the Ahl al-Bayt (Family of the Prophet) and played a central role both during and after the Massacre at Karbala (680), where her brother al-Ḥusayn ibn 'Alī, and 72 of her nephews and other brothers were killed by the Umayyads. For a time, she was the effective leader of the Ahl al-Bayt and served as the primary defender of the cause of her brother, al-Ḥusayn. AtKufa, she defended her nephew—'Alī ibn al- Ḥusayn—from certain death by the governor of the city and, when presented to the Yazīd ibn Mu'āwiya at Damascus, gave such an impassioned and forceful speech in the royal court that forced the caliph to release her and the prisoners taken at Karbala.

Her strength, patience, and wisdom make her one of the most important women in early Islam.

Her shrine at Damascus remains a major place of visitation by both Sunnis and Shi'as, a fact that emphasizes the universality of her legacy among Muslims.

<u>Al-Malika al-Ḥurra Arwa al-Sulayhi(d. 1138).</u>

Her full name was Arwa B. Ahmad B. Muhammad al-Sulayḥī. From 1067 to 1138, she ruled as the queen of Yemen in her own right. She was an Ismā'īlī Shi'i and was well-versed in various religious sciences, Qur'an, hadith, as well as poetry and history. Chroniclers describe her as being incredibly intelligent. The fact that she ruled in her own right as queen is underscored by the fact that her name was mentioned in the khutba (Friday sermon) directly after the name of the Fatimid caliph, al-Mustanṣir- billah. Arwa was given the highest rank in the Yemeni Fatimid religious hierarchy (that of ḥujja) by the Fatimid caliphal Mustanṣir. She was the first woman in the history of Islam to be given such an illustrious title and to have such authority in the religious hierarchy.

It was also during her reign that Ismā'īlī missionaries were sent to western India, where a major Ismā'īlī center was established at Gujrat (which continues to be a stronghold of the Ismā'īlī Bohra faith). She played a major role in the Fatimid schism of 1094, throwing her support behind al- Musta'lī (and later al-Tayyib), and it is a mark of her immense influence that the lands under her rule— Yemen and parts of India—would follow her in this. Indeed, Yemen became the stronghold of the Tayyibī Ismā'īlī movement.

Her reign was marked by various construction projects and the improvement of Yemen's infrastructure, as well as its increased integration with the rest of the Muslim world. She was perhaps the single, most important example of an independent queen in Muslim history. Durgavati was a brave woman of India during the 47th century of Kaliyugas i.e. 16th century A.D. who fought with alien invaders with utmost courage and heroic bravery. Lest her living body may be vilified with the touch of the aliens she, with her sword, sacrificed herself and attained.

<u>Durgavati of India</u>

After the death of King Dalpatishah of Gadha Mandala, there came a crisis in the state. The Mughal ruler, Akbar, sent a huge army to capture the state of Gadha (fort) Mandala. Mounting an elephant, Maharani Durgavati fought with utmost bravery and provided constant encouragement and inspiration to her army. Unfortunately, because of internal disunity and her army being too small in comparison with the invaders, she did not succeed in self-defense.

<u>May Angelou</u>

Poet, Author, and Civil Rights Activist Born on April 4, 1928, in St. Louis, Missouri, writer and civil rights activist Maya Angelou is known for her 1969 memoir, I Know Why the Caged Bird Sings, which made literary history as the first nonfiction best-seller by an African- American woman. In 1971, Angelou published the Pulitzer Prize-nominated poetry collection Just Give Me a Cool Drink of Water 'Fore I Die

She later wrote. the poem "On the Pulse of Morning" — one of her most famous works—which she recited at President Bill Clinton's inauguration in 1993. Angelou received several honors throughout her career, including two NAACP Image Awards in the outstanding literary work (nonfiction) category, in 2005 and 2009. She died

on May 28, 2014.

<u>Queen Rania</u>,
Business Leader, Women's Rights Activist,

Queen Rania *of Jordan*
is best known for her advocacy work in public health, and education and as an outspoken opponent of the practice of "honor killings."

Born in Kuwait (1970)and forced to flee during the first Gulf War in

1991, Queen Rania's early life was much like thousands of other Palestinians. In 1993 she met Prince Abdullah II bin al-Hussein of Jordan at a party and the two were married six months later. Rania is a strong progressive female voice in the Arab world and a powerful advocate for education, health, and women's rights.

Rania's youth, royal status, and glamorous beauty instantly made her something of an international icon. She was photographed at fashion shows and high-society social events, usually mingling with a beautiful coterie of the global elite. Through it all, however, Queen Rania remained remarkably grounded, using her position to advocate on behalf of a variety of causes she believed to be important. A progressive female voice in the Arab world, Queen Rania became a powerful advocate for reform in education and public health, the development of a sustainable tourism industry in Jordan, youth empowerment, and cross-cultural dialogue between the West and the Arab world. Perhaps most notably, she worked as an outspoken opponent of the traditional practice of "honor killings," the murder of women by members of their own family for perceived violations of Islamic moral code.

Christina Koch

With 289 consecutive days in space, the National Aeronautics and Space Administration (NASA) astronaut made history on Dec. 28, 2019, by surpassing Peggy Whitson's record for the longest spaceflight in a single mission by a woman. By the time Koch returned to Earth in February 2020, she had spent 328 days in space the second highest in a single mission by an American astronaut. With fellow astronaut Jessica Meir, Koch set another milestone during the mission the first all-female spacewalk.

Simone Biles

At the Stuttgart World Championships held in October 2019, Biles became the first gymnast to win five gold medals at a single world championship since 1958. The medal haul, which brought her world medal total to 25, also helped her break Belarusian Vitaly Scherbo's career total of 23 to become the world's most decorated gymnast.

Sarah Thomas

Thomas, an American football official, made history as the first female referee to officiate a National Football League (NFL) playoff game on Jan. 13, 2019. Before the remarkable first, Thomas had already created history as the first woman to referee a major college football game in 2007. Two years later, she became the first woman to officiate in a bowl game, and 2011 was the first woman to officiate in a Big Ten stadium as a line judge. In 2015, she was hired as the first full-time female referee in NFL history.

Nadia Murad

An ethnic Yazidi from Iraq, Murad shared the Nobel Prize for Peace with Congolese gynecologist Denis Mukwege in 2018 for their "efforts to end the use of sexual violence as a weapon of war and armed conflict." She was kept as a captive by the Islamic State (ISIS) who attacked her village when she was 19. In 2015, Murad managed to take refuge in Germany, where she works as an activist helping women and children who are victims of abuse and human trafficking.

Tarana Burke

The civil rights activist founded the "Me Too" movement in 2006 to raise awareness about sexual abuse and to build solidarity among survivors of sexual harassment. The use of #MeToo as a hashtag became a global phenomenon in 2017 in the wake of allegations of sexual abuse against Hollywood producer Harvey Weinstein. Today, the hashtag is used across the world to highlight cases of sexual harassment or assault. In 2017, Time magazine included Burke among "The Silence Breakers," a group of women it named as its 2017 Person of the Year.

Peggy Whitson

On April 24, 2017, Whitson, the first woman to have commanded the International Space Station (ISS) twice, broke the record for the most cumulative days spent in space by any NASA astronaut by clocking more than 534 days. By September that year, she accumulated a total of 665 days throughout her career the most by any woman worldwide. Whitson also set other records as the oldest female astronaut at age 57 and the woman astronaut with the most spacewalks (10). She retired from NASA on June 15, 2018.

Chan Yuen-ting

She made history as the first female coach to lead a men's soccer team (Eastern Sports Club) to a professional top-flight league championship victory in May 2016. For the feat, Chan, who was 27 years old at the time, was named among the top women of the year by the BBC and received the Asian Football Confederation (AFC) Women's Coach of the Year award. Her achievement was also recognized by Guinness World Records.

Michelle Payne

Payne became the first-ever female jockey to win the Melbourne Cup in the horse race's 155 years of history on Nov. 3, 2015.

Agnès Varda

One of the leading figures of the French New Wave film movement, Varda (1928-2019) became the first woman to receive an honorary Palme d'Or in May 2015. The prize is given to directors whose works have had a global impact. Varda's work on social issues and feminist topics, and her unconventional methods in film direction brought about a fresh trend in the world of arts.

Malala Yousafzai

In 2014, Yousafzai became the youngest Nobel laureate at the age of 17 when she was jointly awarded the Nobel Peace prize with India's Kailash Satyarthi "for their struggle against the suppression of children and young people and for the right of all children to education." The Pakistani activist grabbed the world's attention when she was shot in the head in 2012 by the Taliban for advocating a girl's education in her native Swat Valley. Yousafzai is today counted among the most powerful voices for the rights of children DiacreDiacre became the first woman to lead a men's professional soccer team (Clermont Foot 63) in a major European country (France) on Aug. 4, 2014. Three years later, she was appointed as the manager of France's women's national team – a position she currently holds.

Danica Patrick

One of the most accomplished women in auto racing, Patrick created history when she became the first woman to clinch pole position for the Daytona 500 – NASCAR's highest division on Feb. 17, 2013. In the subsequent race, she finished eighth the best-ever finish by a woman at the event. In 2015, Patrick beat Janet Guthrie's record for the most top-ten finishes (six) by a woman in the Sprint Cup Series. She retired from the sport in 2018.

Tatyana McFadden

In 2013, McFadden became the first female athlete to win six gold medals at the 2013 IPC Athletics World Championships in Lyon, France. She claimed gold in every category: from the 100m meters through to the 5,000 meters events. Winning the Boston, Chicago, London, and New York marathons in 2013, she became the first person to win all four World Major Marathons in the same year. McFadden won four gold medals at the Rio Paralympic Games in 2016, which brought her total Paralympic gold medal count to seven.

Diana Nyad

On Sept. 2, 2013, after breaking several swimming records and gaining major attention for swimming across large distances, the American author and swimmer became the first woman to swim from Cuba to Florida, U.S., a distance of 110 miles (177 kilometers), without the aid of a protective cage. She was 64 at the time.

Rosie Napravnik

In May 2012, Napravnik became the first woman jockey to win the U.S. Kentucky Oaks. She won the same race again in 2014. She also won the Breeders' Cup twice – in 2012 and 2014. Napravnik was seven weeks pregnant when she won the championship for the second time.

Kathryn Bigelow

Bigelow created history by becoming the first woman to bag an Oscar for Best Director in 2010 for the movie "The Hurt Locker" (2009). She was also the first woman to be awarded by the Directors Guild of America in its 62-year history for the same movie. Bigelow's other hits include "Strange Days" (1995), "K-19: The Widow Maker" (2002), and "Zero Dark Thirty" (2012).

Jóhanna Sigurðardóttir

On Feb. 1, 2009, she became the first female prime minister of Iceland and the world's first openly gay head of government. Advocating gay rights and gender equality, Sigurðardóttir set an example by marrying her partner on June 27, 2010 – the day same-sex marriages were legalized in her country.

Anousheh Ansari

On Sept. 18, 2006, the Iranian-American businesswoman became the first female space tourist when a Soyuz space capsule took off with her and two astronauts for the International Space Station from Kazakhstan's Baikonur Cosmodrome. She was also the first self-funded woman to fly to space. Ansari talked about her experiences in her memoir "My Dream of Stars: From Daughter of Iran to Space Pioneer," published in 2010. In 2018, she became the CEO of XPRIZE, a nonprofit organization.

Shirin Ebadi

The first woman judge in Iran, Ebadi was honored with the Nobel Prize for Peace in 2003 "for her efforts for democracy and human rights." The Nobel citation also states that she "has focused especially on the struggle for the rights of women and children." Forced to work as a clerk in following the 1979 Islamic Revolution, Ebadi took early retirement in protest. It was not until 1992 that she was able to obtain a lawyer's license and set up a private practice, which enabled her to represent and fight for the rights of women and children.

Julie Taymor

Taymor received the Tony Award for Outstanding Direction of a Musical for "The Lion King" in 1998, making her the first woman to win the honor. The second award she won for the production was Outstanding Costume Design. Apart from helming Broadway hits such as "The Green Bird" (2000) and "Spider-Man: Turn Off The Dark" (2011), Taymor directed acclaimed films such as "Frida" (2002) and "Across the Universe" (2007).

Eileen Collins

The U.S. astronaut became the first woman to pilot a space mission, serving as second-in-command for Discovery, in 1995. She was given the command of the space shuttle Columbia in 1999, making her the first female shuttle commander.

Aretha Franklin

Franklin (1942-2018) was the first woman performer to be inducted into the Rock and Roll Hall of Fame in 1987, when she was 45. A winner of 18 Grammy Awards, she was ranked number one by Rolling Stone magazine on its 100 Greatest Singers of All Time in 2010.

Svetlana Savitskaya

With her July 1984 mission, Soviet cosmonaut Savitskaya became not only the first woman to have gone to space twice but also the first woman to perform a spacewalk. During the mission, she spent three hours and 35 minutes outside the Salyut 7 space station cutting and welding metals a feat that made her the first person to weld in space.

Junko Tabei

On May 16, 1975, more than 20 years after Mount Everest was first scaled, Tabei (1939-2016) became the first woman mountaineer to reach the summit (pictured, R). The Japanese mountaineer continued scaling peaks, and in June 1992 became the first woman to scale the Seven Summits, the highest mountains of each continent.

Bernice Rubens

The Welsh novelist's (1923-2004) fourth book, "The Elected Member" (1969) made her the first woman to win the Man Booker Prize in 1970. Her other notable works include "Birds of Passage" (1981) "Kingdom Come" (1990), "A Solitary Grief" (1991) and "The Waiting Game" (1997). Some of Ruben's books, such as "Madame Sousatzka"(1962), have been adapted for films and TV series.

Jerrie Mock

Geraldine "Jerrie" Mock (1925-2014) became the first woman to fly solo around the world on April 17, 1964, covering a distance of 23,103 miles (37,180 kilometers) in 29 days 11 hours, and 59 minutes. For her accomplishment, the American was awarded the Louis Blériot silver medal from the Fédération Aéronautique Internationale the first American and first woman to be so honored, and Federal Aviation

Administration's Exception Service Decoration by the then-U.S. President Lyndon B. Johnson in 1964. She published her story in the book "Three-Eight Charlie," released in 1970.

Valentina Tereshkova

Tereshkova was selected from among a group of four trained women to pilot the Vostok 6 in June 1963, making her the first woman to have reached space. Following her successful mission during which she orbited Earth 48 times in three days, Tereshkova started an active political life and represented the Soviet Union at international events.

Jacqueline Cochran

Colonel Cochran (1906-1980) of the U.S. became the first woman to fly at supersonic speeds in 1953. She was also the first woman to fly a bomber across the Atlantic. At the time of her death, she held the records for the maximum speed, distance, and altitude in the history of aviation.

Shirley Dinsdale

Dinsdale (1926-1999) was present at the first Emmy presentation ceremony to receive the first-ever award for Outstanding Television Personality. The ventriloquist broke into radio with "Judy Splinters," her dummy, which also got her a children's TV show after she won the award.

Bodil Ipsen

The renowned Danish actress (1889-1964) debuted as a director with "Afsporet" in 1942 and made nine more films in the next nine years. She went on to win four Bodil awards, which were named after her and fellow actress Bodil Kjer.

Amelia Earhart

Earhart (1897-1939) was a pioneer in the field of aviation and became the first woman to fly across the Atlantic Ocean as a passenger in 1928 and solo in 1932. She was instrumental in the formation of the Ninety-Nines, an international organization for female pilots, of which she was the first president. Earhart, along with Fred Noonan, disappeared over the Pacific Ocean during a circumnavigation attempt in 1937. She was officially declared dead two years later.

Gertrude Ederle

The American competition swimmer (1905-2003) was the first woman to swim across the English Channel, a task she accomplished on Aug. 6, 1926. In her later years, Ederle, who had a hearing problem since childhood, became a swimming instructor for deaf children.

Aloha Wanderwell

The Canadian-American explorer (1906-1996) is regarded as the first woman to drive around the world a feat she started working on when she was 16 – as certified by the Guinness World Records. Driving a Ford Model-T, she began in Nice, France, in December 1922 and reached back in January 1927.

Marie Marvingt

Marvingt (1875-1963) became the first woman to fly combat missions when she decided to become a bomber pilot for France during World War I. Awarded the Croix de Guerre, she was also instrumental in the introduction of air ambulance services.

Harriet Quimby

Quimby (1875-1912) managed to change the scenario for women in aviation and, in 1911, became the first American woman to get a pilot's license. The next year, she became the first female pilot to fly solo across the English Channel. Quimby was killed in an air crash in 1912.

Raymonde de Laroche

The French aviatrix (1882-1919) became the world's first woman to receive an airplane pilot's license in 1910. Despite suffering severe injuries during an air show, she continued flying and won a cup for flying nonstop for four hours. She died in a plane crash in 1919.

Marie Curie

Curie's (1867-1934) discovery of radium and polonium led to her becoming the first woman to win the Nobel Prize (in Physics) in 1903. In 1911, she became the first person and the only woman to win the prize twice when she was awarded for Chemistry. Her work on radioactivity shaped much of the scientific developments in the 20th and 21st centuries.

U.S STATISTICS OF DOMESTIC VIOLENCE AND ABUSED WOMEN

Statistics underscore the prevalence of violence in our communities. We must stand up against domestic violence, sexual violence, human trafficking and child abuse:

Domestic violence statistics

A person is abused in the United States every 9 seconds; (Bureau of Justice Statistics)

On average, 3 women are killed by a current or former intimate partner each day in the United States; (Bureau of Justice, Bureau ofJustice Statistics)

1 in 4 women has experienced severe physical violence by an intimate partner; (National Intimate Partner & Sexual ViolenceSurvey)

1 in 4 victims of intimate partner violence identify as lesbian, gay, bisexual, transgender, or queer; (National Coalition ofAnti-Violence Programs)

66 percent of female stalking victims are stalked by a current or former intimate partner; (National Stalking Resource Center)

Domestic violence costs more than $8.3 billion a year in medical care, mental health services, and lost productivity at companies; (Centers for Disease Control and Prevention)

More than 15 million children witness domestic violence each year in the United States; (Journal of Family Psychology)

3,500 to 4,000 children witness fatal family violence annually in the United States; (National Task Force on Children Exposed to Violence)

SEXUAL VIOLENCE STATISTICS

1 in 4 women and 1 out of 6 men are sexually abused in their lifetime; (Department of Justice)

 In 8 out of 10 rape cases, the victim knows the attacker; (Department of Justice)

1 in 2 transgender individuals will experience sexual violence; (National Intimate Partner &Sexual Violence Survey)

1 in 4 bisexual women will experience sexual violence; (National Intimate Partner & SexualViolence Survey)

2 in 5 gay men will be sexually abused; (National Intimate Partner & Sexual ViolenceSurvey)

Nearly 6 out of 10 sexual assaults occur in the victim's home or the home of a friend, relative or neighbor; (Department of Justice)

13.3 percent of college women say they have been forced to have sex in a dating situation; (Journal of Interpersonal Violence)

Only 28 percent of victims report their sexual assault to the police; (Bureau of Justice Statistics)

Only about 2 percent of all sexual assaults reported to police turn out to be false; (Department of Justice)

Among developmentally disabled adults, up to 83 percent of females and 32 percent of males are victims of sexual violence; (Disabled Women's Network)

CHILD ABUSE STATISTICS

A report of child abuse is made every 10 seconds; (American Society for the Positive Care of Children)

1 in 3 girls and 1 in 7 boys will be sexually assaulted by the time they reach 18; (Department of Justice)

More than 4 children die each day because of child abuse;(U.S. Department of Health and Human Services)

More than 90 percent of child sexual abuse victims know their attacker; ("Sexual Assault of Young Children as Reported to Law Enforcement by Howard Snyder)

Approximately 70 percent of children who die from abuse are under the age of 4; (U.S. Department of Health and Human Services)

About 30 percent of abused and neglected children will later abuse their own children, continuing the cycle of violence;(U.S. Department of Health and Human Services)

LET THE CENTER FOR FAMILY JUSTICE BECOME YOUR LIFELINE

Hope Starts Here!

Let The Center for Family Justice become your lifeline.

Please call us today at:

203-334-6154

Or

24/7 on a

hotline:

Domestic violence: 203-384-955

Sexual assault: 203-333-2233

Vedas (Spanish): 888-568-8332

Prayer Challenge

* * *

"My Father's House Shall Be Called A House Of Prayer."
7 MINUTES WITH GOD PRAYER
CHALLENGE
A place where we are laying down our phones and devices...yes, you heard me correctly, our smart phones and devices for just Seven (7) DEDICATED minutes with God.
Calling on all Prayer Warriors!
We have traded praying for great production.
We are in troubling times. The world and the church are falling apart; we must admit that we owe God an apology and must repent.
Wherever you are in this world, as believers let's agree to pray everyday
@ 7:00 a.m.
Whatever your time zone
INFO@KINGDOMRIGHTS2.ORG
LET'S PRAY!

Stay Connected

Books:

We are excited to announce that Joseph Brice has published three (3) additional books:

* God The Woman & Their Enemy: (Available in English and Spanish)

* Why I Satan Hate The Woman

* Resurrection

- These books are available in Hardback, Paperback, Ebook, and Audio.

- Available on Amazon, Barnes and Noble, Apple Books, Google Books, and Walmart Ebook

- Also available on our own Kingdom Store @kingdomrights2.org

* * *

Available NOW!   On Apple Podcast, Audible, Amazon Music, Spotify, Pandora, iHeart Radio, SiriusXM, and Google Podcast.

Kingdom Podcast: See the Link Below

When It's All Said And Done

https://KingdomRights.sermon.net/main/main/22177375

* * *

Seven Minutes with God Podcast: See the Link Below

Can A Woman Preach?

https://KingdomRights.sermon.net/22180281

Unlock the Power of Women's Voices in Ministry

"Can A Woman Preach?" by Joseph Brice

Discover the transformative exploration of women's roles in ministry with Joseph Brice's thought-provoking audiobook, "Can A Woman Preach?"

In this compelling narrative, Brice delves into one of the most debated topics in religious communities today. With a blend of rigorous scholarship, personal anecdotes, and biblical analysis, he challenges traditional norms and opens the floor for a dynamic discussion on the potential and power of women in the pulpit.

Why This Audiobook?

- **Engaging Content**: Brice's eloquent storytelling keeps you captivated from start to finish. His insightful arguments and passionate delivery make this a must-listen.

- **Thought-Provoking**: Whether you're a member of the

clergy, a theology student, or someone interested in gender roles within the church, this audiobook provides fresh perspectives that will inspire and challenge your beliefs.

- **Expert Insight**: Drawing from extensive research and years of experience, Brice offers a well-rounded view that is both scholarly and accessible.

- **Convenient Listening**: Perfect for busy schedules, enjoy the convenience of listening during your commute, workout, or downtime.

Join the conversation and explore the biblical, historical, and cultural dimensions of women's roles in preaching. "Can A Woman Preach?" is not just an audiobook; it's a movement towards greater inclusivity and understanding within the faith community.

Available now on all major audiobook platforms. Don't miss your chance to be part of this groundbreaking discussion.

Get "Can A Woman Preach?" today and let Joseph Brice guide you through a transformative journey of faith, equality, and empowerment.

ALL options are available on your Apple and Android App Store and Our own Kingdom Rights app. Look for our Logo.

Kingdom Rights Website:

Kingdomrights2.org